Retiring Well on a Poor Man's Budget

1,001 Ways to Stretch Your Income and Enjoy Your Golden Years

Publisher's Note

The editors of FC&A have taken careful measures to ensure the accuracy and usefulness of the information in this book. While every attempt was made to assure accuracy, some Web sites, addresses, telephone numbers, and other information may have changed since printing. All estimates were made with the best data available at that time.

This book is intended for general information only. It does not constitute medical, legal, or financial advice or practice. We cannot guarantee the safety or effectiveness of any treatment or advice mentioned. Readers are urged to consult with their personal financial advisers, lawyers, and health care professionals.

The publisher and editors disclaim all liability (including any injuries, damages, or losses) resulting from the use of the information in this book.

Faith is the assurance of things hoped for, the conviction of things not seen.

Hebrews 11:1

Table of Contents

Build your nest egg:
    save up to $100,000 this year 1
Simple money-saving ways to prepare for the future

Retirement fund:
    how much is enough? 107
Secrets to sizing up your savings

Pensions and 401k plans:
    cash for your future. 131
Smart ways to grow your workplace investments

Build your nest egg:

save up to $100,000 this year

You need smart, simple, money-saving ways to build your nest egg, and that is what you'll find in this chapter. Each section focuses on areas of your life where you can start saving — from housing, utilities, and groceries to health, travel, and leisure.

Each story gives you great budget-boosting tips and even estimates how much you can save in a year. Of course, your savings may total more or less depending on your situation. But by making the effort to cut back in small ways now, you will reap huge benefits down the road.

Banking

Sidestep sneaky fees

 Budget boost this year: $209.50

Banks don't just lend money. They also make money, often on little-known charges and hidden fees. You'd be surprised how much you may save by reading the fine print.

Uncover a "nickel and dime" scheme. If you have each of these charges just once during the year, you would end up paying $131.50.

- Enclosure fee for receiving canceled checks with your monthly statement — up to $3.

- Copies of deposit slips or checks — $2 per copy.

- Insufficient funds — $24 on average.

- Overdraft protection fee — up to $10 to transfer funds to cover the overdraft.

- Overdraft fees — $34 per incident.

- "Research" fees for things like "statement balancing" — $20 per hour rate with a $20 minimum.

- Fee for checking an account after a death in the family — $20 or more.

- Letter of reference — $10.

- Use of ATM in foreign countries — may cost more than $5.

- Using another bank's ATM — $3.50.

Beware "free checking" fees. Free checking isn't really free if you're charged hidden fees like the ones above. But even if you dodge those fees, you may still lose money. For example, your account may start out free. But after awhile, the bank may begin charging a monthly fee unless you meet requirements — like direct deposit of your paychecks into the account. Avoid these monthly maintenance fees and you could save an average of $78 every year.

So check your statement. If you find unexpected fees, call the bank and ask that the fees be waived — or even consider closing that account. Visit *www.bankrate.com* to find accounts that genuinely offer free checking. Or consider opening an account at a credit union. They tend to charge fewer and smaller fees. Contact the Credit Union National Association at *www.cuna.org* or 800-356-9655 to find a credit union near you.

Reveal hidden fees. In spite of Federal government requirements, banks rarely disclose fees and account terms. To help find hidden fees plus opportunities for extra savings, try these seven questions your bank hopes you never ask.

- What fees will I have to pay?

- Will you remove my checking fees if I take out a loan with you or buy a certificate of deposit?

- How long before I can draw on deposits made to my account? This can help you avoid overdrafts, overdraft fees, and overdraft penalties.

- How does the interest accumulate on an interest-paying checking account? Banks that use "blended rates" to figure your interest are probably shortchanging you.

- What is the penalty for falling below the minimum balance? If your bank offers several kinds of checking accounts, avoid choosing one that can sting you if you get too close to the minimum balance.

- Can you truncate my account? This means the bank saves money every month by sending a list of the checks you wrote instead of your canceled checks. That savings should be passed on to you.

- Will you reduce my loan rate if I have my payments made automatically?

ALERT!

Never write checks with a regular pen if you plan to mail them. It could cost you your life savings. Identity thieves steal checks from mailboxes and use common household products to wash off all the handwritten information on the check except your signature. Then they rewrite the check to themselves for any amount they please. To prevent this, use a Uniball pen with the "uni Super Ink" logo or a pen that writes in permanent ink.

Swap stamps for big savings

 Budget boost this year: $79.20

Paying bills no longer requires a checkbook, pen, stamps, and envelopes. Save time and money by paying your bills online instead.

Here are just a few advantages of online bill paying.

- Your checks can't get lost in the mail.

- The online bill paying service may let you schedule automatic payments ahead of time so you never risk late fees or missed payments.

- No danger of bounced checks. Many bank bill paying sites won't let you pay the bill if you don't have enough money in your account.

- Paying bills online takes less time.

- When you bank online, you're protected by plenty of legislation and regulations. It's easier for identity thieves to steal information from bills and credit card statements in your mailbox than it is for them to hack into a bank's Web site.

But online bill paying also saves you money. If the average household pays 12 to 15 bills per month at 44 cents per stamp, switching to online billing could save $5.28 to 6.60 per month — up to $79.20 a year. Pay bills through your bank's online bill paying service, and you may also save on the cost of overdraft fees — $35 on average. Even better, you'll avoid the damage accidentally missed payments can do to your credit. That can mean lower rates on loans and extra savings for you.

You can set up online bill payment with ease just by visiting your bank's Web site. Or, if you prefer to deal directly with companies that bill you, check their Web sites to see if they offer online bill payment. Just be sure to ask whether the service is permanently free before you sign up.

DON'T FORGET

Act quickly if you notice a mistake on your credit card or bank account statement. Under the Fair Credit Billing Act and the Electronic Fund Transfers Act, you have 60 days to report a billing error. This notice must be in writing.

Maximize your savings online

 Budget boost this year: $49.50+

Why wait in line at the bank when you can go online for big savings? Online banks feature higher interest rates than traditional banks, so your money grows faster.

For example, when a well-known national bank was only offering .2 percent on its savings accounts, HSBC was touting a 1.85 percent yearly rate. If you keep $3,000 in your savings account, that higher rate could mean $49.50 in extra interest in just a year. What's more, online bank checking accounts may offer free online bill paying plus genuine no-fee checking — the kind without sneaky fees and hidden prerequisites.

But Internet-only banks like INGdirect.com or HSBC.com are purely online banks — without ATMs or walk-in branches. If you open an account, you can get your money from another bank's ATM — but you may pay a fee to do it. What's more, you cannot visit a bank branch to deposit money. So what can you do?

Your online bank may let you mail in deposits, but mailing takes time. You may also be able to use direct deposit of your paychecks to get money into an Internet-only account. But here's the best way to use these banks. Ask if you can link your local checking account to the online savings account so you can electronically transfer money between the accounts. This gives you convenient access to the high-interest of Internet-only savings accounts.

Before you open an account at an Internet-only bank, make sure it's legitimate. Read and understand the terms of your account such as minimum balance requirements and fees. Check the bank's Web site for a customer service phone number. Also, make sure the Federal Deposit Insurance Corporation (FDIC) insures the bank's accounts. Look through the bank's Web pages for the FDIC logo and visit *www2.fdic.gov/idasp* to search for the bank's name in the FDIC's listings.

SuperSaver

Instead of paying insurance or lawn maintenance bills monthly, ask about discounts for prepaying once a year or every six months. You may even save extra on billing service charges. For example, if you prepay for a six-month car insurance policy, your discount may reach $40, but paying in five installments may cost up to $30 extra in fees. That's a $70 difference. Prepaying also saves money on checks and stamps.

Debt control

Dig yourself out of credit card debt

 Budget boost this year: $600

You can pay down your credit card debt faster at very little cost to you simply by paying twice a month instead of once.

Say you have a credit card with a $2,200 balance, 13 percent interest, and a minimum payment of $44.16. If you pay that amount every month, it will take you six years and nearly $980 in interest to pay off that balance. But if you paid $22 and change every two weeks, you'd pay off the balance in less than five years for a little over $330 in interest — more than $600 total savings. It may sound too good to be true, but it's not.

Pay biweekly. Credit card companies charge interest on your balance on a daily basis. But they are also required to process your payment when it arrives. So if you pay half your minimum payment two weeks early, you lower the amount of interest you'll be charged for the following two weeks and for all future payments. But that's not all.

If you pay monthly, you only make 12 payments a year. But oddly enough, if you pay every two weeks, you make 26 half-payments a year, which is the same as 13 full payments. This happens because most months are several days longer than four weeks and those extra days add up to 29 extra days per year.

But don't stop at biweekly half-payments. Pay the same amount every time — instead of the constantly shrinking required minimum payment — and you'll pay off your balance even faster.

Set up a system. First, check with your credit card company and make sure they allow you to submit half your payment every two weeks. Also, ask what you can do to ensure those extra payments will be processed quickly. Set up a system to ensure your payment will be sent every two weeks. Otherwise, you may risk getting late fees. If you're not sure whether you can remember to pay every 14 days, consider arranging for automatic withdrawal. If you mail the checks in yourself, write the account number on the check, especially if you have no payment coupon to send in.

This method isn't for everyone. Some won't be able to stick with these frequent payments over the long haul while others have balances or interest rates that are too low to make biweekly payments worthwhile.

But if you need to shrink a painful debt faster, stop putting charges on the card and use biweekly payments to become debt-free sooner.

A good credit counselor may help you restructure your debt, negotiate with creditors, and prevent bankruptcy. Crown Financial Ministries is a reputable group that provides Christian-based credit counseling. Go to *www.crown.org* to find contacts in your area. Or check with your church to see if they have trained financial counselors available as part of their ministries.

Curb the urge to splurge

 Budget boost this year: $1,560

We may splurge a lot more than we think we do. According to one study, nearly a third of all consumers make a "sizable" impulse purchase every week at a median amount of around $30. That's $1,560 a year. To keep that money in your pocket, try this.

Grab a pen and several sheets of paper. At the top of each sheet, write the name of one of your credit cards. Every time you use a credit card, pull out its sheet. Write down the date, what you bought, and how much you charged. At the end of every week, total the numbers to find out how much you spent. If you're an impulse buyer, you'll soon see how much money you lose to those purchases. And just knowing that number can help you resist temptation.

Simple strategies to stretch your budget

 Budget boost this year: $1,196

Your budget is so tight you can't imagine where you'll find room to save more. But ideas like these may help you find a few more nooks and crannies where money is hiding. Just a few small sacrifices can add up to big savings over the year.

- Suppose you pay $30 every four weeks to get your hair cut. That's roughly $360 a year. But if you start going every five weeks, you'll only go 10 times per year instead of 12 — for a savings of $60.

- Instead of buying the latest bestseller once month, get a library card. If you spend $20 a month on books, this could save you $240. Check whether you can also borrow CDs and DVDs. That will save you even more by keeping you out of the movie rental and music stores.

- Trade your bottled water for tap water and, when you eat out, order water instead of tea, soft drinks, or coffee. Replacing five bottles of bottled water a week could save you up to $11 per week or $572 a year. Ordering water could save you $234 in a year if you eat out twice a week. That's a total of $806 per year.

- Cancel your magazine subscriptions and read the same magazines at the library instead. If you cancel three magazines, you could save more than $90 a year.

3 ways to raise quick cash

 Budget boost this year: $250+

You can get extra cash without resorting to pawn shops or payday loans. Try these options.

Have a weekend sale. Some statistics suggest that the average yard sale may bring in $250 or more. So hunt through your house for items that are "taking up space." These can be sold for cash. Don't forget to check the attic, basement, closets, junk drawer, and outside shed. If you have Web access, visit *www.yardsalequeen.com* for clever tips that can make your yard sale even more profitable.

Get money by the byte. Some specialty items won't get their full value in a yard sale because people don't realize what those items are worth. But you can sell your one-of-a-kind treasures online even if you don't have a computer. Simply visit a nearby eBay drop-off location, and let them handle the selling for you. Just be aware that they'll charge a commission for the sale.

Find money you're owed. The National Association of Unclaimed Property Administrators currently holds billions of dollars in life insurance proceeds, safe deposit boxes, dividend checks, and similar items that couldn't find their way to their proper owners. These monies are held in state treasuries until their owners can be found. Plenty of scammers try to charge fees to find missing money that might be yours. Stick with reputable sources of information like *www.unclaimed.org* or *www.missingmoney.com*.

> **ALERT!**
>
> Canceling credit cards to avoid charging can be a good idea, but don't go overboard. Closing more than two cards a month can taint your credit report.

Save $ with a higher credit score

 Budget boost this year: $105

Raise your credit score just 30 points and you could save $105 in finance charges every year, says a recent consumer survey — and it may be easier than you think. The survey by the credit bureau Experian found that one-third of all Americans increased their credit scores during a six month period. A few even raised their score by 50 points or more. Use these tips and you might be next.

Pay on time. Several factors control your credit score. The biggest one — counting for 35 percent of your score — is your payment history. Credit scorers look for a history of bills paid on time. So mark your calendar to make sure you never miss a bill, and pay each one as soon as it arrives.

Limit your debts. Keep your total balance well below your credit limit on any credit card. That's because credit scorers give points to people who don't max out their cards. In fact, this affects your credit score almost as much as your payment history. "If you've got a $10,000 line carrying a $2,500 balance, the utilization is 25 percent," says Curtis Arnold, founder of Cardratings.com and author of *How To Profit from Credit Cards*. "Ideally, you want to shoot for 10 percent." He adds, "If you get anything above 30 percent, your score really starts tanking." So keep your balance as far below your credit limit as possible.

Use credit wisely. A history of using credit responsibly counts for 15 percent of your credit score. The longer you use credit wisely, the better your score may become. Keeping the cards with your longest history of responsible use may also help. But don't stop there. Check your credit report for mistakes that might spoil your credit history. To get a free copy of your credit report, visit the Web site *www.annualcreditreport.com* or call 877-322-8228. You're entitled to one free report from each of the three credit reporting agencies every year. If you find an error in your credit report, you can dispute it and have it removed.

Be choosy about new accounts. The more new credit you get in a given period, the worse your score will be. So be picky, and limit or avoid opening new credit card accounts.

Never pay a late fee again

Never pay late or forget to pay a bill again. How? Just set up automatic bill payment or automatic withdrawals from your bank account. This can work for mortgage, rent, utility bills and more. You can even use it for bills that charge a different amount each month. Just be sure to monitor your bank statement and balance closely in case you're a victim of billing errors or an unusually high bill.

Shrink your balance faster

 Budget boost this year: $3,334

A 0-percent credit card offer in the mail could be the perfect way to slash your credit card balance more quickly — but you have other good options as well.

Erase debt faster. Paying zero interest means you're finally free to put all your money toward your balance. For example, if you have a debt of $2,200 at 17 percent interest, and you pay $183.34 every month, you'll pay off the balance in 14 months for $228.60 in interest. But if you transfer that balance to a 0-percent card, make no new charges, and pay $183.34 every month, you'll pay the balance off in 12 months and save $162 on the interest charges — even if you have to pay fees for the transfer.

Save even more. Be picky about which 0-percent offer you choose. Most offers have balance transfer fees that equal 3 percent of the amount you transfer. Fortunately, some offers cap these fees at a set amount. So take the advice of Curtis Arnold, author of *How to Profit from Credit Cards* and founder of Cardratings.com. He suggests you find an offer that lets you keep the 0-percent rate for 12 months and has a balance transfer fee capped at $100 or less.

"They're still out there, although they're becoming harder and harder to find," says Arnold. Check *www.cardratings.com* for help if you haven't found one yet.

But before you take a 0-percent offer, be sure you can pay off the balance by the time that wonderful interest rate expires. The rate that follows may jump to 30 percent or higher.

Explore different options. But what if your balance is too high to pay off in 12 months or you can't find a 0-percent offer? Then Arnold suggests you find a "for-life" offer such as a card that offers 4.99 percent forever. If you can't find that, consider cards that offer low rates for several years such as 4.99 percent for four years. These can save you a lot — especially if you put no new purchases on the card.

For example, if you have a balance of $7,900 at 17-percent interest and you pay $183 per month, you'll pay $4,401 in interest before you pay off the balance nearly six years from now. If you got a 12-month, 0-percent offer and kept paying $183 per month, you couldn't pay off the balance before the 0-percent rate expired. If the rate rose to 22 percent, you'd pay $2,831 in interest on the remaining balance — plus a balance transfer fee as high as $237.

This deal would still be better than the 17-percent loan, as you would pay $1,333 less in interest. But if you found a card that kept your rate at 4.99 percent for four years, you could pay around $182 every month, pay off the loan in four years and only pay the balance transfer fee plus $830 in interest. You'd save $3,334 over sticking with your 17 percent card and $2,001 more than you would with the 0-percent card. *(See table.)*

Just remember to read the fine print before you apply for cards with zero or low rates. Some cards may require you to make new purchases regularly, possibly at a high interest rate, and that could keep you from paying off your balance for quite awhile.

	Current loan	0-percent offer	For-life offer
Balance	$7,900	$7,900	$7,900
Interest rate	17%	0%/22% after 1 yr	4.99%
Monthly payment	$183	$183	$182
Payoff time	6 years	5 years	4 years
Total interest	$4,401	$2,831	$830
Transfer fee	-	$237	$237
Interest + fee	$4,401	$3,068 ($2,001 savings)	$1,067 ($3,334 savings)

Fight back against high fees

 Budget boost this year: $69.50

We've all seen the Priceline commercials where William Shatner urges people to negotiate for better hotel and flight prices. Well, you can negotiate credit card fees and other terms, too — and you won't need Priceline to do it.

"Card issuers are waking up to the fact that they need to start treating their customers at least halfway the way they would like to be treated," says Curtis Arnold, author of *How to Profit from Credit Cards*. That means if you find unexpected fees in your statement, you could get out of paying them. If you're charged an annual fee, for example, call the credit card company and ask if it can be waived. This often works for most types of cards and can save you $43.50 — the average cost of an annual fee.

And if you're a good customer who almost never has late fees, call the credit card company the next time it happens. They may waive the fee if you ask, saving you an average of $26. If you have no luck with customer service, ask to speak to a supervisor. You may want to go as far as threatening to close your account. That has worked for some people, Arnold says.

Along with fees, you can try bargaining for a better rewards package on your rewards cards or even for a higher credit limit. But be aware that some perks may be easier to work out than others, especially in a rough economy.

"I think it may be tougher going forward to negotiate some things like — for example — your credit line getting cut," says Arnold. "But I think fees, rates, and rewards are still going to be negotiable."

Pull off an interest-rate miracle

 Budget boost this year: $490

Imagine what would happen if your credit card interest rate dropped from 18 to 13 percent. If you have a $3,000 balance and pay $60 a month, you could save $490 in interest charges even if you only kept the lower rate for the next year. If you kept the rate permanently, you could save $1,242.37 in interest.

So how do you pull off this miracle? Simply ask your credit card company to lower your rate. Start by saving credit card offers you get in the mail, noting the rates they offer. Then call your credit card company and tell them about the lower rates, say you're thinking of switching, and ask if they can give you a better rate.

At least one survey suggests you have a 50 percent or higher chance of getting that lower rate just because you asked. You may have even better odds if you've checked your credit report, avoided late payments on any card, kept this particular card for several years, and kept your balance well below your credit limit.

Even if you get the lower rate for a short time, you'll see a dramatic cut in your interest payments.

ALERT!

A rewards card can actually cost you money. Why? The interest rate is usually 1 percent higher than a standard credit card rate. So if you keep a balance on that card, your interest charges may cost you more dollars than your rewards can pay back.

Stop a rate hike cold

Budget boost this year: $3,219

You've never missed a payment on your credit cards, but suddenly your interest rate jumps by 9 percent. Instead of paying hundreds or thousands in extra interest payments, try this.

Call the company. "Be courteous when you call," says Curtis Arnold, author of *How to Profit from Credit Cards*, "but you want to mean business." He recommends a direct approach. "Call their bluff and say, 'I am not going to tolerate this. I've been a good customer.' Don't raise your voice, but if you threaten to close out your account and take your business elsewhere, you'll get transferred," Arnold says. "A lot of these bigger banks have account retention departments and their whole purpose is to keep you as a customer, because a little-known industry secret is that it costs up to $200 to $300 in marketing fees to replace you."

If that doesn't work, consider transferring your balance to a card with a lower rate. See the story *Shrink your balance faster* for more details on how to do this and when it's worthwhile.

Opt out. "Opt out" means you are given the chance to refuse the rate hike. You can never again put any new charges on the card, but you will keep your current interest rate on the existing balance until you pay it off. For example, if you have a $2,500 balance, a $50 monthly minimum payment, and a 13-percent interest rate, you'll pay off the balance in around six years at a cost of $1,120.22 in interest. But if your rate rises to 22 percent, you'll take 11 1/2 years to pay off the balance and spend $4,339.09 in interest. Opting out could save you a whopping $3,218.87 in interest.

"Unfortunately, opt out notices are mistaken for junk mail and get trashed," Arnold says. "So if you see any evidence of a rate hike, watch your mail closely." Arnold also recommends keeping a close eye on your accounts so a rate hike won't sneak by you.

New credit card rules mean that companies should begin notifying you of rate hikes 45 days ahead of time, but it never hurts to be vigilant. Also, remember that you must opt out in writing and clearly indicate that you want to retain your existing rate. Do this quickly because the opt out offer may expire.

Weigh your options. Opting out is offered by most — but not all — major credit card issuers, but it isn't for everyone. "You want to weigh your other options before you opt out," recommends Arnold. Opting out may nick your credit score, particularly if this is your oldest card or one of your larger credit-limit cards. So try other options first.

But don't assume you should never opt out. "It's a great thing to exercise, particularly if your other options have been exhausted or you have no other options," says Arnold. "If they jack your rate from 9.99 percent to 19.99 percent and you can't find any good transfer offers, opt out may be your best option."

6 reasons not to trust a debt service

 Budget boost this year: $2,000+

Just when you're about to drown in debt, you get the break you need. A debt resolution company sweeps in promising to get rid of half your debt. All you have to do is pay a fee up front. But you may be shocked at how much can go wrong with this plan.

Know the pitfalls. While you can find legitimate credit counseling agencies to help with debt problems, questionable agencies are also easy to find. Debt resolution, debt negotiation, and debt settlement companies can be especially scary, and here's why.

- They can further damage your credit.

- They won't solve the collections calls problem. If you refer calls to your debt settlement company, some creditors may turn your case over to a collections agency earlier than planned. Some creditors even sue to get their money back, which may cause your debt resolution company to drop you like a hot rock. They're not qualified to represent you in court.

- You'll pay a lot. Disreputable companies charge huge upfront fees, sometimes thousands of dollars.

- They may make things worse. Questionable companies may dip into money intended for your creditors and pay themselves instead. That can lead to late fees and extra interest charges.

- You may save enough to pay back the debt, but can you afford the taxes? Any time one of your creditors agrees to erase part or all of your debt, that's "forgiven debt." Forgiven debt counts as income to the IRS. That means you owe taxes on it.

- You may be breaking the law. If you live in Georgia, Louisiana, Mississippi, New Jersey, New York, West Virginia, Arizona, New Mexico, Hawaii, Maine, North Dakota, or Wyoming, working with a debt settlement company may be illegal if the company is a for-profit firm.

Settle your own debts. Call your creditors, tell them your situation, and ask for a lower interest rate. Or, if your situation is more dire, admit that you won't be able to pay your bill this month, and ask if something can be worked out. If a debt resolution company asked you to pay $2,000 in fees, but you work out a deal with creditors on your own, you will have just saved $2,000 — or even more.

ALERT!

Universal default means a late payment on one credit card — or anything else that taints your credit report — may raise the interest rates on all your credit cards. Supposedly, this becomes illegal in July 2010, but watch out. Only universal default rate hikes on your existing balance will be outlawed. The credit card companies may still use universal default to raise your rate on future charges as long as they notify you first.

Food & groceries

Save big at the supermarket

 Budget boost this year: $1,920+

Enjoy a carefree retirement, knowing you don't have to cut back on food. By shopping smarter, you can trim 50 percent off your grocery bill. Can you really cut your grocery bill in half? Yes, but only if you know the sneaky secrets grocery stores take advantage of. In fact, 50 percent to 67 percent of all grocery purchases are "impulse buys" — stuff you don't really want or need. Find out how the stores lure you in, and how to steer clear of their traps.

If you normally spend $100 a week, you may only need to spend $50. Here are some basic tactics to cut down on wasteful spending at the supermarket.

- Never shop on an empty stomach. If you're hungry, you'll be too tempted by snacks, treats, and expensive extras.

- Make a list. Take time to come up with a grocery list, then stick to it.

- Get in and out quickly. The more time you spend in the grocery store, the more money you'll spend.

- Patrol the perimeter of the store to find essentials, like produce, meat, bread, and milk. This will help you cut down on high-priced, prepackaged foods in the middle aisles.

- Beware of strategically placed items. Don't fall for the candy, gum, and magazines at the checkout counter or the displays at the ends of aisles. Remember, costlier items tend to be at eye level. Look up and down for big savings.

But that's just a start. Here are a few more ways to trim $50 to $150 a month off your food bill.

Choose store brands. A University of New Hampshire study looked at a one-week shopping list for a family of four and compared the cost of store brands and name brands. The shopping bags with name brands cost $181.72, while those with store brands cost only $136.76. That's about $45 less, or a whopping 25 percent savings. If you use the same strategy, you can slash $25 from your average $100 weekly bill. That's a monthly savings of $100 — and a yearly savings of $1,200.

Use unit pricing. This is the best way to select the best buys. You can compare different sizes, brands, and forms of a product. The unit price is usually on the shelf below the product. Remember, bigger doesn't always mean better. Sometimes smaller packages offer better value.

Combine this tactic with good preparation — like completing a weekly menu plan and grocery list using grocery store ads as a guide — and you can save 15 percent. That's $15 a week off your average $100 bill, which comes to about $60 a month and $720 a year.

Track prices. Keep a notebook to track prices from store to store — and even from week to week at the same store. That way, you can spot deals and stock up on one item when it's cheapest. When you buy just a few common items at their lowest prices, you can save 47 percent.

Practice portion control. You may not need as much food as you think. Smaller servings stretch your food dollar. You can buy less food and make what you bought last longer.

Break the rules. Just because the sale is "two-for-one" or "buy four for $10" doesn't always mean you have to buy that amount. You should still get the sale price for one item.

Catch errors. After taking the time to find savings, don't lose them thanks to a costly slip-up. Watch the scanner as the cashier rings up your items, and check your receipt for mistakes. You may even get a full-price refund if the sales price doesn't register.

Best place to buy everyday items

 Budget boost this year: $156+

Your local grocery store might have the best meat and produce in town, but your neighborhood dollar store carries perfectly good household items, snack foods, and more for 40 to 90 percent less. If you normally spend $30 a month on these items in your supermarket, that's a savings of $12 to $27 a month, or $144 to $324 a year.

- Save cash and buy bargain brand cleaning products. They contain the same basic ingredients from one brand to the next.

- Get your greeting cards, gift wrap, and gift bags on the cheap any time of year. No one will know the difference but you and your bank account.

- Snag great deals on snack food, which usually has a long shelf life. You'll often find the same name brands in dollar stores as in grocery stores, but at better prices. Look for food in tightly sealed containers.

- Shop for off-brand shampoos and hair sprays at discount stores, and spend the extra cash on high-quality conditioner.

- Save a mint on spatulas and other kitchen gadgets by foregoing the gourmet cooking shops in favor of dollar stores.

Despite all the savings, there are five things you should never buy at the dollar store. Some are a waste of money, no matter how low the price, while others could wreck your health.

Batteries. The ones in dollar stores are usually made from carbon zinc and won't last nearly as long. Choose alkaline batteries instead.

Toothpaste. Toothpaste laced with a poisonous antifreeze ingredient ended up in dollar stores around the country in 2007, prompting a massive recall. Play it safe and buy the name-brand kind at a super-market or drugstore.

Electrical products. Sure those holiday lights are dirt-cheap, but so are the wires and insulation inside them. Beware electrical items at dollar-store prices. The safety hazards they pose wipe out any savings.

Kids' toys and jewelry. The cheap versions are usually made in China and are more likely to contain lead.

Vitamins. The government doesn't regulate the quality of vitamins and supplements. The cheap ones may not contain the nutrients they claim or dissolve properly once swallowed.

Cut your weekly grocery bill 20 percent

 Budget boost this year: $1,000+

Spend some time seeking out coupons, and you'll spend considerably less at the supermarket. In fact, the Promotion Marketing Association's Coupon Council says 20 minutes of clipping can cut your weekly grocery bill 20 percent — $1,000 or more every year.

Watch sale cycles. Supermarkets put different categories of items on sale each week. One week you might see great deals on paper products, the next week on chicken. These run in 12-week cycles, but manufacturers don't want you to know this.

Keep track of the sales trends each week for 12 weeks, and you'll fig-ure out when the items you use typically go on sale. Then maximize your coupon savings. Instead of buying only what you need for the week, plan ahead and use your coupons to load up on the super-sale groceries featured each week. This coupon user's secret could save you hundreds. Here's another hint — items about to go on sale for the week often have a coupon in the weekly newspaper insert.

Get carded. More stores are moving toward loyalty cards — a card or key fob you swipe at checkout to get the sale price on products.

Sign up for one, and many stores will also mail you extra coupons and discounts on your total grocery purchase.

Go online. Sunday newspapers are no longer the only — or even the best — source for coupons.

- Print coupons straight from your computer at Web sites such as *www.coupons.com*, *www.smartsource.com*, *www.coolsavings.com*, and *www.ppgazette.com*.

- Check the manufacturer's Web site for printable coupons and free samples of new products.

- Head to *www.couponcravings.com* and *www.becentsable.net* to learn about freebie offers and in-store specials.

- Load coupons directly onto your store loyalty card at *www.shortcuts.com*, and you'll never forget to use a coupon again.

Double up. Target, Walgreens, and other retailers often run coupons good only at their stores. What you may not know is that you can use a manufacturer's coupon on top of the store coupon for even bigger savings.

SuperSaver

When you shop can be just as important as where you shop. The best days to shop for items is during the week they're on sale in the 12-week sales cycle. You'll chuckle at the spendthrifts who shop on other days. They just paid a whole lot more.

When it comes to produce, always buy it on Saturdays. Stores have just restocked their bins to gear up for weekend crowds, so it's freshest then.

Slash your food budget in 5 simple steps

 Budget boost this year: $1,800

Groceries for your family for just $2 a day per person? Discover this frugal family secret and see how it's done in the real world.

Steve and Annette Economides, who have five children, spend only about $350 a month on groceries, toiletries, and cleaning supplies. Here's how they do it.

- Plan carefully. The Economides family outdoes Santa Claus because they make a list and check it three times to make sure they only buy what they need. They also plan menus in advance to help focus their grocery list.

- Use coupons. They clip coupons and keep them organized for trips to the store.

- Scour the shelves. Using walkie-talkies, the Economides family makes a coordinated effort to search the store for last-minute bargains, like two-for-one or buy-one-get-two-free deals.

- Freeze extras. Having a lot of freezer space lets the Economides family store items they find on sale but can't eat right away.

- Stay away from credit cards. The Economides family never uses a credit card and never has to pay costly interest payments — but they do budget wisely. Figure out your monthly expenses. Once those are paid, divide your remaining funds into a house emergency fund, a recreation and vacation fund, and a fund for saving or charitable giving.

The U.S. Department of Agriculture says the average senior spends about $50 a week on groceries. That's $7 a day. But, as the Economides prove, you can pay less for groceries. If you follow the Economides' plan and spend only about $2 a day, that's a $5 savings every day. These practical tips can help you save up to $1,800 a year.

It's a telltale sign you're getting a good deal when supermarkets place a limit on sale items. The store may be selling the items at — or even below — cost. They set limits to prevent owners of smaller stores from buying a big supply of the discounted items and reselling them at a higher price. Luckily, you can take it to the limit for unbeatable savings.

Outsmart spoilage with simple storage strategies

 Budget boost this year: $440+

It doesn't matter if you get a great deal on fruits and vegetables if they go bad before you use them. How you store your food can have just as big an impact on your budget as how much you pay for it. Throwing away food is like throwing away money.

In 2006, the average American spent $592 on fruits and vegetables. Say a quarter of it spoils before you use it. You just lost $148. The same goes for dairy products, which cost about $368 a year. If one-fourth of your milk curdles or your cheese gets moldy, you're out $92. Meat, poultry, fish, and eggs cost about $800 a year. Wasting a quarter of those items means you wasted $200. These losses can really add up. But, with smarter food storage strategies, you can turn these losses into savings.

Protect your produce. Make the supermarket your last stop on your trip home so your produce doesn't sit in your car too long. And always buy fruits and vegetables in good shape — not bruised or damaged. Know which items, like tomatoes and bananas, stay better at room temperature, and store fruits and vegetables separately in your refrigerator. Wash greens when you get home, then wrap them in a paper towel and store them in a zip-lock bag. They should keep an extra three or four days.

Rotate food in your refrigerator so more perishable items get eaten first. When it comes to fruit, eat grapes and bananas first, then move on to pears, apples, and oranges, which tend to last longer. If you notice any mold on your fruits or vegetables, toss them right away so they don't contaminate other produce in your refrigerator.

Make meat last longer. Ground meat will keep one to two days in the refrigerator. After that, put it in the freezer. You can buy meat in bulk and freeze it — but it's important to label it so you know how long it's been there. For the best flavor and texture, use it within three months. One good trick is the double-wrap technique. Wrap small portions individually so you can thaw out what you need, then put the whole thing in a freezer bag.

Help for your herbs. Don't let the herbs from your herb garden go to waste. After washing and drying them, place them on a clean paper towel and microwave them for 30 to 40 seconds. Crumble the dried herbs and store them in an airtight container for up to three months. You can also store herbs, either chopped up or whole, in the freezer. Keep them in an airtight container or freezer bag. Just break off what you need and return the rest to the freezer. If you have leftover fresh ginger, the best way to store it is in your refrigerator, unwrapped.

Sidestep slip-ups. Avoid common food-storage mistakes with these foolproof fixes.

- Make sure lids and caps are very tight. Squeeze air out of bags before sealing. Sloppy wrapping could let in air and moisture.

- Rewrap supermarket meat, poultry, and cold cuts. The store wrap may look good, but it could have tiny holes.

- Match the size of your container to its contents. Too much room between the food and the lid could lead to spoilage or freezer burn.

- Keep your refrigerator set at 37 degrees Fahrenheit and your freezer at 0 degrees. If they're too warm by even a few degrees, food spoils faster.

- Use the refrigerator door compartment, which is usually 3 to 5 degrees warmer than the inside, for vinegar-based condiments, like mustard, ketchup, and relish. Keep eggs, milk, and other more delicate items in the back of the refrigerator where it's colder.

- Cool your leftovers before refrigerating them. If you put piping hot food in the refrigerator, it will warm up the foods around it.

- Pay attention to use-by dates, as well as the look and feel of your leftovers. Don't just rely on your nose. Food can be bad without smelling bad.

- Wrap smelly food thoroughly. You shouldn't be able to smell it through the wrapping or container. Otherwise, foods like milk or eggs may absorb the odors.

- Label and date your containers and take inventory regularly. You don't want to lose track of what you have — or how long you've had it.

SuperSaver

Don't get boxed in at the supermarket. Buy items in bags rather than boxes if you have a choice. Bagged foods generally cost less. Rice and cereal are two good examples of this strategy.

Pinch pennies with a perfect pantry

 Budget boost this year: $675

Why go out to eat when you can just go to your pantry? Having the right pantry items on hand saves you trips to restaurants or the grocery store and trims your takeout and delivery costs.

According to the U.S. Bureau of Labor Statistics, the average American spent nearly $2,700 on food away from home in 2006. If you eat at home just one-fourth of the time using a well-stocked pantry, you'd save $675.

With a good pantry, you'll always be able to whip up a quick, delicious, and low-cost meal right at home. As an added bonus, fewer trips to the store means less money spent on gas and less wear and tear on your car. Stock up on these essential items to save money.

- Super staples. Every kitchen needs the basics, including salt, pepper, olive oil, vegetable oil, all-purpose flour, and granulated sugar. Most likely, you have these already. Just make sure you don't run out.

- Canned goods, such as chicken and beef broth, canned tomatoes, tomato sauce, tomato paste, canned beans, and tuna.

- Starches and dry goods, like spaghetti and other pasta, egg noodles, rice, lentils, and split peas.

- Potatoes, onions, and garlic.

- Condiments, including white vinegar, balsamic vinegar, apple cider vinegar, soy sauce, Worcestershire sauce, salsa, and hot sauce.

- Spices. Every meal needs some seasoning. Keep dried basil, bay leaves, cayenne, chili powder, cumin, cinnamon, oregano, and paprika in your spice rack.

- Refrigerated items, such as eggs, milk, butter or margarine, ketchup, mustard, mayonnaise, and cheese.

- Frozen vegetables, like corn, spinach, and peas. Keep ground beef and chicken breasts in your freezer, as well.

- Baking needs, such as cornmeal, brown sugar, confectioner's sugar, honey, baking soda, baking powder, vanilla extract, cornstarch, rolled oats, nuts, raisins, and chocolate chips.

Of course, you don't have to stock your pantry all at once. You can build it gradually, taking advantage of sales, coupons, and other deals. Replenish your supplies as necessary when you make your regular trip to the grocery store.

Not sure what to make for dinner? Try an online recipe finder. With this handy tool, you can get some hints based on what you already have in your pantry. For instance, try RecipeMatcher at *www.recipematcher.com*. Just enter the items you have, and you'll get options — and with a loaded pantry, you should have plenty.

Great reasons to stop buying bottled water

 Budget boost this year: $75+

Bottled water is no safer than tap water, although it may seem to taste better. In fact, about one-fourth of bottled water is simply bottled tap water. It is, however, a lot more expensive than tap water, and the plastic used to make the bottles may leach harmful chemicals called phthalates into the water itself.

If your local water tastes funny, or if you worry about its safety, buy an inexpensive faucet or pitcher water filter. Switching from bottled water to a Brita faucet filter could save you upward of $75 a year. Look for a filter certified by NSF International, and be sure to maintain it properly, replacing the filter as recommended. Otherwise, it could actually worsen the water quality.

If you like the on-the-go convenience of bottled water, invest in a stainless steel travel bottle. Wash it between uses, and reuse it again and again.

While you're at it, ditch those pricey to-go coffees from gourmet shops, and make your own at home. The humble Eight O'Clock

brand coffee outranked all the fancy ones in *Consumer Reports*
recent taste tests. And at around $6 per pound, the price can't
be beat.

Household & utilities

Slash heating bills without sacrificing comfort

$ *Budget boost this year: $75+*

Lowering your thermostat just 5 degrees in winter can slash your heating bills $75 to $300 a year, depending on the type of fuel you use.

If you use natural gas, dropping the temperature 1 degree cuts your
usage by 5 percent, a modest $16.24 in savings each year for the
average household. Bundle up and lower the temperature 5 degrees,
and the savings stop being so modest — $81.20 a year, on average.

Best of all, you can save money no matter what kind of heating you
have — natural gas, electricity, fuel oil, or kerosene. See how fast the
dollars add up.

Lower temperature 5 degrees in winter and save

Fuel type	Natural gas	Electricity	Fuel oil	Kerosene
Drop in heating costs	25%	30%	20%	25%
Approximate savings per year	$81.20	$75.61	$318.24	$87.45

Remembering to turn down your thermostat before bed or every time you leave the house is tricky. That's why experts recommend installing an inexpensive programmable thermostat. Set your temperatures in summer and winter, and you'll save consistently all year long. The typical American household spends nearly $1,000 a year on heating and cooling costs. Setting a programmable thermostat can cut that amount an average of $180 annually.

Max out your savings by sticking to these settings. In winter, keep the thermostat set below 70 degrees in the mornings and evenings. Roll it back to 62 degrees when you leave the house and at night while sleeping. In summer, cut your electric bills the easy way. Keep the thermostat set above 78 degrees in the mornings and evenings. Bump it up to 85 degrees when you leave the house and 82 degrees at night while sleeping.

Make money off the power company

 Budget boost this year: $20+

Have the power company pay you, for a change. You heard right. Secret load management programs reward you with money on your electric bill.

On hot summer days when air conditioners run overtime, the power company strains to produce enough electricity to meet people's needs. Building more power plants can ease the pressure, but it's also expensive. Electric companies would much rather pay you, instead.

Sign up for their load management program and get instant credit on your utility bill. The power company installs a radio receiver on your air conditioner. When electricity use in your community starts to overwhelm the system, they send a signal to the remote, shutting off the AC for a few minutes. Each time they flip that switch, you earn more credits.

Georgia Power pays customers $20 to let them install the receiver, then another $2 every time they flip the "off" switch, usually a few times each summer. If the company hits the switch five times a summer, the customer earns $30 the first year, plus $10 each additional year. Call your utility and ask if they offer a similar deal.

Look for the star to cut utility costs

 Budget boost this year: $388+

The next time you need to replace anything from a light bulb to your dishwasher, invest in a product with the Energy Star label for serious cash savings. Energy Star products are guaranteed to use less energy than regular models, making them good for your wallet and the environment. If you replace all the appliances listed below with Energy Star appliances, you could save $388 or more on utilities in a year.

- Retire your old clothes washer for a new Energy Star model and trim $50 a year in utility costs by using less energy and 7,000 fewer gallons of water. Over the washer's lifetime, you'll save $550, enough to buy a brand new dryer.

- Replace your rattling pre-1992 refrigerator and save more than $100 a year. Energy Star refrigerators use 20 percent less energy than other new models and an incredible 40 percent less than those made before 2001.

- Exchange your old gas furnace for an Energy Star model and lower your heating bill 12 percent, almost $40 a year — more if you live in a cold climate.

- Install an Energy Star tank water heater and cut utility bills $30 a year, or $360 over the heater's lifetime. Large families net even bigger savings.

- Swap your old ceiling fan for an Energy Star model and cut power bills $15 a year per fan. Screw in compact fluorescent light bulbs (CFLs) for even greater savings.

- Change out a 12-year-old central air conditioner for a new Energy Star model and slash 30 percent off your cooling bills for an average savings of $123 each year.

- Ditch your pre-1994 dishwasher in favor of an Energy Star model and shave $30 a year off utility bills. These machines use 41 percent less energy than regular new models and save $90 in hot water bills over their lifetime.

Your utility companies and federal and state governments are teaming up to help you pay for Energy Star appliances. Many utilities offer rebates and low-interest financing on energy-efficient appliances. Call your utility company and ask about available programs, or search online at *www.energystar.gov* or *www.dsireusa.org*.

Federal and state governments kick in tax-based incentives, too. Head to the Web site *www.dsireusa.org*. Click on your state for state tax incentives or on the FED link for federal tax incentives. Need more help? Try the searchable database of tax incentives at *www.energytaxincentives.org*.

No computer? No problem. Call the IRS at 800-829-3676 and request Form 5695. This tax form and its instructions explain which improvements qualify for the federal energy-efficient property credit. For state tax credits, contact your state's department of revenue or taxation and ask which energy-efficient appliances and improvements qualify. Keep the store receipts, warranty information, and other product or service documents in case the IRS has questions.

Maximize your energy savings

A family living in an average, 1,800 square-foot home in Washington, D.C., built in the 1970s, would save a whopping $595 a year on utilities just by upgrading to Energy Star appliances. That's $6,701 in savings over the appliances' lifetimes.

Best of all, they wouldn't have to upgrade all at once. Simply replacing worn out appliances when they break down with new, Energy Star models can make a huge difference in the long run, without blowing the family budget. Some appliances will even pay for themselves.

Appliance	Annual savings	Appliance's lifetime savings
Clothes washer	$68	$596
Gas furnace and programmable thermostat	$290	$3,675
Tank water heater	$28	$364
Two light fixtures	$21	$279
Ceiling fan with CFL bulbs	$32	$258
Central air conditioner with programmable thermostat	$95	$1,002
Dishwasher	$29	$250
Refrigerator	$8	$85
Spare freezer	$9	$83

Get free energy-saving home improvements

 Budget boost this year: $358+

You can get $6,500 worth of energy-saving improvements made to your house for free and save more than $358 a year on your energy bill through the Weatherization Assistance Program — regardless of whether you rent or own, live in an apartment, mobile home, or single-family home.

This program works to make the homes of low-income families more energy-efficient, reducing their energy bills — as well as their need for government assistance. So far, 5.6 million families have benefited from Weatherization Assistance. Your family could be next.

Early in its history, the program focused on cheap improvements, like adding weatherstripping to doors and windows. Now, it does much more. If you qualify, you'll get a sophisticated home-energy analysis and whole-house solutions, such as insulating the attic and walls. An expert will also measure carbon monoxide, mold, and moisture levels and fix these hazards.

States have different standards for who qualifies. People receiving Supplemental Security Income or Aid to Families with Dependent Children automatically qualify. Some states give preference to seniors, but you still need to meet income limits set by your state.

The National Energy Assistance Referral (NEAR) project can put you in touch with weatherization assistance programs in your area. Call NEAR toll-free at 866-674-6327. If you don't qualify for weatherization help, you may still qualify for the Low Income Home Energy Assistance Program (LIHEAP). It offers short-term help paying utility bills and may provide some free weatherization. Contact NEAR for LIHEAP information, too.

Save hundreds on energy bill — with a spray can

 Budget boost this year: $230

Sealing air leaks with spray foam, caulk, and weatherstripping is one of the most cost-effective ways to cut energy use and keep more money in your pocket. Plug those leaks and trim 10 percent off your energy bill, for an average savings of $230 a year. Beat the summertime heat and winter cold — and power bills — with these energy-saving tips. Use the extra money on your vacation instead of your bills.

Spot sneaky leaks. Incense isn't just for churches. Light a stick and hold it next to windows, doors, plumbing and ceiling fixtures, attic hatches, and electrical outlets. If the smoke blows sideways, you've found a leak. Look, too, for dirty spots in exposed insulation. These indicate a hole nearby where air sneaks into and out of your house. Dirty spots on ceiling paint and carpet may point to leaks at wall/ceiling joints and wall/floor joists.

Seal them tight. Canned spray foam plugs leaky holes in exterior walls, while caulk and weatherstripping make doors and windows airtight. Line exterior doors with a flexible sealing gasket along the bottom. Seal exposed air duct joints and connections with aluminum tape and mastic, available in home improvement stores. While you're at it, wrap R6 or higher insulation around exposed ducts in unheated attics and basements.

Check the attic. Poorly insulated attics lose lots of heated and cooled air. Take a peak in yours. If you can look down the length of it and easily see the floor joists, you need more insulation. Most attics need 10 to 14 inches, depending on the type of insulation used. Blow it in loose or buy fiberglass batts or blankets to bring it up to snuff.

THE NEXT STEP

Energy audits are a lot more fun than IRS audits. And unlike tax audits, they can save you money. Plus, easy-to-use online tools let you do one yourself, for free.

- Home Energy Saver at *hes.lbl.gov*

- Energy Guide at *www.energyguide.com*. Click on "Analyze your use," then on "In-Depth Analysis."

- Alliance to Save Energy's Home Energy Checkup at *www.ase.org/content/article/detail/971*

Slash your electric bill with CFLs

 Budget boost this year: $50

Compact fluorescent light (CFL) bulbs use one-quarter the electricity of regular bulbs and last up to 10 times longer, saving on energy and replacement bulbs. Replace the five bulbs you use most often, and save $50 a year off the cost of electricity and replacement bulbs. That's $375 over the life of these bulbs. CFLs can even cut your cooling costs, because they put out 75 percent less heat than incandescent lights. Plus, they are less of a fire hazard.

For recessed canister lights, buy reflector CFLs, not the spiral-shaped type. Lights on a dimmer-switch or in a 3-way fixture also take special CFLs. Just like regular bulbs, CFLs come in different shades of light. Look for the Correlated Color Temperature (CCT) on the package. Buy bulbs with a CCT between 2700K and 3000K for a soft-white appearance, and those with 3500K or higher for a "bright" or "daylight" look. And don't go by the wattage listed on CFL packages. Instead, shop by lumens, the amount of light the bulb puts out.

SuperSaver

Bigger isn't better when it comes to window ACs. It's just more expensive. An AC's cooling capacity is measured in British Thermal Units, or BTUs. Figure out how many BTUs you need, then buy the right unit.

- Multiply the room's square footage times 20 BTUs.

- Add 600 BTUs for each additional person who will use the room, not counting yourself.

- Add another 10 percent for sunny rooms, or subtract 10 percent for shady rooms.

- Add 4,000 more BTUs for kitchen units.

Plug the leak in your bank account

 Budget boost this year: $50

Ever poured money down a toilet? If your toilet ever leaked, you have. The same goes for faucets and shower heads. The average American home loses 11,000 gallons of water each year. One in 10 loses three times that much. Experts say simple repairs can save the typical family 10 percent on their water and sewer bills — about $50 a year.

Some leaks are easy to spot. Noise from a dripping faucet or running toilet are sure signs. Others are silent and harder to detect. Try these tricks to catch leaks in the act.

- Turn off your ice maker and don't run any water for two hours. Check the reading on the water meter at the start of two hours and again at the end. If the number has changed, chances are you have a leak.

- Review your January or February water bill. A family of four should use less than 12,000 gallons of water a month during the winter. Higher usage suggests a leak.

- Drop food dye in the toilet tank and let it sit a few minutes. If the coloring shows up in the bowl, you have a leak. Flush before it stains the bowl.

If you decide to tackle plumbing problems yourself, remember to turn off the water before removing pipes and fixtures. Take the pieces with you to the hardware store to make sure you get the right size replacements.

Pull the plug on runaway water bills

 Budget boost this year: $90

Toss old, water-hogging toilets and save big bucks. Flushing toilets make up the biggest use of water inside your home. Chances are, if your home was built before 1992, your bank account would benefit from buying high-efficiency toilets. Models sold today need as little as 1.3 gallons per flush — less than half the water of old toilets.

The savings are significant. For each 3.5 gallon toilet you replace, you could reap $90 a year in water and sewer savings, or $2,000 over the toilet's lifetime. Replace three and knock $270 a year off your water bill.

The Environmental Protection Agency gives its WaterSense label to low-flow toilets that need only 1.3 gallons per flush, but 1.6-gallon models are also easy to find. Look for rebates, too, from your local utility or watershed management agency.

Can't afford a new, low-flow toilet? Make your own. Place a clean, empty 2-liter soda bottle inside the tank of a 3.5 or 5 gallon toilet. Let the bottle fill with water, then replace the tank lid. Now every time you flush, you'll save 2 liters of water. These handy tips can further cut your use.

- Switch from water sprinklers to drip irrigation. One-third of the water used by the average home goes toward landscaping. Drip irrigation uses as little as half the water sprinklers do, saving you $1,150 over the system's lifetime.

- Buy a faucet aerator for $5 and save thousands of gallons of water every year.

- Install a low-flow shower head and cut shower water use in half. Low-flow heads use 2.5 gallons per minute, while regular heads use 5 gallons.

Go tankless to save

 Budget boost this year: $115+

The average American home spends $400 to $600 a year just on heating water for showers, dishes, laundry, and other chores. That's why switching to a tankless water heater can knock $115 or more off your energy bill each year. They heat water only as you need it, instead of storing it and constantly keeping it hot.

They cost a little more to install than traditional storage water heaters, but the money you save will soon pay you back. They also last longer, up to 20 years, nearly twice as long as tank heaters. Plus, there's no danger of them springing a leak and flooding your home.

Talk your way to lower phone bills

 Budget boost this year: $240+

Telephones can eat up a big chunk of your budget. Going without is out of the question, but you can cut your cost in half without sacrificing service.

Do away with long distance. With all the choices out there, who needs regular long-distance anymore? Calling cards, toll-free services, and dial-around plans offer cheaper rates in many cases. Consider these companies for starters.

- TEL3Advantage, a dial-around long-distance service. Visit them online at *www.3longdistance.com* or call 800-441-0295.

- GetPIN, a long-distance service that uses Personal Identification Numbers (PINs). Go to *www.getpin.com* or call 877-GET-PIN1.

- Calling Cards Home, a calling card provider with different plans based on how many long-distance calls you make. Check them out at *www.callingcardshome.com*.

Once you find a service you like, cut back your landline phone to the basic, local-calling package and watch your phone bill drop by half. Keep in mind, store-bought calling cards usually have expiration dates and charge connection fees, so you may not be getting as good a deal as you thought. And if you lose the card, you lose the minutes, too. Also, check for hidden fees in any card or long-distance service before signing up.

Switch to a cell phone. Ditching your landline and going completely cellular can net you a pretty penny. If you already have a cell phone, you can save $30 to $50 a month, or $360 to $600 a year by getting rid of the landline. If you don't yet have a cell phone, you'll at least break even by getting one.

Many national cell phone carriers offer free long distance with a basic calling plan. Not a bad deal, as long as you don't use more minutes than your plan allows. Exceed your minutes and you'll pay through the nose.

Prepaid phones, like TracFone and Net10, take the surprise out of cell phone bills. Long distance may not be free, but it's likely cheaper than with a landline carrier. Read the fine print carefully. You may use up your money faster with daytime calls than evening calls. Fees and roaming charges may apply, too, which can eat into your prepaid cash.

Not all rural areas support 911 cell phone service, so consider carefully before canceling your landline if you live in these areas.

Buy in bundles. Bundling phone, cable, and Internet services can shave $20 a month off these bills, for a total of $240 a year, in addition to any rebates you get for bundling. As with anything, read the fine print before you sign up. The low introductory rates may shoot up after a short lead-in period, and you may have to sign a contract. Taxes and hidden fees can also push the rates higher than advertised.

Get back to basics. Drop the fancy bells and whistles from your home phone. Ask yourself if you really need caller ID or call waiting, or the ability to surf the Internet on your cell phone. Call the service provider to find out how much you'd save by ditching these extras. A basic landline phone usually runs about $22 a month, but added extras can easily double the price.

A wet cell phone isn't the end of the world. Try drying it out before you replace it. Remove the battery and wipe off any water. Shake out the phone, then unscrew the back. Gently clean the insides with a cotton swab dipped in rubbing alcohol or a cleaning spray made for electrical contact. Let the phone sit until completely dry. Wait another 24 hours before turning it on again.

Earn money on old cell phones

 Budget boost this year: $100

You could make up to $100 in cash or gift cards by trading in your old cell phone, thanks to a new crop of companies. With Flipswap, for instance, you can exchange your phone at a brick-and-mortar store for credit or online for cash.

Head to the Web site *www.flipswap.com* and type in your ZIP code. You'll get a list of nearby Flipswap businesses that accept used cell phones, including Best Buy. Take your phone in, and the store will accept it as a trade-in or give you store credit. Be warned, not all phones have value. If yours doesn't, simply tell the store to trade it for a tree. Flipswap will recycle the phone, and CarbonFund.org will plant a tree on your behalf.

If you want cash, trade it in online. Go to the Flipswap Web site and type in your phone's make and model. The site will tell you its value, and you can choose how you want the money — as a check, Amazon.com gift card, or charity donation. Next, print out the pre-paid postage label and mail in the phone. Shipping is free, but Flipswap recommends buying tracking or insurance for the phone.

This company has some competition, and shopping around could net you a better trade-in deal. Compare Flipswap with offers from *www.greenphone.com* and *www.cellforcash.com*.

Phones are refurbished and sold around the world, or recycled if they can't be reused. Take a few smart precautions before swapping in your phone. Erase everyone in your Contacts list and delete all text messages, photos, and personal information.

Housing

Top tips for making your home irresistible to buyers

 Budget boost this year: $13,700

Small improvements bring the biggest returns when selling your house. Forget massive renovations like adding bedrooms or baths. These rarely pay for themselves. It's the little things, like cleaning and decluttering your home, that reel in big bucks. Best of all, they're cheap or free.

HomeGain.com, a Web site for homeowners trying to maximize their home's value, surveyed more than 2,000 real estate agents around the country. They found that these inexpensive improvements give you the biggest bang for your buck.

Clean and declutter. Simply deep-cleaning your home and getting rid of excess stuff could boost your sale price almost $2,000.

- Don't just do your regular cleaning. Get down and dirty, scrubbing tile grout and removing stains. At the least, your kitchen and bath should sparkle.

- Sell or store extra furniture to make rooms seem bigger.

- Remove all appliances from your kitchen counter, including your toaster and microwave, to create a spacious-looking kitchen.

- Move everything out of stairwells and hallways, and clean all the junk off your front and back porches or patio.

- Tackle your closets, pantries, storage rooms, bathroom vanities, and cabinets. Organize, donate, or toss items to get these areas looking clean and uncluttered.

- Take down personal photographs and possessions while your house is on the market.

Create a sense of light. Spending $200 to $300 here can net you up to $1,500 in return. The right lighting can make a room feel larger and more comfortable. Increase the natural light coming in by opening blinds and curtains and taking down dark, heavy drapes. Clean windows inside and out, and trim back any trees or shrubs that block the light. Get outside lights working and turn them on at night.

Paint the town. Next, invest in a little paint. It's a low-cost improvement with a huge impact. HomeGain says painting the inside alone can boost your home's value nearly $2,200. Paint the interior light, neutral colors that will appeal to everyone. Whitewash or paint over dark paneling.

Set the stage. Home staging is the art of dressing up your house to its best advantage by decluttering, rearranging furniture, and adding little touches that make a house feel like a home to would-be buyers. Putting just $400 to $500 dollars into staging can return as much as $2,400 when you sell.

Simply rearranging furniture can help, but consider renting more modern furnishings if yours are old or in bad shape. Invest in inexpensive touches, like luxurious bedding and fresh flowers, to reel in the offers. You can hire a professional home stager to either advise you or do it for you.

Clean the carpet. Save yourself a chunk of change by cleaning your carpet instead of replacing it. If it's not faded or noticeably damaged, simply rent a carpet shampooer from the store or hire a pro. You'll earn back about $2,000. Tack down loose carpet, replace worn patches, and be sure to remove any pet smells.

Fix up the floors. Raise your home's sale price as much as $2,000 by sanding and refinishing hardwood floors, cleaning and waxing linoleum, and driving finished nails into creaky areas to silence them.

Solve electrical and plumbing problems. Nothing spells trouble to buyers like lights that won't turn on, doorbells that don't ring, or toilets that run constantly. Spend a few hundred dollars now fixing these problems upfront. You'll save yourself the hassle of fixing them after the home inspection, plus sell your home faster and for up to $1,600 more.

THE NEXT STEP

Picking out paint colors, tile, and other materials may feel like the hardest part of any remodel, but these Web sites make it easy — for free.

- Get help choosing colors, tiles, counters, cabinets, and more at *www.move.com*.

- See how paint colors will look before buying them at *www.behr.com* and *www.sherwin-williams.com*.

- Find general how-to and decorating advice at *www.hgtv.com*.

- Uncover expert advice on doing it yourself at *www.diynetwork.com* and *www.thisoldhouse.com*.

9 no-nonsense ways to add value to your home

 Budget boost this year: $2,150

How your home looks on the outside will decide whether buyers bother to see the inside. Make a good first impression and increase your home's value up to $2,150 with some simple outdoor cleanup and landscaping. The best part is it doesn't have to cost a fortune. You can do most of it yourself and spend just a few hundred dollars on plants and repairs. If you plan to sell soon, tackle these projects right away.

- Cut back overgrown trees and shrubs that hide your house.

- Keep the lawn mowed, shrubs trimmed, and walkways edged while your home is on the market.

- Weed flower beds and pull out dead and dying plants.

- Rake leaves and clean up trash in your front and back yards.

- Stack firewood neatly for a quaint, cozy look.

- Repair the fence and take down warning signs, such as "Beware of Dog."

- Keep walkways and driveway swept and weeded.

- Replace your welcome mat.

- Add colorful potted flowers and plants around the front door and porch.

If you're selling in a few years instead of right away, you have time to really perk up your home's curb appeal. Hire a landscape designer to draw up a three-year or five-year plan for your yard, then do the work yourself. You'll pay a few hundred dollars for a professional's help but save thousands of dollars in labor. The result — a professionally designed yard for a fraction of the cost.

THE NEXT STEP

Find the best interest rates on a new home loan with the handy Homebuyer's Mortgage Kit. It lists recent mortgage rates and application fees, explains the meaning behind points and fees, and can help you choose the right type of loan for you. Call HSH Associates, Financial Publishers at 800-UPDATES to order the kit for $20, plus shipping and handling.

Secrets to selling your home without an agent

 Budget boost this year: $6,000+

Skipping the real estate agent and selling your house yourself can save $6,000 to $12,000 on a $200,000 home, or 3 to 6 percent of its value. The savings come because you don't have to pay a selling agent, although you may still owe the buyer's agent their cut.

People taking the "For Sale By Owner" route (FSBO) get at least as much money for their homes as agents do, although their homes tend to take longer to sell, according to a study from Northwestern University and the University of Wisconsin-Madison.

Going it alone takes a lot of hard work, time, and energy. You will have to set an asking price, market the house yourself, hold open houses, and be available to show it at any time of day. On top of that, you'll need to negotiate with the buyers and hire a real estate attorney to handle the legal documents.

Start by deciding if it's worthwhile. To figure out how much you could save going FSBO, first find out your home's value. Then multiply it times 0.03, since you may only save yourself 3 percent of its value. If you decide to take the plunge, begin with this advice.

Set a realistic price. Don't set the price based on how much you want for your home or how much money you need. Set it based on hard facts — what similar homes have sold for recently in your area. You can do this several ways.

- Hire an appraiser to do the work for you. For a few hundred dollars, you will have hard evidence of what your home is worth in the current market.

- Find the latest sales prices at the county records office. Look for homes with a similar number of square feet, bathrooms, bedrooms, and other details.

- Get a ballpark figure at Web sites such as *www.zillow.com* and *www.homegain.com*, but don't rely on these prices alone. They aren't accurate enough to determine your asking price.

List with MLS. Sticking a sign in your yard won't sell your house. Too few people will see it. If you're serious about selling, you need to list your home with the Multiple Listing Service, the same database real estate agents use. Pay a licensed Realtor a flat fee to list it for you at Web sites such as *www.flatfeemlslisting.com* or *www.owners.com*. FSBO sellers who list their home through the MLS could save more than $5,000 in commissions on a $222,000 home.

Protect your interests. Look out for yourself. Before you accept a buyer's offer, get a good-faith deposit of at least $1,000, along with a pre-approval letter from their lender.

Hire legal help. Pay an experienced real estate attorney or title company to finalize the deal and draw up the closing documents. It pays to make sure the sale is airtight.

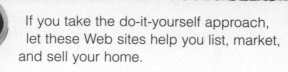

If you take the do-it-yourself approach, let these Web sites help you list, market, and sell your home.

- www.forsalebyowner.com

- www.owners.com

- www.salebyownerrealty.com

- www.homesbyowner.com

- www.10realty.com

Take advantage of free foreclosure counseling

Budget boost this year: $2,528+

You've seen the ads of foreclosure counseling companies that promise to negotiate with your lender and save your home — for a fee, of course. Don't plunk down precious money. The Office of Housing and Urban Development (HUD) offers free counseling that will do the same thing.

For-fee companies typically charge two to three months worth of mortgage payments. If you own a $200,000 home and your mortgage payment is $1,264 a month, you'd save between $2,528 and $3,792 by getting free help. Call 800-569-4287 to get in touch with HUD-approved housing counselors. They can explain your options if you have defaulted on your loan, have credit issues, or face foreclosure. Plus, they'll help you organize your finances and represent you in negotiations with your lender.

Try these tactics if you have spoken to a housing counselor and your lender still won't work with you.

- For conventional home loans, call the Homeowner's Hope Hotline at 888-995-HOPE, operated by Hope Now, an alliance of housing counselors, mortgage companies, investors, and others that offers free help preventing foreclosure.

- For loans insured by the Federal Housing Administration (FHA), contact the FHA's National Servicing Center at 888-297-8685.

- For VA-insured loans, call 800-729-5772 and ask to speak with a Loan Service Representative.

Whatever you do, don't ignore the problem. Return phone calls and letters from your lender. They may be willing to negotiate your mortgage in order to save your home. The longer you wait and the further you fall behind, the harder it will be to work out a deal.

A housing counselor can probably help only if you have missed one or two payments. You may need an attorney if you are further behind. Luckily, a number of programs offer free or low-cost legal aid.

- Call your state's Bar Association and ask about pro bono — or free — help for homeowners.

- Area Agencies on Aging also offer free legal advice to people over age 60. Find your local AAA by calling 800-677-1116.

- The Legal Services Corporation (LSC), a private, nonprofit corporation, hires staff attorneys to help people who cannot afford a lawyer. Check your telephone directory for an LSC office near you.

ALERT!

Foreclosure is frightening, but don't let con artists prey on your fears. Scammers may contact you posing as "mortgage consultants" or a "foreclosure service," claiming they can stop the foreclosure immediately if you just sign one document. Unfortunately, you may be signing over your deed, and you'll instantly lose possession of your home. Seek professional advice from an attorney, real estate agent, or HUD-approved housing counselor before signing anything.

10 ways to save on home insurance

 Budget boost this year: $76+

Easily shave hundreds of dollars off your homeowner's policy. You must ask your agent about these 10 home insurance discounts. These breaks could be saving you money every month for the rest of your life.

- Install smoke detectors to get at least 5 percent off your premiums, or $76 annually off an average $1,519 homeowner's policy. Quitting smoking could lower them even further.

- Bundle your policies — home, auto, life — with the same insurer for another 5 to 15 percent ($76 to $228) savings. Shop around first to make sure you'll save money by switching insurers.

- Alert your insurer to neighborhood changes that make your home safer, like having a fire hydrant added within 100 feet of your home or getting a nearby fire department substation.

- Have a home security system and deadbolt locks installed and save at least 5 percent — $76 a year. Ask your insurer which alarm systems qualify.

- Pipe in a sprinkler system to cut your premiums. Combine it with high-quality burglar and fire alarms for a possible savings of 15 to 20 percent off your policy, or $228 to $304 annually. Not every insurance company offers a sprinkler system discount. Check first and buy the one they recommend.

- Update your heating, electrical, and plumbing systems. Improving those more than 10 years old could net you a discount.

- Stick with the same insurer, as long as you are happy and getting a good deal. You could earn long-term customer discounts, like 5 percent off premiums after three to five years ($76 savings), and 10 percent off after six years ($152 savings).

- Tell your insurance agent when you retire. Since retirees are home more, they're less likely to be burglarized and may spot fires sooner. They also tend to have more time to maintain their homes — all of which can save you up to 10 percent a year ($152) if you are at least age 55.

- Keep your credit rating high. A strong credit history and high score can cut your insurance costs. Pay bills on time, and keep credit card and debt balances low.

- Disaster-proof your home based on your region. Retrofitting an older home to withstand earthquakes in earthquake-prone areas or adding storm shutters or hurricane-resistant glass in other areas can really cut your insurance costs.

Cheap ways to burglar proof your home

 Budget boost this year: $1,440

Burglars look for the easiest house to break into. If it takes more than four or five minutes to get in, they give up and move on. Make yours a challenge without shelling out $1,200 to buy and install an alarm system, plus $240 or more a year for monitoring.

- Don't rely on window thumb locks alone. For double-hung windows, drill a hole at an angle where the upper and lower frames overlap. Drill through the top of the lower frame and part-way through the bottom of the upper frame. Insert a removable nail or eyebolt to "pin" the window closed.

- Install deadbolt locks, not door chains, on exterior doors.

- Slide a dowel or broomstick into the track of sliding glass doors.

- Give the spare key to a trusted neighbor instead of hiding it outside the house.

- Install outdoor lights, like flood or landscaping lights. Outfit them with motion detectors or leave them on at night.

- Keep trees and shrubs trimmed back from the house so they don't give thieves cover to break in.

- Arrange valuables inside your home, including flat panel TVs, computers, or antiques, so they can't be seen from the window.

Medical & health

Great vision deals for the uninsured

 Budget boost this year: $200+

Most health insurance plans and Medicare don't pay for much eye care. So what can you do?

Buy online. Beat the high prices of expensive eye-care boutiques by shopping the discounters. You'll get a great pair of glasses at a fraction of the price, easily saving $200 or more. Here are a few to try.

- *www.zennioptical.com.* Prescription eyeglasses for just eight bucks? You bet — and you can get them no matter where you live. Bifocals start at $25, while progressive lenses are as low as $37. Simply pick the frames and lenses you want, enter information about your prescription, and place your order. You'll pay $4.95 per order shipping and handling, and you may have to wait a few weeks before your glasses are delivered. But it's a great deal compared to the local optical shop where you'd probably spend around $200 to $400.

- *www.39dollarglasses.com.* If you want cheap glasses but don't want to wait, try this Web site. You get frames, lenses, and even next-day delivery if you want.

- *www.eyebuydirect.com.* Again, glasses are inexpensive at this discount site. Plus you'll get a money-back guarantee.

Check out 3 for free. These groups can help you get an eye exam and provide glasses free or at a greatly reduced price.

- Vision USA. This program, run by the American Optometric Association (AOA), provides free eye care to uninsured and low-income workers and their family members who need it. Contact Vision USA at 800-766-4466 or *www.aoa.org*.

- Lions Club. The "Give the Gift of Sight" program can help you find free or discounted eye care. Call 800-747-4448 or see *www.lionsclubs.org* to get contact information for your local Lions Club office.

- EyeCare America. The American Academy of Ophthalmology sponsors the Seniors EyeCare Program, which finds eye exams for people who can't afford it. To qualify, you must be 65 or older, not have seen an ophthalmologist within three years, and lack vision insurance. Contact 800-222-3937 for more information.

ALERT!

> It's OK to use those cheap over-the-counter reading eyeglasses for short periods if you break or lose your regular glasses. Wearing nonprescription glasses may cause eyestrain but shouldn't cause any permanent damage. But for long-term use, experts say it's better to get prescription lenses.

Clip coupons for cheaper drugs

 Budget boost this year: $180+

A recent survey found one in seven Americans has skipped a needed prescription because they couldn't afford to fill it. Low prices on common generic drugs have helped many people get their medications on the cheap — as little as $4 a month. But what if your drug is not available in a generic? Then it may be time to start clipping coupons.

Check out these two Web sites where you can get coupons for brand-name drugs.

- *www.optimizerx.com.* You'll have to register and sign in, but the service is free. Then you'll be routed to various offers for discounts on the drug you need.

- *www.internetdrugcoupons.com.* Find a coupon for the drug you need, and you may get up to 40 percent off name-brand drugs.

What does that mean in real dollars? If you're a man who takes Flomax every day, a 40 percent-off coupon could save you around $33 a month or $396 per year. Or you may find a special for $25 for a 30-day supply, a savings that adds up to $696 per year. If you take Lipitor for high cholesterol, you can cash in with a coupon that takes $180 a year off your drug costs.

Take your coupon to several stores to see where you can get the best deal. Just remember that you can't use coupons for generic drugs or any drugs you get through a state or federal program, including Medicare.

SuperSaver

Check your health insurance policy to see if you get a discount for belonging to a gym. This benefit is sometimes offered because healthier people cost less to insure.

Online MDs save time and money

 Budget boost this year: $510

How would you like a private visit with your doctor from the comfort of your home, paid by your insurance no less? If you have a computer, such an unlikely scenario is entirely possible.

"Virtual" doctor visits work best for mild conditions or to find out if you should go to an emergency room or simply schedule a visit with your regular doctor. To meet a doctor online, both you and the physician need a Web cam — a camera attached to the computer so you can see each other on the screen. Picture the videophone from the old George Jetson cartoons, and you'll get the idea. The doctor will check your medical chart before the visit, so she'll know your history.

Some health insurance companies are joining the trend of offering online doctor visits. If you use Blue Cross/Blue Shield in Hawaii, your online doctor visit costs just $10. Even people without health insurance can save money by seeing a physician online rather than getting help at their local emergency room. Besides avoiding the usual long wait, you can easily save $510 without leaving the house. You'll pay a small fee of around $50, but that beats the average ER visit cost of $560.

Quick clinics offer low-cost option

A drugstore health clinic is a cheap choice if you prefer to see someone face to face. Many drugstores offer clinics staffed by nurse practitioners. You can find help quickly for common illnesses, get flu shots, and have a prescription filled all at once. Walgreens, CVS Pharmacy, and Wal-Mart are all expanding in-store health clinics. You can use your health insurance or pay less than $60 for a typical visit.

An even cheaper option for routine health care is your local health department. You can get shots or tests, like blood pressure screening or a prostate test, for next to nothing.

Easy way to save on hospital bill

 Budget boost this year: $1,200

The less time spent in a hospital, the better. That's true for your wallet as well as for your happiness.

If you can avoid checking in to a hospital over a weekend or on a holiday, you may save as much as $1,200 a day. That's the typical cost for one day in the hospital. You probably won't get treated over a weekend. Instead, you'll just lie in bed and wait for the next regular working day. So unless it's an emergency, don't check in early. If you're scheduled to have tests or elective surgery, check in as close to the procedure as possible.

THE NEXT STEP

Some experts say you'll get better care at a hospital that treats lots of people with your particular condition. If you have computer access, you can easily get that information. Navigate to *www.hospitalcompare.hhs.gov*, and enter information about your condition and how far you're willing to travel. You'll get a list of specialty hospitals. You'll also find survey results about patient satisfaction, quality of care, and Medicare treatment.

Personal & leisure

Unbeatable way to read for free

 Budget boost this year: $306

Clear your shelves of old books you'll never read again, and save money on new books. You can get all the reading material you want for next to nothing by swapping books through PaperbackSwap.com.

Get in the game. Here's how it works. Register at the Web site *www.paperbackswap.com*, and post at least 10 books you're willing to swap. This gets you two book credits. You can use these credits to request books from other members. With more than 3 million books available, you're sure to find something you want to read. After you request a book, the other member pays for the postage and sends it to you for free. In return, you ship your posted books out when another member requests one. Because you can use media mail, postage often costs less than $2.50.

Savor the savings. Books aren't cheap. The average family of four spends around $136 a year on reading material. You can easily spend $15 on a single paperback book. If you swap and read two books a month instead of buying them, you'll save more than $306 a year.

Bag the bonus benefits. It's not all about saving money. Joining PaperbackSwap.com nets you these other rewards.

- less clutter as you find new homes for old books

- option to trade in regular-print books for large-print versions

- search engine that helps you find other titles by your favorite author. You can also find new authors by searching within a genre.

- free birthday and Christmas presents for family and friends

- opportunity to also swap hardcover books, audio books, and textbooks

THE **NEXT STEP**

Read part of a new book for free, then decide if you want to buy it. Sign up at *www.dearreader.com* and you'll get excerpts of a new book sent to your e-mail every day. It's five minutes of daily reading, one new book a week. You can pick a genre that interests you, like classic literature or general nonfiction. You'll also see daily columns by club founder Suzanne Beecher.

Skip hidden fees and watch movies for free

 Budget boost this year: $200

Think you're saving money by renting movies to watch at home rather than going to the theater? Maybe so, but you can do better. You pay around $4 to rent a movie every Friday night. That's $200 gone at the end of the year.

When you think about it, that rental charge may be just the tip of the iceberg. Look out for these other fees.

- Late fees. Even at certain Blockbuster franchises that advertise "no late fees," you'll still pay for tardiness. After a certain amount of time, you automatically buy the overdue movie. Goodbye $40.

- Restocking fees. That's what you pay instead of a late fee if you return a long-overdue Blockbuster movie. You're probably out around $1.25 per movie.

- Fees for additional days. Renting from Redbox — DVD vending machines in certain big stores — costs just $1 a day. But if you return the movie late, you pay for each additional day.

- Use it or lose it. Netflix lets you pick a plan for rentals, paying as little as $4.99 per month to rent up to two videos. It's a great deal when you use it. But skip a month, and you're still out the five bucks.

Instead, head to the public library and save $200 a year by letting your tax money work for you. Your library probably has lots of VHS tapes and DVD movies you can take home for free — just like library books. You may not be able to see new films right when they're released, but so what? You'll still have a steady supply of new-to-you entertainment. Just return them by the due date so you don't end up paying library fines.

Watch a movie when you want — no hassle, no cost. Try these Web sites that offer free viewing of full-length movies and TV shows. Some require registration, and some include commercials. Watching movies on your computer works best if you have a high-speed Internet connection rather than a slower dial-up connection.

- *www.hulu.com*

- *www.watch-movies-links.net*

- *www.snagfilms.com*

- *www.veoh.com*

Usher your way to fabulous shows

 Budget boost this year: $1,200

Live theater, concerts, and comedy shows are expensive, but you can often get in for free if you're willing to do a little work.

Ushering is a fairly easy job. You just have to arrive early to take tickets and hand out programs. You'll also help the guests find their seats, then perhaps clean up after the show. In return, you get to see the performance without paying for it, although you may have to sit in whatever seat is available or even stand. You may even get a free drink or snack from the concession stand during your shift.

Just how much do you save? It's not uncommon for a ticket to an off-Broadway show or big-name concert to sell for $100 or more. If you see just one show a month as a volunteer usher, that savings adds up to $1,200 a year in your pocket — plus you get high-quality entertainment.

Ushering is a great way to see shows for free in many theaters across the country — even in New York City. But you probably can't see an actual Broadway show this way, because most Broadway theaters hire union ushers. Call the box office of a theater you want to work at to see what is needed.

Save your dimes on dining out

 Budget boost this year: $600

A recent Zagat survey found the average diner eats out 3.3 times a week and spends $33.23 on dinner. That can really add up.

Take restaurant food home. Next time you crave that special version of pasta Alfredo from your favorite Italian restaurant, pick up the phone. You can enjoy your favorite meal and some real savings as well. Just bring it home to eat, and you'll skip the extras that can inflate your bill. For example:

- Drinks. Alcohol and soft drinks can really run up your tab.

- Salad. You can probably make a better one at home.

- Appetizer and dessert. Who needs these diet-busters, anyway?

- Tip. That's 15 percent saved, just for carrying your own plate to the table.

Restaurant entree portions are usually more than you need in a single meal. Take one portion home, and split it with your favorite dining companion, or save the leftovers for another meal.

How much can you save? Let's say you took your husband out for Italian food, sharing an appetizer and ordering two salads, entrees, desserts, and glasses of wine. Add a tip, and you'll easily spend $80. But get your takeout entree to split, and add all the extras at home, and you'll probably pay around $25. That's a $55 savings — on basically the same meal. Do it once a month and you save more than $600 a year.

Go out with a plan. But what if it's the whole restaurant experience that you enjoy? You can't really get that at home. Try these other tips to help you save when you eat out.

- Look for a restaurant with early-bird specials or senior discounts.

- Go out for breakfast or lunch rather than dinner.

- Find a local culinary school with an on-site restaurant.

- If you take the grandchildren, find a restaurant with a children's menu or "kids eat free" night.

- Clip a coupon from your local newspaper or the Internet.

SuperSaver

Do you like to try new foods but hate to pay high restaurant prices? How about organizing a gourmet dinner club? Once a month, members take turns making a meal for the rest of the group. Or, the appointed "chef" can make the main course and have others bring side dishes. It's more fun than a restaurant and is sure to produce some memorable meals.

8 cheap dates for you and your honey

 Budget boost this year: $540

Just because your nest is empty doesn't mean you can't take your lovebird on a date. Try these free or nearly free ways of spending time together. You'll bring back the romance in no time.

- Have a picnic at a local park. You can stargaze if it's nighttime or people watch during the day.

- Be a tourist in your own town. Get a guidebook from the library, and see what you've been missing.

- Visit a local winery that offers free tasting and tours.

- Share some exercise and fresh air by enjoying a hike or bike ride.

- Cook a homemade meal together, then go out for coffee and dessert.

- Visit an inexpensive museum, historical site, botanical garden, or zoo. Look for the occasional free day that most offer.

- Attend a poetry reading or lecture.

- Find a local horse show, and watch owners ride and exhibit their beautiful animals.

All of these ideas beat the typical dinner-and-a-movie date. With movie tickets around $7 and a nice dinner easily topping $80, you'll save $90 by using a little creativity. Enjoy a "cheap" date six times a year, and you'll keep $540 in your annual budget.

Cut the high cost of dry cleaning

 Budget boost this year: $468

You try to avoid buying clothes labeled "dry clean only," but sometimes you can't resist. You can still save money by cleaning some of those items yourself.

Pick up a kit. Not all garments labeled for dry cleaning really need professional care every time. Home dry-cleaning kits like Dryel, FreshCare, and Dry Cleaners Secret can help you save money. Most kits include a bottle of stain remover, some cleaning sheets, and a few dryer-safe plastic bags. You place a dry-cleaning sheet in a plastic bag with a couple of garments, then put it all in the dryer for 10 to 30 minutes. Remove the garments immediately and hang them to prevent wrinkling.

The kits are best used to freshen up garments. You'll pay around 60 cents per item of clothing when you use a kit, compared to around $5 per item at the dry cleaner. If you take two sweaters or shirts to the cleaners every week, you'll save nearly $9 by using a kit instead. That's a whopping $468 a year.

Take care with your cleaning. Sometimes the labels mean business, though. Clothing expert Steve Boorstein, who offers advice at *www.clothingdoctor.com*, urges caution when you ignore the label's dry-cleaning advice and instead wash your delicate items.

- Check the fabric content. Some cotton, rayon, microfiber, and polyester can be washed.

- Skip the stains. An oily stain is hard to get out, so leave that to the professionals.

- Consider your emotions. Fading, shrinking, and bleeding of dyes can happen in the wash. If you're truly attached to an item of clothing, don't try doing it yourself, Boorstein says.

Save on gifts without playing Scrooge

 Budget boost this year: $150

You want to give friends and relatives gifts they will appreciate and cherish. But you don't want to waste money, especially in these tough economic times. Try these tricks to keep your costs down and your generosity up.

Give your time. Offer to babysit, do some housecleaning or gardening, cook a meal, organize a collection of digital photos, create a scrapbook, whatever you do well. Use your special skills, and give a present that's more personal than anything you could buy. It won't cost you a penny.

Master the art of regifting. You can avoid spending money on gifts by regifting — passing along an unwanted gift to someone who will appreciate it. You'll also free yourself of clutter and guilt. Follow these regifting rules to avoid hurting feelings or looking cheap.

- Regift only items that are new, unused, and in their original packages.

- Good choices include CDs, DVDs, and books.

- If you pass along gift cards, be sure they're unused, have no fees subtracted, are good for at least another year, and can be used at a store where the receiver enjoys shopping.

- Never regift an item that was handmade for you.

- Keep track of who gives you a gift so you don't accidentally regift it to that person.

Don't waste money on trimmings. You can brighten up your gifts by wrapping them with items you have around the house. Try these:

- fabric remnants

- leftover wallpaper

- tissue paper from the dry cleaner

- yesterday's newspaper. Add a red ribbon for color, and spray on hairspray to add a glossy finish.

Say you typically give six gifts a year, averaging $25 each. By using one of these alternative ideas, you've saved $150 in a year.

Shape up for less

 Budget boost this year: $1,022

Health clubs offer a ton of exercise equipment and fitness classes. They also bring in crowds and can easily cost you $95 a month for membership. Build your own personal gym at home, and get the equipment you need without the crowds — or the big expense.

Even if you don't aim to bulk up like Mr. Universe, you still need exercise to stay fit, avoid losing muscle mass as you age, and prevent a serious fall later. Studies show older women can increase their muscle strength with a little effort, just like when they were younger.

Gather these items in your home gym, and you'll be set for a full-body workout.

- Yoga mat — around $20. Along with helping you remain stable during yoga, a mat provides cushioning.

- Hand-held weights — $30 for two sets. If that's too pricey, you can use large cans of tomatoes or other items from your pantry for free.

- Exercise video — roughly $15. Watch an expert to learn proper weight-training techniques or be guided through a yoga course. Even cheaper — check out a video from your public library.

- Stability ball — around $23. You'll use this for a core workout or training your back and abdominal muscles.

- Resistance bands — $30 a set. Exercising with weights relies on gravity to work your muscles. But these elastic bands or tubes let your muscles work in many directions.

You can put together all this equipment for around $118, and use it as much as you like. Compare that to $1,140 for an annual gym membership. You've just saved $1,022.

Cut and color at a fraction of the cost

 Budget boost this year: $850

Getting your hair cut and colored at the salon is a steal — for your hairdresser. You can easily pay $120 every time you get the full treatment. But there is another way, and you'll still look great.

First, be brave and do the color yourself. Women have been coloring their own hair for ages, and the price is right — around $13 for a bottle of color at the grocery store. It's even easier if you can convince a friend to help you out.

Then, go to a local beauty school for a haircut. A cosmetology student may take longer to cut your hair since she's learning, but it's worth your time. And she'll probably do a fine job — her instructor is watching. The best thing about the beauty school? The price — around $12 for a haircut.

All told, you save $95 every six weeks when you update your hair. That's easily $850 more in your pocket every year.

Don't let good makeup go to waste. Try these tricks to use every bit.

- Add a few drops of water to the bottle of foundation when it gets low. Shake it up, and you'll still get smooth coverage. Substitute several drops of lotion in oil-based foundation.

- When the lipstick tube gets low, use a lipstick brush or cotton swab to get at the last bit.

- Empty the remains of a broken powder compact into a cup, break up the clumps, and mix in some baby powder.

Just say 'ahh' to an at-home spa

 Budget boost this year: $300

Massages, facials, and other beauty treatments make you look and feel good. But they cost so darn much at the spa, and even the price of home equipment and fancy supplies can add up. Try these substitutes.

Pamper your feet. Electric foot massagers can average $80, while a quality hand-held massaging tool can go for $40. It's easy to cut costs here.

- Get a shallow baking pan and spread a small towel in the bottom.

- Cover the towel with marbles.

- Keep it nearby when you sit to relax in the evenings. As you roll your bare feet over the marbles, your tired dogs will get a lift.

For a nice leg massage, dig out an old rolling pin and roll the kinks out of your calves. Total saved, about $120.

Mix up a recipe for beauty. A drugstore beauty mask costs around $3.25 every time you use it. Make your own.

- Mix a ripe ba   up of oatmeal and a dash of milk.

- S   , and leave it on for 15 minutes.

- Rin   ur mo urized skin.

The homemade   costs just over 50 cents per use, so you save about $2.75 a week or $140 a year.

Steam your skin. Finally, save the $40 yo   pay for an appliance to give your face a steam treatment. You   a better job for no cost.

- Boil water and pour it into a shallow bowl.

- Mix in some herbs, like crushed rosemary or a few drops of mint extract.

- Lean over the bowl with your face about 8 inches from the surface. Drape a towel over your head to catch the steam.

- Enjoy the treatment for 10 minutes. Your pores will be opened and your skin moisturized.

Shopping

Step up and claim your senior discount

 Budget boost this year: $920

You've earned it — your senior discount, that is. Even if you feel too young to qualify for deals, some retailers will give you a discount at age 60, 55, even 50 years old. Check out these bargains and money-saving deals for seniors.

Senior deals aren't always advertised. Stores have changed their policies to save money, so you may need to ask rather than expect an automatic discount. Some retailers give senior discounts only on certain days of the week, commonly slow days like Tuesdays and Wednesdays. Or you may need to join a club to get your discount.

Think outside the box. Go beyond the "typical" senior deals, and you'll find discounts in many places you spend money.

- Fast-food restaurants. A discount of 10 percent at Arby's, Burger King, or Wendy's doesn't give you the same dollar savings as a deal at a pricier establishment, but take what you can get. You'll also score deals like free coffee — normally $1.35 — at many McDonald's restaurants during breakfast hours. If you join your pals for a cup of joe every weekday morning, you'll be $350 ahead at the end of the year.

- Supermarkets and department stores. Retailers like Belk, Banana Republic, Kohls, and even Goodwill let you save green with your gray. And everyone wants to save on groceries, so head to Kroger, A&P Supermarket, or Whole Foods to save 10 percent. If you normally spend $100 a week, you can keep an extra $520 in your pocket this year.

- Entertainment. Movie theaters like AMC and Regal Cinema and video stores like Hollywood Video want your business. When you get 30 percent off the price of a regular movie ticket, you end up paying about $4.90. Take your wife to the theater once a month, and you save $50 in a year.

- Car services and hair cuts. Jiffy Lube gives seniors special deals, while SuperCuts offers a senior discount of $2 off a hair cut.

Benefit from the bust. In tough economic times, even businesses that don't usually offer senior discounts may try this method to get you in the door. For example, ask your plumber, roofer, or accountant if you can have a senior discount. The chance to take a big bite out of your cost is worth the effort.

Sweet talk your way to a better deal

 Budget boost this year: $72

Asking for a discount is not just for yard-sale shopping. Even a big retailer may give you a lower price if you negotiate. Here's how.

Do your homework. Look on the Internet or in store circulars to see prices for the item you want. Some stores are actually eager to match or beat a competitor's price.

Pick the right time and place. Look for a situation when you can reasonably expect to get a better deal. For example, don't bother trying to haggle for that hot new electronic game system that's flying off the shelves. Stick with items in less demand. But if you happen to know that a newer version of the game system is about to be released, or if you find a nice shirt that's missing a button, it may be a great time to try for a bargain.

Wait until the store is not crowded so salespeople aren't rushed. And if you see a floor model you like — a couch in a furniture store or a camera in an electronics store — give it a shot.

Talk to the person in power. Don't waste your time with someone who can't make a deal. But a floor manager usually can give a discount of up to 15 percent.

Reap the rewards. Let's say you talk your way into a 15-percent discount on that shirt with a missing button. If the regular price is $40, you save $6 — just for asking. And you can make that repair in minutes using the extra button that comes sewn inside the shirt.

Use your bargaining expertise once a month for something similarly priced, and you'll save $72 a year.

Save a bundle on like-new buys

 Budget boost this year: $360

Want a high-end appliance, computer, or stereo component? Buy refurbished from the manufacturer, and you can get exactly what you want without paying a high price.

Descriptions like "reconditioned," "refurbished," or "open box" typically mean the item was purchased, then returned to the store. The manufacturer has inspected it and returned it to like-new condition. That doesn't mean the product was defective. Maybe it was the wrong color, or maybe the customer just changed her mind. You probably won't see any difference between a reconditioned item and one that's new, and you should get the same warranty as when buying new.

Expand your options. You can find great deals on reconditioned computers, televisions, and stereos. Apple, Dell, and other manufacturers sell products this way, and discounters like *www.tigerdirect.com* and *www.newegg.com* are great places to check. But you can also find steals on household appliances like vacuum cleaners, washing machines, and kitchen mixers. Want a long-arm sewing machine or other big-ticket item? Check with the manufacturer, and you can probably find deals on nearly new models.

Enjoy enormous discounts. It's worth investigating reconditioned products because of the huge savings possible. Some sources say you'll save 30 percent or more, while others claim you'll pay around half the regular price. If you are in the market for a laptop, sewing machine, and navigation system this year, here is an example of what you'll find.

- An HP Pavilion notebook computer, regularly $699.99, sells for $579.99 through the recertified section of *www.newegg.com*. That's $120 savings on a laptop.

- A Janome sewing machine is more than half off in the refurbished section of *www.overstock.com*. With the regular price of $249.99 slashed to $99.99, you save $150.

- Save $90 on a Magellan GPS car navigator when you buy it recertified from *www.tigerdirect.com*. Pay $59.99 recertified compared to $149.99 new.

Use due diligence. Keep these cautions in mind when you shop the reconditioned market.

- Find out exactly what the term "reconditioned" means from the store where you're shopping.

- Compare prices with new and sale merchandise to be sure you're getting a deal.

- The best prices often come straight from the manufacturer.

- Check the return policy. You should be able to return an item within 15 days of the sale.

- If possible, go to a brick-and-mortar store to purchase so you can see and try the item before you buy.

SuperSaver

Those stainless steel refrigerators and stoves look sleek and modern. Save yourself — leave them in the store. Instead, pick a more traditional model in black, white, or beige. It will probably cost you much less, and it will look new longer. The stainless steel exteriors need constant wiping, don't hold refrigerator magnets, and are easily dented.

Claim your rightful rebate

 Budget boost this year: $60

The savings sound great — get cash back when you buy a new appliance or computer. Rebates put money in your pocket, but only if you follow the rules carefully. Otherwise, you may never see any savings.

- Save all paperwork and packaging that come with a product until after you've mailed in the rebate. You may need some odd things from the package and contents just to fulfill the instructions.

- Read the instructions and fine print carefully to make sure you qualify for the rebate, preferably before you buy the product.

- Make copies of your store receipt, the item's bar code, forms, product containers, serial numbers, and even the mailing envelope. Mail the originals with the rebate form.

- Don't skip steps or questions on the rebate form, even if they don't apply to you. For example, if the form asks for an e-mail address and you don't have one, write "no e-mail" in the space.

- Don't use your post office box as an address on the rebate form.

- Staple together all items the form requires and send them in.

- Mail in your rebate right away. You may have as little as seven days before the deadline. Use certified mail and ask for a receipt.

- Mark your calendar so you'll know when to call and start asking questions if your rebate check doesn't arrive.

Sounds like an awful lot of work, but rebates can be well worth the trouble. If you can save $30 on a KitchenAid stand mixer that sells for $279, you've saved more than 10 percent. That's worth a little paperwork. Make the effort just twice a year, and you put $60 back in your pocket.

Get help shopping around. Reviews from some of the major product information Web sites, including *www.epinions.com* and Consumer Reports, are gathered at *www.consumersearch.com*. You just look in the product category you're shopping for, select the item you want, then see a summary list of reviews. You'll also see typical prices at certain online stores, so you can go directly to the best deal.

Head to the highlands for low furniture prices

 Budget boost this year: $3,600

More than half of the furniture sold in the United States is made near Hickory and High Point, North Carolina. That makes this mountain area an ideal spot to shop for furniture bargains. If you are decorating your new retirement home or simply need to replace your living room set, you may want to consider a trip to this beautiful area.

Save at the source. With so much of the furniture made locally, it's no surprise you can save 40 to 50 percent off the regular price when you buy in North Carolina. And don't think it's only solid wood furniture. You'll also find low prices on sofas and other upholstered furniture and all types of accessories. Even better, if you make it to the North Carolina sales in October or April, you'll save up to 70 percent on floor samples. That's because you're hitting the stores just after the semiannual furniture markets for interior designers and other professionals.

Check out dealers with good reputations such as Furnitureland South, Boyles Furniture, and Hickory Park Furniture Galleries. You can find details about the stores before you travel by checking Web sites like *www.highpointfurniture.com*.

Don't be scared by shipping. Believe it or not, the cost to ship from North Carolina will probably be less than you would pay locally. You can consolidate items that you've bought from various stores into a single shipment. Expect to pay about a dollar a pound for shipping. Alternately, you can take your own truck or rent a trailer to take home your goodies.

Save by the truckload. Generally, you'll save 40 to 50 percent off the regular price. So if you're considering buying $1,000 sofa, you'd easily save $400 by shopping in North Carolina. One customer from New York paid $800 for a chair in High Point — the same chair she saw at home for nearly $1,300. That's $500 saved. Or what about paying $900 for a fancy armoire that normally sells for $3,600? You'd save $2,700.

If you don't want to travel to North Carolina, you can still score some savings by shopping online from the same retailers. Order items at a discount, and have them shipped straight to you.

SuperSaver

Look for bargains on high-end furniture from model homes. Builders pay interior designers to select nice furniture that gives each model the right look. But when a neighborhood fills up and the houses are sold, furniture in the model homes must go. Builders have already written off the loss, so you may get deals for as little as one-tenth the cost of the item.

Secret to slashing your clothing costs

Budget boost this year: $937

A patriotic poster from World War II reads "Use it up — wear it out — make it do!" If only Americans still followed that policy, lots of money could be saved. But most of the clothing tossed nowadays still has plenty of wear left in it. That's why you can grab great clothing bargains if you're willing to shop at resale and consignment stores.

Go high end. Everyone knows about thrift stores, like Goodwill Industries and other charity stores. Consignment stores are different. They typically limit what they accept and sell, offering only high-quality — even designer — items in great condition. Sellers earn money through the stores only if their items sell.

You'll find general consignment stores that have clothing, shoes, and accessories for the whole family. You'll also find specialty shops, like bridal store White Chicago. The chain Once Upon a Child sells clothing for children, while teens can get the latest styles at Plato's Closet. With more than 20,000 resale shops in the country, you're sure to have a store near you that's worth checking out.

You can find a consignment store that's affiliated with the National Association of Resale & Thrift Shops (NARTS), a trade group in the industry, at *www.narts.org*. Look in the nicest part of town for the best-quality goods. As you search for a consignment store, think about why people might be getting rid of certain items. For example, you may find great winter clothes at stores in Florida when you're visiting. People often move there and realize they don't need cold-weather items anymore.

Snip your costs. You can easily save 50 percent with careful consignment store shopping. Government statistics say a family typically spends around $1,874 on clothing annually. That means you can save $937 in a year, look great, and have fun doing it.

Be wary in your bargain hunt. Consider these tips from NARTS on buying secondhand clothing.

- Do your research so you know the retail price of what you're shopping for. Then you'll recognize a good deal.

- Look at all items carefully. Be sure there's no damage or stains you're not willing to live with.

- Try on all items. Don't buy if it doesn't fit or it can't be altered. Some alterations — like hemming a skirt — are simple and cheap. But others — like enlarging a jacket that's too small — may be nearly impossible.

- Know the good-quality brands, and check the materials and workmanship of items you're considering. Buying high-quality clothing may be worth paying more for if it lasts longer.

- Explore several consignment stores in your area. They're all different, and you may find one you really like.

THE NEXT STEP

If you have Internet access, you can shop online for resales of good-quality clothing. Try these sites.

- *www.eBay.com* — Bid on designer clothing and accessories. Search for specific items of clothing, size, and NWT (new with tags) to find great deals on exactly what you want.

- *www.shopgoodwill.com* — This site has auctions similar to eBay. You'll see designer clothing and accessories that are current and in good condition.

Smart ways to save on shipping

 Budget boost this year: $60

Shopping for clothes through the Internet is convenient, not to mention a great way to find bargains. But the shipping charges are often ridiculously high. What's worse is when you have to pay twice for shipping because you need to return something that doesn't fit. Try these tactics to take some of the sting out of shipping costs.

Shop locally, buy globally. Try on clothes at a store near you, then buy online when you see a better price. This tactic works if you live near a store that also sells clothing online, such as Sears, J.C. Penney, or Ann Taylor. You can wait for an end-of-season sale and order the item you want — knowing it will fit. You may be able to return something to your local store if it doesn't work out.

Hire a virtual model. Get out your tape measure, and build yourself an online model. Tools like My Virtual Model at *www.mvm.com* let you type in your measurements, include your hair color and facial features, and create yourself on the screen. Then you take your model to shop online at stores like Lands' End, Sears, and H&M Clothing. Your virtual model tries on the clothing, so you'll know what fits and how outfits look on you. Be honest when you input measurements so the system works.

Skip the fees altogether. Pick a store that doesn't charge for shipping, and you don't have to worry about this extra cost. Shop for shoes for the entire family at *www.zappos.com* or *www.piperlime.com*. You can buy the size shoes you think you need, try them on after they arrive, then return them for free if they don't work.

Join a club. If you love a certain store, look into the benefits of getting a preferred customer card.

- Chico's Passport Club gives you free shipping, 5 percent off your purchases, and special birthday discounts.

- Coldwater Creek's OneCreek program offers free return shipping on mail-order purchases, a personal shopper, discounts, and a birthday surprise.

If you can avoid paying for shipping, you'll probably save around $6 per item of clothing you buy. If your family buys just 10 items in a year, that's a savings of $60.

Get help from Medicare if you need special shoes for medical reasons, including diabetic foot problems like peripheral neuropathy, foot amputation, or poor circulation. If you qualify, Medicare will pay 80 percent of the cost of one pair of therapeutic shoes and three sets of insoles every year. Ask your doctor about this program, which requires a prescription for the shoes.

Taxes

Easy way to get a pay raise

 Budget boost this year: $2,500

Americans of all income levels willingly hand out monthly loans averaging $200 at 0-percent interest — and you may be one of them.

If you get a big tax refund every year, then you're essentially lending Uncle Sam money from every paycheck without getting paid interest. Considering the average tax refund is around $2,500, that means you're handing the government more than $208 of your hard-earned money every month. Think what you could do with that money if you kept it.

- If you applied $208 every month to $2,300 of credit card debt at 14 percent, you could pay it off in a year and save $995 in interest. That's far better than spending six years paying the minimum payment.

- You could put that money into an emergency fund so you wouldn't have to use your credit card or raid your retirement funds the next time an unexpected medical bill comes up.

- You could invest half of it in a 6-month CD and then have that money — plus interest — available for use again around tax-refund time.

- Even if your checking account only offers 1-percent interest, depositing $208.33 every month would make you $11.49 richer in a year.

So how can you take your money back from the government? If your annual income doesn't vary much and you aren't planning any big life changes this year, consider lowering your paycheck withholding. It's like getting a raise without having to ask the boss. To do this, you'll need a fresh copy of the W-4 form. These documents may be a big help as well.

- A copy of last year's tax return.

- IRS Publications 505 and 919. Get these free from *www.irs.gov* or by calling toll-free 800-829-3676.

Your W-4 form has worksheets to help you figure out the appropriate number of withholding exemptions to claim. Follow the instructions on that form, or consult a tax adviser. You can also use the withholding calculator at *www.irs.gov*. Be careful not to withhold too much or too little. Too much will keep that tax refund rolling in, and too little could get you penalized by the IRS. When you're done with the W-4, make two copies, and give one to your payroll or human resources representative. Keep the other for your records.

SuperSaver

Americans miss up to $400 in savings because of deductions, tax credits, and income exclusions they don't claim. So be sure to check last year's tax return to see what deductions and tax credits you normally take — or use tax software like TurboTax or TaxCut to help you find new ones.

Earn top dollar on your charity donations

 Budget boost this year: $900

You can save a lot on taxes just by donating used clothes and household items to charity, according to William R. Lewis, CPA and author of the booklet *Money for Your Used Clothing*. The key is to accurately estimate the items' worth.

Learn how to estimate. "In surveys that we've done, people — prior to using our book — usually estimated their used-clothing donations at $300 or $400 because if they claimed over $500 they had to complete IRS Form 8283," Lewis says. "We again did surveys after taxpayers used our booklet, and they were averaging between $2,000-$3,000 in deductions because they had a proper method to do it."

Lewis notes that someone in the 25-percent federal tax bracket who pays a 5-percent state income tax could see a huge tax saving by using his guide. "Thirty percent of $3,000 would be about a $900 actual savings — money in their pocket," Lewis estimates.

Follow the rules. Naturally, the IRS expects you to jump through some hoops to get your deduction. Here are some crucial "hoops" you should know about.

- Your donations are only deductible if the items are in good used condition or better. That means you can deduct donations of "gently used" or "like new" clothing — not old, ripped jeans.

- You must donate to a qualified charity, but you must not exceed your allowed deduction limits. For details, see *Give More to Charity and Less to the Tax Man* in the *Outsmart the IRS* chapter.

- The IRS requires you to get a signed, dated receipt from the charity — unless you deposited the items in the charity's drop box.

- You must itemize on your tax return instead of taking the standard deduction.

- You must keep IRS-specified records to qualify for any charitable deduction. IRS record-keeping requirements vary depending on such things as how much you donate and whether you receive anything from the charity. See IRS Publication 526 for details.

Avoid IRS penalties. The IRS expects you to estimate the fair market value of each item you donate. Rather than the price you paid for the item, you must use the price you'd pay if you bought the item at a thrift store. To help avoid penalties for overestimating, Lewis's book provides two extensive listings of fair market values for specific clothing and household items — one list for "gently used" and another for "like new."

"We provide the detailed description and fair market value that the IRS requires in order for you to complete form 8283," explains Lewis. Estimates of fair market value are also available at *www.goodwill.org* or *www.salvationarmyusa.org*.

And remember, if you donate more than $500 worth of items, you must fill out Form 8283 to send with your tax return. To do this, you'll need such information as how you came to own the items, what you paid, when you got them, and contact details for charities you donated to. For detailed information, see IRS Form 8283 and the instructions for completing it.

For details on tax deduction rules for charitable donations, see IRS Publications 526 and 561, available free from *www.irs.gov* or by calling toll-free 800-829-3676. For a useful workbook with fair market values and user-friendly instructions on getting your deductions, order the *Money for Your Used Clothing* booklet from *www.mfyuc.com*, or call 866-417-7678.

Transportation

Pay less at the pump

 Budget boost this year: $636

Slash gas costs by as much as $1.06 a gallon just by heeding these smart rules of the road. If you travel 15,000 miles this year and average 25 miles per gallon, you'll save $636.

Avoid aggressive driving. Jackrabbit starts, speeding, and hard braking reduce your gas mileage a whopping one-third on the highway and 5 percent on city streets. With gas at $1.84 a gallon, you'd save up to 61 cents per gallon by ditching these bad driving habits.

Slow down. Generally, every five miles you drive over 60 mph tacks another 24 cents to every gallon of gas you put in your car. You'll improve gas mileage between 7 and 23 percent just by obeying speed limits. That'll save you up to 42 cents per gallon — more, if it also saves you a traffic ticket.

Lighten up. Dump the junk in your trunk. Every 100 additional pounds cuts your gas mileage up to 2 percent, or 4 cents per gallon. Small cars lose more mileage than large ones.

Turn off your engine. Idling for more than 60 seconds wastes more gas than turning off the engine and restarting. The larger your engine, the more gas you lose. Plus, excessive idling can damage the engine and contaminate oil.

Use cruise control. On the highway, it helps maintain a constant speed, which saves gas. Don't bother with it in hilly areas. There, cruise control tends to waste fuel.

Take the back way. Taking a slightly longer route with few stops actually uses less fuel than a shorter route with lots of stop lights or stop signs. Take the highway on long trips. Four-lane highways are generally more fuel-efficient than two-lane roads.

Combine trips. Running a single, quick errand wastes gas because the engine doesn't have time to warm up, and engines gulp more gas when they're cold. Combine several short trips into one afternoon of errands to keep the engine warm between stops, especially in winter. A car can burn 50 percent more fuel in winter than summer on the same short trip.

Invest in a block heater if the temperature regularly dips below freezing where you live. These gadgets warm the engine and fluids in winter, boosting fuel efficiency 10 percent in cold weather. Put the heater on an automatic timer, and set it to switch on two hours before leaving.

THE NEXT STEP

These three Web sites can help you find the cheapest gas around, without driving all over town.

- *www.gasbuddy.com*

- *autos.msn.com/everyday/gasstations.aspx*

- *www.gaspricewatch.com*

Drive farther on far less gas

 Budget boost this year: $473

Make fuel efficiency your top priority the next time you're in the market for a car. Switching from a vehicle that gets a modest 20 miles per gallon to one that nets a miserly 30 mpg will save you $473 a year on gas. That's more than $2,300 in only five years. Can't afford a new car? Take care of the one you have now. These small savings will really add up.

Fix the big problems. Pay attention to that Check Engine light, and take your car to the mechanic as soon as it comes on. Fixing a serious issue like a faulty oxygen sensor can boost your gas mileage up to 40 percent — a 74-cent savings on every gallon.

Breathe easier. Clogged air filters make your engine work harder to create the same amount of power. Harder work means wasted fuel. Changing out a choked-up air filter is cheap and easy to do, plus it cuts up to 10 percent off fuel costs, or about 18 cents a gallon.

Keep it tuned. Fixing a noticeably out-of-tune car that failed its emissions test cuts fuel use by 4 percent, a savings of 7 cents per gallon.

Pump up tires. Keeping tires properly inflated shaves 3 percent off gas costs, or 6 cents every gallon. Check your tire pressure regularly, especially in cold weather and after a sharp drop in temperature. Buy a good gauge and measure it yourself since service station gauges often aren't accurate.

Buy the right oil. Check your driver's manual, and use the type of motor oil it recommends. Putting the wrong oil in your car can cut mileage 2 percent, up to 4 cents a gallon. Look for oil labeled "Energy Conserving."

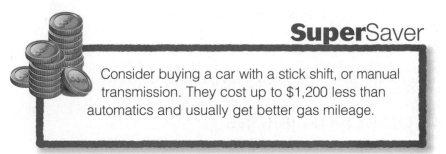

SuperSaver

Consider buying a car with a stick shift, or manual transmission. They cost up to $1,200 less than automatics and usually get better gas mileage.

Take the bus for big savings

 Budget boost this year: $8,481

Give up your car and take the train or bus, and you could save $8,481 a year on gas and parking, according to the American Public

Transportation Administration. That could pay for all your food for a year and still leave $2,000 in your pocket. The Transit Calculator can tell you exactly how much you could save. Visit the Web site *www.apta.com/services*, and click on the Transit Calculator link.

Senior discounts and senior passes, offered by most transit agencies, make riding the rails even more affordable. In some cities, seniors ride free. Contact your city, local transit agency, or your state's department of transportation, and ask how to get a discount.

In some cases, you can get paid to ride. The government allows employers to pay their people up to $115 a month tax-free in the form of cash, vouchers, or passes in exchange for ditching their cars and taking public transportation or vanpooling to work.

Buy the car of your dreams for thousands less

 Budget boost this year: $16,575

You can buy your dream car for half the price you think, keeping thousands of dollars in your pocket and dodging a hefty car payment. To find the best car at the best price, simply decide which type of car you want, then buy one that's three years old instead of brand new.

This tactic stretches your money farther, while still netting you a car with modern safety and convenience features. A three-year-old car in good condition with low mileage can sell for half the price of a new one. Consider this. A brand new 2009 Toyota Camry LE retails for $27,870. A 2006 Toyota Camry LE with 40,000 miles sells for just $11,295 — a difference of $16,575.

You can thank the power of depreciation for netting you such a good deal. Used cars have already seen their biggest drop in value. On average, cars lose nearly a third of their value in the first two years, hence the three-year rule. Follow it, and you'll be able to afford cars you never thought you could. If buying used scares you, consider these solutions.

Play it safe with certified. Certified preowned vehicles cost slightly more than regular used cars but give you peace of mind. You may also score better financing and lower interest rates. The certification usually guarantees a vehicle:

- has no history of major damage.

- has undergone strict mechanical and cosmetic inspections.

- comes with an extra warranty, on top of the original factory warranty.

Buy demos. Demo cars are nearly new, late-model vehicles that dealerships use for test drives or demonstrations. They are still covered by a factory warranty, and they must have logged less than 10,000 miles. Otherwise, they're considered used. While they aren't as cheap as used cars, demo's still cost less than new.

Call in the fleet. A fleet department is the bulk-buying arm of a car dealership. They usually sell to companies, but they will also sell a new car to you. Simply follow these steps.

- Decide which make, model, and color of car you want before you approach the fleet department.

- Go for test drives at the regular dealerships, since you can't test drive through the fleet department.

- Check prices online at *www.kbb.com*, *www.edmunds.com*, or *www.cars.com*.

- Call the dealership and ask for the Fleet Manager. Make sure they route you to the Fleet Manager and not a regular sales manager.

- Ask the Fleet Manager what the invoice price is on the car you want, and negotiate the price.

If you plan to finance, check your credit score before going to the dealership. If you know you have good credit, a car salesman won't get away with sticking you in a bad loan. For the best loan terms, aim for a credit score above 720 and put down at least 20 percent.

Paying cash is best of all, because you'll have no car payment. Start saving before you buy. Figure out what your monthly payment would be if you financed the purchase, then stash that amount each month into a savings account just for the car. Keep saving until you have enough cash to buy one outright. If you follow the three-year-old rule and buy a used car, you'll save enough in no time.

SuperSaver

Secure your own financing before heading to the dealership. You can use the financing deal you have in hand as a bargaining chip and rest easy knowing you're already guaranteed a good rate before you buy.

10 minutes to lower car payments

Budget boost this year: $1,155

Get out from under massive car payments in as little as 10 minutes by refinancing your high-interest car loan. It's much easier than refinancing a home loan, in part because there is no appraisal. The new loan amount is based solely on the balance of your current loan.

Let's say you have a $20,000 car loan originally financed for five years at 12 percent interest. Your payments would total $445 a month, and you'd pay nearly $6,700 in interest over five years. That's a lot of money you can't afford to lose.

Now consider this. If you refinanced that loan after the first year into one with four years left at 6 percent interest, you would not only owe $48 less each month — a $576 annual savings — but you'd also pay $579 less in interest each year, for a total savings of $1,155. The earlier you refinance, the more you save.

Shop around for the best rates. Most lenders won't refinance their own auto loans, but plenty of others will be happy to help you. The Internet makes comparing rates quick and easy. Start with *www.bankrate.com* to check rates from lots of lenders in one place. Or visit lenders directly at *www.up2drive.com* or *www.capitalone.com/autoloans/refinance*. Watch out for any points they may try to tack onto your loan.

Once you refinance, cut your interest payments further. Even though your monthly payments dropped, keep paying the old, higher amount toward your loan. The extra money will go toward principal, paying off your loan faster and saving you more money.

Get 200,000 miles or more out of your car

 Budget boost this year: $20,000

Squeeze another six years out of your car, even if it already has 100,000 miles on it. With a few inexpensive upkeeps, you can skip buying a new car and save $20,000 to $30,000.

Modern cars can last 250,000 miles with few major repairs. The simple secret that will keep most cars on the road for 200,000 miles or more — follow the manufacturer's maintenance schedule. Taking proper care of your car can also keep insurance rates low.

Dig out your owner's manual, and decide if you should follow the normal or severe schedule. If you do most of your driving on paved highway roads with little dust, then stick to the normal driving schedule. You should follow the severe schedule if you:

- idle for long periods

- take mostly short trips (under 10 minutes)

- do lots of stop-and-go city driving

- drive in extremely cold weather or in dusty areas

- tow a trailer

Now that you know your schedule, it's time to get down to business. These four chores are especially important. Remember to perform them regularly, and you'll add miles and years to your car's life.

Change the oil. The best fix is sometimes the easiest. Changing your oil is the single best way to make your car last longer. Follow the maintenance schedule for your car, or play it safe and change the oil every 3,000 miles or three months, whichever comes second.

Rotate the tires. Front tires wear down in different places and at different speeds than rear tires. Rotating all four helps them wear evenly and last longer. Your car owner's manual will tell you how often to have them rotated. Get this service done for free and save yourself $20 to $30 each time.

- Buy your next set of tires from a place that offers free lifetime rotation, balance, and alignment. You may pay a one-time fee for this package deal, but it will quickly pay for itself.

- Have your regular mechanic rotate the tires while he has them off for another service, such as brake repair. He probably won't charge extra.

Check the pressure. Under- and over-inflated tires wear out faster than those with proper air pressure. They're also less safe. Check your tire pressure often, preferably when tires are "cold," before you drive anywhere. Don't forget to check the spare. After all, a flat spare tire won't do you any good.

Don't use a pencil gauge, those popular, pocket gauges shaped like a pencil. They are notoriously inaccurate. Don't rely on the gas station gauge, either. They are often broken or missing. Instead, invest in a good digital or dial-type pressure gauge.

Change out the fluids. Engine oil is important, but it's not the only fluid your car needs. Check your owner's manual, and change the coolant, transmission, and differential fluids as recommended. Change and flush brake and power steering fluids every three years or 75,000 miles, or more often if the manual suggests it.

Some cars aren't worth repairing. Don't feed a money pit. Bite the bullet and buy a new one if the old one:

- needs repairs that cost more than it's worth.

- spends more time in the shop than on the road.

- has been in a flood or serious accident.

Insure your auto for less

 Budget boost this year: $1,125+

Cut your car insurance costs by as much as 50%. You could save between $675 and $1,275 a year on a $1,500 insurance premium.

Ask for an age discount. People between the ages of 55 and 70 usually qualify for 10 to 20 percent discount on premiums, just for being seniors. Ask your insurance agent if you qualify. It could save you $150 to $300 a year on a $1,500 policy.

Update your agent. How much driving you do plays a big role in the cost of your policy. Let your agent know if you drive less these days — for instance, if you retired, started carpooling, or began working from home. You could cut premiums 5 to 15 percent — $75 to $225 — each year.

Raise your deductible. Bump it from $200 to $500, and slash premiums 15 to 30 percent, or $225 to $450. Up the deductible to $1,000 and shave as much as 40 percent off your premiums for $600 in savings.

Cut collision. Dropping collision coverage on clunkers can help cap insurance costs. Check your policy to find out how much you pay just for collision coverage. Multiply this cost times 10. If the answer is higher than your car's value, drop the coverage. Just keep your comprehensive, liability, and bodily injury coverages.

Bundle up. Insure your home and all your cars with the same company to save 15 to 20 percent on car insurance, or $225 to $300 a year.

That's not all. Cut costs even further with a few smart steps.

- Let your agent know if your car has special safety features, such as airbags, antilock brakes, or an anti-theft device.

- Brush up on driver's ed. Senior driver refresher courses, such as AARP's 55Alive, can earn you a discount.

- Keep your credit in tip-top shape. People with good ratings and a long, stable credit history tend to have fewer accidents and, therefore, score lower rates.

- Shop around, checking rates with several companies before settling on one.

- Tell your agent if you have worked for the same employer for many years. It may earn you another discount.

- Ask about group insurance discounts through membership in professional, business, or alumni associations.

- Park inside your home's garage or in a locked parking lot, to lower your premiums.

ALERT!

Gas-sipping small cars may save on fuel but break you on insurance. They tend to have higher theft rates and are involved in more accidents with larger personal injury claims — all of which can make them more expensive to insure. Check with your insurer before buying your next car.

Drive away with cut-rate car-rental deals

 Budget boost this year: $200

Shop smart and sniff out deals, and you could save $33 or more per day on a car rental. If you travel and rent a car for two long week-ends this year, that's about $200 in savings.

Book early. Lock in a low rate by booking early, before peak travel season arrives, but don't prepay for the rental. Keep shopping for a better one even after you book, especially as your trip approaches. If the price of your car drops, call the local rental agency — not the national phone number — and ask for the lower rate. Or simply cancel the first booking, and snag the better rate.

Rent online. Big travel Web sites such as *www.expedia.com*, *www.travelocity.com*, and *www.orbitz.com* often negotiate special deals with national car rental companies. Compare costs at these sites, or search lots of travel sites and rental agencies at once through *www.kayak.com* and *www.sidestep.com*. Deep-discount travel sites such as *www.hotwire.com* and *www.priceline.com* sometimes offer super-low rates. Still other Web sites focus solely on rental cars, including *www.breezenet.com*, *www.carrentalexpress.com*, and *www.carrentals.com*.

Find discount codes. Use your AAA membership, credit card, or employer to get promotional codes for car rental discounts. If you can't find a code this way, try the Web site *www.rentalcodes.com*.

Avoid the airport. You'll pay more renting a car near the airport than in surrounding cities or suburbs, maybe $8 or more a day. That's because local and state governments tack "tourist" taxes and fees onto rentals close to airports. Take a taxi, train, or shuttle to a suburban or city-center car rental agency, instead.

Know the gas policy. Find out before you take the car how the agency charges for fuel. If they charge for a full tank upfront, then bring the car back on empty. On the other hand, if they want you to refill it before returning, then be sure to refill it yourself at a local service station. You'll pay a premium for gas sold at the rental agency.

Skip the added insurance. Declining the rental agency's extra insurance coverage could save you up to $25 a day. You probably don't need it if you already have home and auto insurance. Ask your insurance agent if your policy covers rental car damage, replacement, and loss of use.

Travel & recreation

Deals and discounts for DIY travel

 Budget boost this year: $475+

Who says you need a travel agent to put together a great vacation? With a little planning and some patience, you can enjoy the vacation of your dreams without spending a bundle.

Shop online for the best deals. With travel search engines, you can compare prices on various airlines and hotels and find cut-rate, first-class vacations without paying a travel agent. Try these popular sites.

- Travelocity.com

- Expedia.com

- TripAdvisor.com

- Sidestep.com searches multiple airline web sites and other travel sites, like Expedia and Hotwire.com — all in a single search.

- BudgetTravel.com. Click on "Real Deals" and see specific trips, flights, and hotels on sale now. But you'll need to be flexible to get the most from these deals. Many are last-minute specials.

- Farecast.live.com and Travelocity's Farewatcher feature alert you to deals for your specific destination.

And don't forget eBay. You can find travel deals there, too. Consider all-inclusive, no-hassle packages auctioned off by travel agents. These package resort stays include airfare, hotel, food, drinks, activities, and more — all in one price.

For example, if you wanted a five-night stay for four people in Bonaventure Resort in Fort Lauderdale, Fla., you'd normally pay $121.25 a night or $606.25 for five nights. But you could get a package deal at eBay for $129.99 — the "buy it now" price — if you agree to attend a 90-minute sales presentation and meet certain qualifications. That's a savings of $476.26.

Live like you're at home. Decide not to spend every second of your vacation living like a king. For example, enjoy one nice meal a day at a restaurant. For other meals, buy prepared food or sandwich fixings from a supermarket deli.

Save big with off-season travel. Vacation during "shoulder season" — the two weeks just before and after the most popular season for a vacation spot. For example, you may save 12 percent or more on hotel rooms by vacationing right before the ski season or immediately after. Try these "off" seasons:

- the week before Thanksgiving for cheaper flights

- December before Christmas for ski vacations

- Europe in late fall or early winter

- Las Vegas during the week between Christmas and New Year

Plan ahead. Visit *www.uptake.com* to search for budget hotels, attractions, and things to do at your planned destination. You can also go to your public library before your trip and check out a travel guide about the city you're visiting.

Never pay full price for a hotel room

 Budget boost this year: $57+

Hotel rooms are negotiable. Seasoned travelers know how to get the same room everyone else gets, but they pay up to 50 percent off. Try these travel-wise tricks to get a good night's sleep on the cheap.

Call twice for a price. First, call the hotel where you want to stay and then call that company's central 800 number. One may give you a cheaper price. Also, check travel discount Web sites, such as Travelocity, Orbitz, and Hotels.com. Just type your destination, travel dates, number of children and adults, and number of rooms. The site finds bargains that fit your request.

Ask for a better deal. Don't accept the first quoted rate. Ask if there are any special deals or discounts — or ask if there's a better price for someone in your group. Special discounts may be available for senior citizens, government workers, and members of AARP, AAA, and the military. For example, the Hyatt Hotels and Resorts senior discount can be as much as 50 percent. In fact, at the Hyatt in Rosemont, Ill., regular rates are $114 a night, so a 50-percent discount would save you $57 a night.

But be careful. Some chains make you join a club and possibly pay a membership fee for the benefits. For example, Hilton gives discounts to members of its Senior HHonors program, but you must pay $55 to join and $40 to renew annually. You'd need to stay at Hiltons regularly to make this worthwhile.

Look into fringe benefits. These free extras are worth considering when choosing a place to stay.

- Free breakfast. Saving the cost of breakfast is like getting your room for that much less.

- Free gas card to help cover travel costs.

- Discounts on local fun. Check the Web site of the hotel you're considering. You may find discounts on tickets to local attractions.

And if you need more than one room, you may save money by getting a suite instead — with two bedrooms, a sitting room, and perhaps a kitchenette.

SuperSaver

Hostels are no longer just for the young. People of all ages can stay at a hostel — a thrifty hotel with dorm-like or single rooms. You'll typically find no-frills accommodations, but the price is always right. What's more, you get to stay with a community of fellow travelers. Check your library to find a hostel in the city you want to visit. Or locate a hostel at *www.airgorilla.com* or *www.hihostels.com*.

Discover affordable ways to fly

Budget boost this year: $160

You can afford to fly — if you learn the cardinal rules of buying tickets. It's worth the trouble, because sometimes driving just takes too long. Add to that the rising price of gasoline and flying becomes truly enticing.

Find cheaper flights. Use meta search engines to shop for tickets online. For example, check out Kayak.com to quickly compare flight prices on more than 140 airlines — but check Southwest separately, since Kayak doesn't include it.

Time your shopping. If you want to fly on a weekend, look online just after midnight Eastern Time on Thursday night. That's when weekend deals are posted. Otherwise, book online around midnight any day of the week to get latest updates and your best chance of discounts. To shop around and know what's a good deal, also visit *www.farecast.com*. There you can check both the history and future projections of prices for the flight you want. But don't stop there.

Compare flights to and from cities near your departure and destination cities. Sometimes an airport just a little out of your way can mean great savings. After you find the cheapest flight using an online search tool, book directly with the airline to avoid extra booking fees.

Be flexible. Fly on Tuesday or Wednesday for cheaper tickets.

Skip flying direct. You'll get better deals if you're willing to take connecting flights. But give yourself at least two hours between flights to be sure you make your connection.

Avoid extra charges. Most airlines charge $15 for your first checked bag and $25 for your second. If you and your spouse each take two checked bags, you'd pay an extra $80 each way ($160 total). Airlines don't charge for a carry-on bag and some experts say — if you're careful — you can pack enough for a week in one bag. Here's how to start

- Pack clothes you can mix and match — or stick with one color.

- Pack wrinkle-resistant clothes and roll them up tightly.

- Wear sneakers for sightseeing and pack one pair of dress shoes.

- If you'll need a coat, wear it on the plane.

- Pack sample-size toiletries.

Here's another clever idea — pack a box instead of a suitcase and ship the box to your destination a few days before you leave.

Cruise your way to a bargain holiday

 Budget boost this year: $1,000

Ocean cruises used to be just for the wealthy. Not anymore. If you know your way around the cruise market, you can enjoy a budget vacation on the high seas.

Get help from the professionals. Consult a travel agent to plan your first cruise. An agent who specializes in cruises can find a low price on a trip that matches your needs and lifestyle. You might also get freebies, like cabin upgrades and credit for on-board extras. Look for an agent affiliated with an organization like the American Society of Travel Agents or the Cruise Lines International Association. But once you have a few cruises under your belt, you can find great deals through Web sites like *www.cruisecritic.com* or *www.cruisemates.com*.

Search for last-minute deals. Cruise lines depend on a strong Wave Season — the period between January and March when lots of cruises are booked for the year. That's a good time to check prices.

Benefit from a down economy. When neighbors are tightening their belts and staying home, you can snap up good deals. Some experienced cruisers say they won't book unless the cruise is $100 a day or less per person. If you notice a price of $80 — or even $40 — a day, it's time to pounce. A down year may help you net a deal like saving $1,000 off the price of a cruise to Europe, or free airfare when you book the cruise.

Book early without fear. If you book a trip and the price goes down before you sail, many cruise lines will refund the difference in price — if you ask. Find out the cruise line's policy before you book.

Don't sink your savings. No matter how low the price of the cruise, costly extras can blow your discount. Cruise lines encourage you to spend, spend, spend on excursions, souvenirs, professional photos, on-board gambling, and drinking. Don't do it.

Take your hobby to the high seas

Consider taking a cruise, even if you don't think you're a cruise person. You can find a great variety of specialty cruises — like quilting, knitting, Elvis enthusiasts, motor-cycle lovers, gourmet cooking, and music. Enjoy your hobby while you cruise, and your spouse enjoys the vacation without having to watch you knit. But check prices. Cruises with expert instructors may cost more.

See the world on a shoestring budget

 Budget boost this year: $235+

The number of seniors is growing as baby boomers join the ranks of the over-65 crowd. That change gives you some pretty good company in the senior-discount aisle. You can travel cheaply if you ask around for senior deals.

Take to the air. Some airlines stopped giving senior discounts, but others remain. Southwest Airlines offers deals of 20 to 70 percent off the regular price of tickets to passengers 65 years or older. Senior one-way fares are limited to $139 or less. Want to visit northern California, but you live in Alabama? A typical full-price ticket would cost about $513, but a senior would pay no more than $278 round trip. That means you'd save $235 by claiming a senior discount.

Other airlines, including Continental, American Airlines, and United Airlines, may give you a senior discount. Ask about it when you book your ticket.

Ride the rails. People who enjoy the romance of trains will love traveling by Amtrak. Even better, if you're age 62 or older you can save 15 percent on most tickets.

Get around town. Traveling by bus, subway, ferry, or commuter train is usually an inexpensive way to go. Add in a senior discount of 50 percent or more, and you're really saving dough. The age to qualify for a senior discount on public transit is different for various locations — it may be as low as age 50 or as high as age 65. And in some cities, you ride free after a certain age.

Super savings at national parks

 Budget boost this year: $100+

Trek to a national park and you'll get a great deal on a visit to the great outdoors. National parks also include dozens of historic sites and buildings within cities. Did you know the Statue of Liberty and Alcatraz Island are both national parks? They're not just for campers and hikers.

Uncover an "inside" bargain. You may think a hotel outside the national park is always cheaper, but check the rates first. Sometimes, staying in the park can save you money.

Sleep under the stars. If you're adventurous and really want to save, consider camping. You can enjoy great views, wildlife, and the beauty of nature for less than $20 a night — and still eat all your meals in the park's lodge restaurants if you wish. Compared with in-park lodgings, this may be as much as $100 cheaper per night.

Claim your senior discount. As soon as you turn age 62, you can buy a Senior Pass at any national park for only $10. The senior pass — formerly the Golden Age Passport — is good for life and gets you free entrance to all national parks, as well as campsite discounts. Entrance to parks can be as high as $25 per car, so this pass may be a great saver the first time you use it.

Be a road scholar with Elderhostel

 Budget boost this year: $800

Seniors who want to learn while they roam may enjoy Elderhostel, the educational travel program for people in their 50s and older. Elderhostel combines travel with casual educational programs. For example, you can learn about Scottish history while staying at a castle in Edinburgh or tour France by bike. Closer to home, you might visit Mount Rushmore or learn about art in New York City. You'll find programs year-round in all 50 states and in more than 90 countries.

Typical prices start around $400 — including accommodations and meals — but can reach the thousands. Of course, you could save money by finding a class in your area. Then you could stay in your home and save on accommodations.

But if you want to travel while learning, scholarships may help shrink the price down to $100. In fact, Elderhostel awards over 600 scholarships each year to people with financial need. These scholarships run as high as $800 and can be used for any American or Canadian program priced at $1,000 or less. To put in your application for a scholarship, visit *www.elderhostel.com* or call toll-free 877-426-8056.

THE NEXT STEP

Get a free guided tour from a knowledgeable native when you visit a new city. Volunteer city greeters will give you a personalized walking tour around various parts of Chicago, New York, Houston, and other cities. You can get to know a certain neighborhood while you make a new friend. Check the tourism Web page of the city you'll visit, and look for a Global Greeters link.

Save thousands with senior scholarships

 Budget boost this year: $402+

School is cool — especially when someone else pays the bills. Your silver hair may be your ticket to taking college courses for little or no money.

Check out your options. Some scholarships are offered for people older than age 25. Other scholarships are only available to people who worked, or still work, in a certain field. You may even be able to get "life credit" for time worked in a profession — meaning you get course credit without taking the course.

When April 15 comes, you may also get a tax break, thanks to the Hope or Lifetime Learning tax credits. You may be eligible for up to $1,650 in Hope tax credits or up to $2,000 for Lifetime Learning credit. See IRS Publication 970 — available from *www.irs.gov* — to find out if you qualify.

Pay zero tuition. Some colleges and universities let people 65 years and older take courses without paying tuition. You must still buy your books and materials, and you may have to pay some fees — especially if you want to earn college credit. But you could save anywhere from $402 to $490 for just one three semester hour class.

On the other hand, you may be able to audit — sit in on a class that interests you — for no charge if space is available. This may be as simple as getting permission from the instructor or department chair. Contact your local university or community college to see what they'll do for you.

Uncover GI benefits. If you're a U.S. military veteran, see if you can still use your veteran's educational benefits. Some may run out after a certain period or the benefits may vary depending on when you served. Check with the U.S. Department of Veterans Affairs to see what's available for you. Even if your federal benefits have run out, your state may give you a full tuition waiver.

Retirement fund:

how much is enough?

3 secrets to sizing up your savings

A retirement planner can probably list a hundred things that will determine how much you need to save for retirement. Here are three you should definitely consider.

- When will you retire? In other words, how many years of retirement should you plan for?

- What kind of lifestyle do you expect in retirement? Do you want an affluent retirement or a simpler, low-cost lifestyle?

- Where will you live during retirement? Some locations cost more, while others can save dollars or even put cash in your pocket.

Your answers can have a big impact on just how much retirement savings you'll need. So don't assume that thinking about such "frivolous" things is a waste of time. Instead, decide what you want, and accept that these are crucial parts of your retirement planning. You'll help make sure your savings last as long as you do.

Retire later for a larger nest egg

When you choose to retire makes a big difference in how much your retirement costs, and here's why.

A person who retires at 70 should probably plan for 25 years of retirement, but a person who retires at 62 should prepare for at least 33 years. That's assuming you only live until age 95. Some experts say you should plan as if you'll live to 100 so you don't outlive your money.

For example, say you start saving at 25 and expect a yearly retirement income of $40,000 after taxes and inflation. You'd need to save $15,250 a year to retire at 62, $12,625 a year to retire at 66, and $10,375 a year to retire at 70. This calculation assumes your money earns 6 percent yearly and that you get no Social Security or other income, so your exact numbers may vary. But even so, building your retirement nest egg is much easier if you don't have to retire early.

Critical ages to remember

One key to a happy retirement is knowing the critical ages that affect your nest egg and retirement benefits. According to the Employee Benefits Security Administration, these are six of the most important ones.

- 50 – starting age for extra "catch-up" contributions to 401k and other retirement accounts

- 59 – minimum age to avoid tax penalties on withdrawals from retirement accounts

- 62 – minimum age to receive Social Security benefits

- 65 – starting age for Medicare

- 66 – people born between 1943 and 1954 become eligible for full Social Security benefits

- 70 – must take minimum withdrawals from most retirement accounts by this age to avoid tax penalties

Don't outlive retirement savings

You don't want to run out of money during retirement, but how can anyone predict their retirement expenses years ahead of time? You may get a good estimate if you start by considering what kind of lifestyle you want in retirement. Imagine the details, including where you'll live and how you'll spend your days. This "daydreaming" is important. Why? Because most retirement calculators ask how much yearly income you'll need during retirement. And that amount will strongly depend on the lifestyle you choose.

To roughly estimate the retirement income you need, ask yourself if you would need more or less than your current income to live the retirement lifestyle you want. Although taxes, inflation, medical costs, and investment returns will also affect your retirement numbers, estimating your lifestyle costs is still a good place to start. It can help you determine whether you are heading for trouble or are right on track for your dream retirement.

ALERT!

Inflation may not seem like a big deal, but it can really affect your retirement. Conventional wisdom suggests prices double roughly every 20 years. So the same groceries that cost you $50 at age 45 may cost $100 at age 65 and $200 at age 85. When calculating the amount of money you'll need during retirement, plan for higher prices in the future.

Choose the perfect place to retire

Deciding where you're going to spend the next 30 years of retirement is a big decision. Use these tips to help you choose wisely.

Narrow down your choices. Make a list of what you'll gain by moving plus things you'll be sorry to lose. Include both financial changes and intangible things like friends and organizations you belong to. Visit *www.bestplaces.net* and *www.retirementliving.com* for information about cities and towns you might like.

Once you have several locations in mind, take these steps.

- Start reading their local newspapers online or at the library.

- Visit local Web sites such as those for government offices, utilities, and realtors.

- Look through their local Yellow Pages to see what shops, restaurants, and services are available. Check for local information pages or a "new residents" page in the book.

- Contact the local Chamber of Commerce and local and state tax offices.

- Ask your librarian for help in getting cost-of-living, home price, and tax information as well as other details you may need.

Get your questions answered. While researching retirement spots, get answers to these questions.

- Is the new locale the kind of place where you can quickly make friends? Or is it close to friends and family already?

- Will moving to a particular location help stretch your retirement nest egg or keep you from running out of money during retirement? Examine the cost of living, housing costs, health care costs, taxes, and so on. See *Dig deep to find tax-friendly state* in the *Outsmart the IRS* chapter for details on getting tax information.

- Does the climate match your lifestyle and preferences? How prone is the area to natural disasters, and how well can you to cope with them as you get older?

- If you choose a rural area or small town, is a good-sized city nearby?

- Can you pursue your favorite pastimes and hobbies easily and inexpensively in the place you're considering? Are there affordable adult education opportunities, recreational options, and cultural events if you want them?

- Can you find a home you like that will fit both your budget and lifestyle? Could it accommodate your needs if you developed an illness or disability?

- How much do the place's typical lifestyle and living conditions match your preferences?

- Are crime rates low?

- Can you find doctors willing to take you as a patient? Good hospitals? Will your medical insurance be accepted? Can you get affordable long-term care if you need it?

- Can you find banks, libraries, and other "essentials" that meet your needs?

- How will this affect your Medicare costs and services? Visit *www.medicare.gov* to find out how much Medicare premiums will cost in your new location.

- Is an airport or train station close by? If you eventually can no longer drive, what transportation would be available to you?

Find the best fit. When you've narrowed your list of possibilities to two or three, visit each one and compare it to where you live. Visit your final candidates more than once and at different times of the year. Consider renting for as long as three months before making a final decision. You may even want to try living on your projected retirement budget while you do it.

Relocate to cut your costs

Move from New York City to Little Rock, Arkansas, and your cost of living may drop by 51 percent, according to Sperling's BestPlaces.net. That means some people can get more mileage from their retirement dollars simply by retiring to a new place.

If you live where taxes, housing, and local and state expenses are high, consider moving to a place where these costs are low. Cheaper costs may reduce the total amount you need to save for retirement or keep you from outliving your nest egg. This doesn't mean you should ignore other factors when deciding whether to move or where to go, but make sure you consider costs like these before making your choices.

Smart reason to stay put

Roughly 90 percent of those over age 60 stay put in retirement. Here's one way retiring "in place" may save plenty of money. If you stay in a house you've lived in for years, you're more likely to finish paying off your mortgage before retirement. However, if you relocate and cannot pay cash for your new house, you may add a new 30-year mortgage expense to your retirement budget.

Relocating and taking on a new mortgage would only be worthwhile if:

- savings in your cost of living, taxes, home maintenance expenses, and utility bills would cover the mortgage cost.

- home maintenance and the daily activities of living in your house would become too expensive or difficult as you age.

ALERT!

Don't take a check from your 401k when switching jobs before retirement. You'll owe loads of taxes even if you put the money in an IRA. Instead, do a "trustee to trustee" transfer to roll your 401k into an IRA so your money can keep right on growing.

9 common retirement mistakes to fix now

Are you making common mistakes that are sure to ruin your retirement? Find out with these nine important tips on Social Security, home ownership, pensions, and more — and avoid gaffes like these.

Mistake #1: Buying more home — or home maintenance — than you can afford. Before you buy your dream home, run some numbers to see if it will still fit your budget when you're retired. Include your mortgage payment, home upkeep costs, property taxes, and insurance costs.

Mistake #2: Believing Social Security is enough. You've probably heard how much trouble Social Security is in, so don't depend on Social Security alone. Instead, squirrel away additional retirement savings in IRAs, 401ks, or other tax-deferred or tax-free retirement accounts.

Mistake #3: Assuming you'll get all the pension you expect. A number of companies have ended their pension plans or made other changes that limit the dollars you'll get. Even government may not pay as much as you expect. So make sure you can still retire when you want to and with adequate funds. Open other retirement accounts where you can stash extra money.

Mistake #4: Assuming you have enough income for retirement. Check each of your planned sources of retirement income, and find out what monthly payout you can expect. Add up these sources to figure out whether your monthly retirement income will truly be enough.

Mistake #5: Assuming your dollars will go far enough. Statistics suggest that at least one member of a retired couple will make it to age 90, if not both. Make sure you have enough dollars to get that far.

Mistake #6: Believing your medical costs won't go up. Some experts say you'll need only 70 to 80 percent of your current income when you retire, but medical costs could change that. Medicare may not cover everything, especially if you need nursing home care. You should also plan how you'd handle the costs of long-term care, a disability, or a chronic or serious illness. So plan for higher income needs and start taking better care of yourself.

Mistake #7: Forgetting to plan for taxes and rising prices. When figuring the size of your yearly income in retirement, be sure to cover the tax bite from property taxes, income taxes, and so on. Also, compare the price of gasoline or a movie when you were a teenager to what each one costs now. Plan your retirement as if the price of everything will keep going up over the years.

Mistake #8: Tapping your 401k before retirement. Don't cash out or take loans from your 401k for anything less than an emergency. You'll miss out on money your retirement dollars could be making for you — thus shrinking your retirement nest egg.

Mistake #9: Assuming that you can keep working. An economic downturn, health problems, or a disability may decide when you quit working. So make a financial plan for what you'll do if you must stop working earlier than expected.

Secrets to an accurate estimate

Paper worksheets and online calculators make calculating your nest egg amount look easy. But unless you've done a little legwork, the numbers you put in may be little better than a wild guess — and the number you get out may not be much better. Use these tips to get an accurate estimate of how much you need to retire so you won't run out of money when you need it most.

Figure retirement expenses first. Finding a paper worksheet or online calculator isn't hard. In fact, you'll see good sources for them in the next story. Some calculators ask what percentage of your current income you will want in retirement. Others ask for a monthly or yearly number.

Some experts suggest your retirement expenses will be so low that you can live on as little as 70 percent of your working years' income. But others warn that the poor outlook for Social Security and the rising costs of health care, taxes, and inflation make this figure unreasonably low. Perhaps a wiser approach is to figure your retirement expenses before you estimate the income you will need.

Make your own "expense report." To estimate annual expenses, figure your monthly retirement costs, and multiply by 12. See the list in the following table to be sure you include all your expenses. Also, consider how some expenses may be larger during retirement.

For example, health insurance may cost more or cover less in the future — and medical costs rise faster than other prices — so plan for higher out-of-pocket medical expenses. Some experts even suggest you may need up to 120 percent of your current income to cover long-term care and other health-related costs.

Keeping points like these in mind can help you estimate expenses — and income — more accurately.

Input the correct numbers. Some calculators require an estimate for each source of income you'll have in retirement. Don't just guess what these should be. Get the correct numbers ahead of time.

- For your Social Security amount, check the mailing you get from the Social Security administration around your birthday, or visit *www.socialsecurity.gov* and click on "Estimate your Retirement Benefits." Experts suggest you may not end up getting your full benefit, so consider planning for only a portion of your expected benefit.

- Check with past and present employers to determine whether you'll receive pension payments from them and how much you can expect. Be aware that some retirement calculators may not include pensions as an income source.

- To learn how much you have in your IRA and how much you contribute each year, check your IRA statements, or call the bank or broker with whom you opened the IRA.

- See your 401k paperwork, Web site, benefits administrator, or human resources office to learn how much you have in your 401k and how much you contribute monthly or yearly.

- Don't forget additional sources of income such as salary or wages, tips, investment income, rent, alimony, and inheritance.

You may also be asked for a rate of inflation. Experts recommend 3 percent. And if you're asked for a rate of return on your retirement investments, assume 6 to 8 percent, or try the calculation with varying rates of return.

For more on calculating the size of your nest egg, see *Make your money last a lifetime* in the *Scam-proof your savings* chapter.

Key long-term costs to consider

Don't sabotage your retirement budget by forgetting to include an important expense. Use this checklist to help you include more easy-to-miss costs.

utilities	electricity, natural gas, heating oil, water, sewage, trash collection, cable, Internet, cell phone
home	mortgage, insurance, maintenance, property tax, repairs
food	eating out, groceries
car	insurance, gas, auto-related taxes, car payments, maintenance
clothes	clothing, dry-cleaning
personal	haircuts, other personal care
health care	health and dental insurance, long-term care
travel expenses	hotel, air fare, on-the-road expenses
charity	donations, costs of volunteering
events and fun	entertainment and hobby costs
yearly commitments	subscription costs, dues, memberships
life events	birthdays, weddings, anniversaries, graduations, births
small replacements	small kitchen appliances such as food processor, mixer, coffee pot
medium replacements	electronics, including computer, TVs, DVD players

large replacements	appliances, home "systems" like air conditioning, furnace, roof, carpeting, flooring, water heater, lawn mower, cars
reserves	emergency fund
daily household expenses	toiletries, cleaners, OTC medicines, light bulbs, batteries, other small goods
holiday-related	Christmas gifts, stocking stuffers, Valentine's flowers, gift-mailing costs, holiday foods, holiday entertaining, decorations, gift wrap
investments	fees and other costs
monthly debts	credit card bills, other loan repayments
insurance	life, home, and other insurance

Savvy ways to plan for the future

Only 42 percent of Americans have calculated how much money they need for retirement, according to the U.S. Department of Labor. If you're not one of them, you run the risk of running short. Use paper retirement worksheets or online calculators to help you catch up

Calculate the old-fashioned way. If you don't have a computer, don't worry. The Employee Benefits Security Administration offers *Taking the Mystery Out of Retirement Planning*. Designed for people about 10 years from retirement, this free booklet contains worksheets to help you figure out how much you need. To get it, call toll-free 866-444-3272, or have someone download it for you from *www.dol.gov/ebsa*.

The American Savings Education Council (ASEC) offers a retirement worksheet called the Ballpark E$timate for anyone looking to save for retirement. To request a free paper copy of the Ballpark E$timate, send a self-addressed stamped envelope to:

EBRI Publications
1100 13th Street, NW Suite 878
Washington, D.C. 20005

Put the Web to work. For online calculators and worksheets, try these sites:

- *www.aarp.org/bulletin.* Click on "Your Money."

- *www.smartmoney.com.* Click on "Personal Finance," then "Worksheets," and then "Retirement Worksheets."

- *www.schwab.com.* Click on "Advice and Retirement," then "Retirement Planning."

- *www.troweprice.com/ric4*

- *www.asec.org* to try the interactive Ballpark Estimator

Try more than one. No single retirement calculator is perfect. Any given calculator may make one of the following mistakes.

- Assume a particular rate of return on investments or a particular tax bracket. If their assumption doesn't apply to you, they may not give you the most accurate result.

- Fail to consider that medical costs rise faster than other prices, or leave long-term care out of their equations.

- Underestimate the effect of taxes on your retirement dollars.

- Underestimate how long you'll live — meaning how long your retirement will be.

- Not include pensions as an income source.

And, of course, some calculators are designed by people who are selling something, so beware calculators that suggest you buy anything.

The bottom line is, you need to try several calculators and compare the results. They will at least give you a rough estimate of how much you need to save. But don't hesitate to go deeper into the planning process by figuring your retirement expenses or consulting a financial professional. A little extra planning could have a big payoff.

Why it's never too late to save

Either you haven't saved for retirement or you haven't saved nearly enough, and it's only a few scant years away. Don't give up hope. Thanks to the "power of compounding," it's almost never too late too save.

Suppose you are just 15 short years away from retirement and you choose to put more money into retirement by eating out less. This adds an extra $19 to $20 to your savings every week. At the end of one year, you have nearly $1,000. If that $1,000 earns an average return of 6 percent every year, it will turn into $2,261 by the end of year 15. This happens because your original money earns money and then the earned money also earns new money. Here's how it works.

Year	Interest earned	End-of-year total
1	$0	$1,000
2	$60	$1,060
3	$63.60	$1,123.60
4	$67.42	$1,191.02
5	$71.46	$1,262.48
6	$75.75	$1,338.23
7	$80.29	$1,418.52
8	$85.11	$1,503.63
9	$90.22	$1,593.85
10	$95.63	$1,689.48
11	$101.37	$1,790.85
12	$107.45	$1,898.30
13	$113.90	$2,012.20
14	$120.73	$2,132.93
15	$127.98	$2,260.91

Even better, if you save $1,000 each year for all 15 years, you won't just increase your nest egg by $15,000. Assuming a 6 percent return, you'll earn $24,537.

If you decide to work a few extra years, you may save even more. But even if you don't, it's not too late to save thousands before you retire.

5 simple steps to success for late savers

Retire rich even if you're a late starter with these tips.

- Learn how to avoid sneaky investment expenses that siphon money away from your retirement nest egg. See *Slash fees to save big bucks* in the *Mutual Funds: low-risk moneymakers* chapter for details.

- Save a few quarters or dollars every day.

- Discover how to pay down your money-stealing debts.

- Put more of your money where it can cut your taxes, reduce your spending, and boost your retirement savings.

- Find extra retirement money in your home, yard, and budget.

To find out how to put these tips to work for you, read on.

Uncover your invisible savings

You have more money to save for retirement than you might think. You just have to know where to look.

Start tracking your expenses aggressively. Write down every penny you spend for a week or even a month. If you only track your daily expenses for a week, keep track of your once-a-month expenses for the entire month. When you're done, look over your records.

- Find your sneak expenses — the small "insignificant" costs you wouldn't even miss if they were gone. You may be surprised at how fast these pile up. Now consider how much you could save by eliminating them. If you save just 50 cents a day, you'll have an extra $180 in one year. If you can save $5 a day, you'll have $1,825 in a year.

- Highlight your luxury expenses — such as dining out, using specialty goods, or splurging. Determine which of these you could spend less on, replace with something cheaper, or even eliminate. If this boosts your savings to $10 a day, you'll have $3,650 in a year. Add that money to your bank account or investments, and it will earn you even more money.

"Invisible" savings may still lurk in your paycheck, yard, and home. Here's how to find them and add to your nest egg.

- Go through your attic, garage, closets, the backyard shed, and any other place where you store things you never use. Sell your unwanted items in a yard sale, garage sale, or on eBay.

- Use direct deposit to divert some of your paycheck into savings accounts or retirement accounts. If you never see the money, you can't spend it. This one easy trick can help you save money every month for the rest of your life.

Cut taxes and build a better nest egg

Imagine shrinking your taxes, saving more for retirement, and easily avoiding the temptation to overspend. Here's how.

Your 401k contributions can automatically be deducted so you won't be tempted to spend that money. What's more, both 401k contributions and traditional IRA contributions can reduce your taxable income so you pay less in taxes.

Money in IRAs and 401ks can help expand your retirement savings because it grows tax deferred. That means your nest egg grows faster because taxes don't take a bite out of your gains every year. So find out the maximum amount you can contribute to your IRAs and 401k. If you're over 50, also ask about extra catch-up contributions. Then set your payroll deductions, or make other arrangements to contribute as much as possible to your retirement accounts.

Erase debt to increase savings

You may not think credit card debt is damaging your retirement savings, but consider this. If you have $5,000 in credit card debt, a 13-percent interest rate, and a monthly payment near $150, you will spend $1,237 in interest charges before you pay off the debt in 3 1/2 years. That's more than $1,000 that could have gone towards retirement.

So don't just make the minimum payment. Pay as much as possible each month to help pay off your credit cards sooner. Or pay biweekly to shrink your balance even faster. See *Dig yourself out of credit card debt* in the *Build your nest egg: debt control* chapter for an explanation on how to do it. And just as important — avoid accumulating any new credit card debt if you can't pay it off in the same month.

4 tactics for tackling debt

Credit card debt is bad enough, but you may have lots of other debt that keeps you from saving for retirement. Try these tactics to help you get rid of it.

Stop digging a hole. If you're trying to get out of a hole, stop digging. That means stop adding to your debt. Seek ways to avoid taking on new loans, new credit cards, or any new purchases that require loans or credit card payments.

Discover money you might not know you had. See *Uncover your invisible savings* earlier in this chapter for ways to do this. If this isn't enough, you may also consider working overtime or finding a second job for a time. Use this money to pay off your debts.

Try a debt-busting secret. List all your debts from the highest interest rate to the lowest. Pay the minimum payment on all of them except the one with the highest interest rate. Put any extra dollars you have towards paying down that one high-interest debt. But when you pay it off, act as if you haven't. Here's what that means.

Say you pay $150 per month on Debt #1 and you finally finish paying it off in March. Your next-highest interest rate debt has a minimum payment of $25. So when April comes, you not only pay the $25 on Debt #2, but also add the $150 that formerly paid Debt #1. That means you're paying off $175 per month of Debt #2. When you finish paying off Debt #2, you'll simply roll that $175 over to help pay off Debt #3. Like a ball rolling down a hill, your debt reduction will pick up speed until there's nothing left to pay.

Beat debt a different way. If you get discouraged or if you know you'll have trouble sticking with the plan above, try this instead. List all your debts from smallest to largest. Pay the minimum payment on all of them except the smallest. Put any extra dollars you have towards that smallest debt so you can pay it off more quickly. When you pay off Debt #1, add its payments to the minimum payment for your next-largest debt — just as with the earlier technique. When you pay off the second debt, roll that payment over to the next debt — and keep going until you're debt free.

THE NEXT STEP

You've finally paid down that last credit card. But instead of spending that money, consider continuing the payments — but make them to a retirement savings account instead. If this would cause you to exceed the legal limits of accounts like IRAs or 401ks, just put that money into another account you've earmarked for retirement.

Cut your credit card debt faster

Pay less interest while avoiding debt-raisers like extra fees, lost motivation, and temptation. Use all the tips below, and you may spend fewer months — or years — paying off your credit cards.

- Find out how much total credit card debt you owe. Calculate how long it will take to pay it all off — including interest charges.

- Pay on time. Avoid the added strain of late fees.

- Pay cash for everything. When you don't have cash, don't buy.

- Call your credit card company and ask if you can get a lower rate. Some companies will say yes in order to keep you as a customer. Other companies may say no, but you won't lose anything by asking.

- If one credit card charges a higher rate than your other cards, try this. Transfer the balance on the high rate card to your lowest rate card. But ask about balance transfer fees first. They can cost up to 3 percent of the amount transferred.

For more debt-busting details, see the *Build your nest egg: debt control* chapter.

SuperSaver

Put your credit cards in water in the freezer, so each one freezes in its own block of ice. You'll have to wait for a card to melt to use it and, by that time, the temptation to purchase may have passed.

Healthy living saves health-care costs

What's the #1 thing you can do to ensure you'll stay independent for life? Keep yourself healthy. It's also a good way to save for retirement and avoid outliving your money.

Keep your money. Nearly half the people in a recent AARP survey asked their doctors what diet and lifestyle changes they could make to lower their number of medications. They have the right idea. Studies suggest that a good way to keep your independence — and your money — is to help prevent costly illnesses and disability by taking better care of yourself. Take diabetes for example.

- The average annual health costs of people with type 2 diabetes are three times as high as the health costs of the average American.

- Complications from diabetes can cost up to $10,000 per year, with $1,600 of that coming straight from your pocket.

- Treating simple diabetes costs the U.S. health system $37 billion per year. But treating diabetes plus complications when people don't follow their treatment plan costs more than $57 billion annually.

- Research suggests that eating a Mediterranean-style diet — full of veggies, fruits, nuts, legumes, whole grains, and fish — could help you avoid diabetes and its costs.

Keep your independence. Disability and conditions like Alzheimer's can take away your ability to live independently, but research shows that simple wellness habits can help prevent these problems.

- Adults can lower their odds of disability just by participating in a walking exercise program, says a University of Georgia study.

- People who take brisk walks more often are less likely to develop dementia, an Italian study found. Doing household chores, yard work, and gardening also help.

- Overweight seniors who exercised regularly developed less disability than normal weight or overweight seniors who were inactive, according to a study in the *American Journal of Public Health*.

- Strokes can also cause disability, but a University of South Carolina study found that you can lower your risk of stroke, heart attack, and heart disease just by taking up four healthy habits: exercising, controlling weight, eating at least five fruits and veggies a day, and not smoking.

So if you want to save more of your money, try taking better care of yourself. It could save you a bundle in health-care costs and help you enjoy the independent, fun-filled retirement you've dreamed of.

Make the right mortgage decision

You're anxious to pay off your mortgage before you retire, but you've heard you might be better off keeping it. Before you make a decision, consider your payoff pros and cons.

Pros:

- Paying off your mortgage lifts a significant financial burden off your shoulders.

- If you decide to sell your home, you will reap a higher overall profit.

- You can save thousands in interest charges. For example, if you have $150,000 left to pay on a 6-percent, 30-year mortgage and you have 20 years of payments left, you could save more than $9,000 in interest just by paying an extra $50 per month. If you can pay $100 extra a month, you'll save more than $24,500. If your mortgage has no prepayment penalties, you will reduce the number of years spent paying your mortgage, so you can be mortgage-free in retirement.

Cons:

- You no longer have the benefit of deducting mortgage interest on your tax return.

- Paying off your entire mortgage at once may reduce the amount of cash you have on hand for emergencies, such as health problems or a furnace that must be replaced.

Some experts say you should keep your mortgage if you can get a higher rate of return on your investments than the interest rate on your mortgage. In other words, if your investments are paying 10 percent, but your mortgage rate is only 6 percent, you should keep your money in investments. Your investments most likely are making more money than you're losing in mortgage interest.

But if the stock or bond markets have a bad year, you may have to sell an investment at a loss in order to keep paying your mortgage. You also may be forced to withdraw money from your IRA or 401k to make the payments. Unfortunately, taking money from these accounts raises your taxable income and may boost your income enough to trigger hefty taxes on your Social Security benefits.

For some people, the mortgage payoff decision will be complex. In that case, you may want to consult a financial advisor to help you make the right choice for your situation.

The nuts and bolts of refinancing

Refinancing may help you save extra dollars for retirement and give you more money during your retirement years, but it won't help everyone. Before you call a loan officer, do some research to find out whether refinancing is right for you.

Do the math. Some experts say it's time to refinance if your new loan rate would be one percentage point lower than your old one — such as a drop from 6 percent to 5 percent. But the lowest rate may not be the rate you'll get. If you don't have a lot of equity in your home or a high credit score, you may want to check out *www.TrueCredit.com*. Click on Mortgage Simulator, and for a small fee, you will get an estimate of the rate you'll qualify for.

Another way to determine the suitability of refinancing is to divide your total expected closing costs by your expected monthly savings. For example, if your closing costs are around $4,000 and you expect to save $125 per month, it will take roughly 2 years and 8 months of cheaper payments to recoup the costs of refinancing. You must keep the house for at least that long for a refinance to be worthwhile.

Keep in mind that you're also restarting the clock on your mortgage. If you've paid 10 years of a 30-year mortgage, and you must refinance into another 30-year mortgage to get a cheaper payment, run some numbers to determine how 30 more years of mortgage payments will affect your current and future budgets.

Beware the pitfalls. Housing lenders have become much more cautious recently, so you may find new refinance hurdles like these.

- You may need a higher credit score to get a good rate.

- You may need as much as 20-percent equity in your home to refinance. Whether you meet that percentage is determined by the value of your home, so you must pay for a home appraisal even if you don't end up qualifying for the loan. Before you contact a loan officer, get a rough estimate of your home's value by calling a real estate agent or by visiting a realty Web site such as *www.zillow.com*.

- If you owe more than your home is worth, or if your home value has plummeted, you may not qualify for a refinance loan.

- If your home value has fallen less sharply, you may qualify but have to pay extra costs.

- If you have more than one mortgage on your home, the second mortgage lender must agree that the second mortgage will be subordinate to the new loan — meaning the second mortgage remains the "second payoff" loan. Some lenders refuse to do this.

Pensions and 401k plans:

cash for your future

Pick pension payout carefully

Many financial advisors will tell you to take your pension as a lump sum distribution, rather than a monthly payment. They want you to invest that money through them, so they can earn a commission. It's good advice for the financial advisors, but it's bad advice for a lot of retirees. Both lump sums and monthly payments have their drawbacks. Find out which one is right for you.

Test your risk tolerance. If you don't like to gamble, you probably won't like the risk that comes with a lump sum. Getting all that money at once sounds great, until you realize you have to invest it yourself, too — and smartly so it lasts the rest of your life. If your stocks or bonds do poorly, you could outlive your money.

Monthly payments don't run this risk. First, the responsibility for managing your money and investing it wisely rests with the pension provider, not you. Second, traditional pensions guarantee a monthly income for life. You can't outlive your payments, no matter what happens in the stock market.

Look at life expectancy. According to T. Rowe Price, a 65-year-old man has a 50-percent chance of living to age 85, while a woman has the same chance of living to age 88. With people living longer than ever, monthly payments make sense, since you can't outlive them. However, if you don't expect to live long due to serious health problems or a family history of them, then taking the lump sum may be a better choice.

Eye your employer's health. The company's financial health can play a big role in your decision. You may want to "take the money and run" in a lump sum if you know your employer is struggling to fund its pension, or otherwise fighting to stay afloat financially.

Get good advice. This decision is too big to rush into. Start by talking to the Human Resources manager where you work. Ask how much your lump sum would be. You might find out it would be smaller than you think, thanks to a 2006 law that changed the way lump sum distributions get calculated. Next, ask if taking a lump sum would affect your retirement benefits, such as health insurance.

Unfortunately, you may not get a choice about how to take your pension. If it's worth $5,000 or less, your employer may automatically pay it out as a lump sum without your consent.

ALERT!

Watching your old employer sink beneath the financial waves isn't the end of the world. The Pension Benefit Guaranty Corporation takes over troubled pensions to ensure retirees don't go down with the ship. That's the upside. The downside is, your monthly payments could decrease, since PBGC only guarantees pensions up to a certain amount.

Protect spouse with survivor benefits

You face a lot of choices about your pension plan when you retire. One seems to be a no-brainer, but it's more important than you think. If you decide to take your pension in monthly payments rather than a lump sum, you get to choose whether you want a single-life or a joint-and-survivor annuity.

It's tempting to pick the single-life option. You'll receive more money every month until your death. After that, though, the payments stop, leaving your spouse with nothing. The joint-and-survivor option, on the other hand, gives you a smaller monthly pension check but continues benefits for your spouse if you die first.

Many retirees choose the bigger check now and worry about the future later. But you may be setting up your "better half" for poverty. Trying to guarantee income for you spouse in other ways can backfire.

- Term life insurance policies sound like good protection. However, if you outlive the term, your spouse gets nothing when you die.

- Pension maximization insurance is basically life insurance, and the policies aren't cheap. Buying one as a backup for a single-life pension can eat up the bigger monthly payment. Plus, if the insurance company loses money on its investments, your payout can shrink, and if you fall behind on the policy payments, you lose coverage.

Despite these drawbacks, single-life pensions may be a good choice if your spouse is terminally ill or likely to die before you, or has their own source of income. Before retiring, talk to the Human Resources manager where you work to find out which type of pension you currently have and to change it, if necessary.

SuperSaver

The old saying, "don't put all your eggs in one basket" applies to retirement plans, too. Don't count on your pension alone for retirement. Your employer could change the terms on you, or the fund could go bust.

Diversify your savings, instead. Open other retirement accounts, such as a traditional IRA or Roth IRA. If something happens to your pension, you'll still be safe.

Free pension help for veterans

Now veterans and their families who meet certain age, income, and military service requirements can get free help applying for the Department of Veterans Affairs Improved Pension program.

Applying for the pension can involve a maze of paperwork and government bureaucracy. Project VetAssist is helping to change that.

This nonprofit organization gives veterans and their surviving spouses step-by-step help in signing up for the program. You'll need computer access, but the rest is easy. Simply visit *www.vetassist.org,* or e-mail them with questions at *info@VetAssist.org.*

Smart ways to recover missing money

Old employers may be holding retirement money that's rightfully yours. Here's how to track down pensions and retirement accounts to get your full due.

Be proactive. Head to your company's Human Resources department before you retire, and find out what money and benefits you're entitled to. Then do the same with past employers. Make a list of every place you worked for more than one year. Call the Human Resources department of each, and ask if you are entitled to any retirement benefits. If so, make sure they have your current address, marital status, and beneficiary information.

Track down missing pensions. Not every company keeps good records. Perhaps you know you had a pension, but the employer can't find any record of it. PensionHelp America can aid in solving the mystery. Visit *www.pensionhelp.org*, and click on PensionHelp to get aid from nearby pension counselors, or look for the missing pension plan yourself by clicking on PensionSearch.

No computer? No problem. Call the U.S. Department of Labor's Employee Benefits Security Administration toll-free at 866-444-3272 for help resolving pension problems.

Find folded plans. You can still get your money, even if your employer or pension plan folded. The Pension Benefit Guaranty Corporation will help you find the troubled plan. Call them at 800-400-7242, or go their Web site at *www.pbgc.gov.*

Unearth forgotten 401ks. Figuring out which employer or firm is in charge of an old 401k isn't always easy. Search for the plan on the

Web site of the National Registry of Unclaimed Retirement Benefits at *www.unclaimedretirementbenefits.com.*

Draw pension while still working

You can start collecting pension benefits while still working if you are 65 or older, or if you are 62 and your pension plan allows it. In return, you switch from full-time to part-time, drawing a reduced salary and making up the difference with pension benefits. Ask Human Resources if your employer offers phased retirement and if it would affect your current health benefits or future full-retirement benefits.

Grow your savings, slash your taxes

Stop tucking money under the mattress. Put it in a 401k to grow it faster and slash your taxes. Unlike pension plans, this type of retirement account lets both you and your boss stash cash tax-free for your retirement.

Get better returns than a bank. Think of it as a savings account with tax benefits. You sign up for one through your employer and decide how much money you want to put in it each year. The money comes directly out of your paycheck before taxes and gets deposited in the 401k account. Some employers help you save by kicking in matching contributions.

With any luck, the money in a 401k account accrues faster than it would in a savings account. That's because you can invest 401k savings in stocks, mutual funds, bonds, and other investments that generally earn more interest than a savings account. An outside company manages the 401k funds. You tell them how to invest the money, and they send you statements explaining how much money those investments earned each year.

Enjoy tax-free savings. Best of all, you don't pay taxes on the money you put in or on the interest it earns until you retire and start withdrawing it. That's a big deal. With a regular savings account, you pay taxes every year on the interest you earn. With a 401k, you don't, which enables your nest egg to get bigger, faster.

Here comes the next tax break. Putting part of your paycheck in a 401k lowers the amount of income you pay taxes on. If you earn $40,000 and put $7,000 in your 401k, you only pay income tax on $33,000, which lowers your tax bill.

This type of retirement account is an all-around winner. Find out if your employer offers one. If so, start contributing. The IRS limits how much money you can put into these accounts each year, but the limit goes up annually. In 2009, you could tuck up to $16,500 in your 401k. People over age 50 can stash an extra $5500 to help them "catch up."

MAKING IT WORK

Pretend you have $20,000 in a savings account earning 2 percent interest. You're in the 25 percent federal tax bracket, and you pay 8 percent in state taxes. If you were to leave it there for 20 years, you would end up with $26,100. Not bad. Now, pretend you didn't have to pay taxes on the interest earned every year. The same money turns into $29,719 in 20 years — $3,619 more.

That's essentially what happens with a 401k, only on a much larger scale because 401k accounts typically earn more interest than savings. Imagine putting the same $20,000 in a 401k earning 7 percent interest. You never add more money. You simply leave it there for 20 years. At the end, you would have a whopping $77,394, all thanks to tax-deferred growth at a healthy interest rate.

Earn free money for retirement

What would you do if your boss offered you an extra $1,500 a year, every year, with no strings attached? You wouldn't have to work more hours or take on more responsibility. Participate in a 401k plan at work, and that's exactly what can happen.

Some companies match their employees' 401k contributions, usually up to a certain percentage of their income. You may get a dollar-for-dollar match or a portion, like 50 cents on the dollar.

It's free money. You get it just for participating in the program, and you'd be crazy not to take it. All that extra cash going into your 401k could grow your nest egg twice as fast as if you alone were funding the account.

Ask your Human Resources department about the company's 401k program and matching contributions. Find out the matching limit, and make sure you contribute at least that much of your paycheck to your 401k. Your goal should be to max out the employer match. Otherwise, you're missing out on free money.

MAKING IT WORK

Say you make $40,000 a year, and your employer will match your 401k contributions dollar-for-dollar, up to 5 percent of your income. To max out the match, you decide to contribute 5 percent of your paycheck — $2,000 — to your 401k every year. With the match, your boss kicks in another $2,000 annually.

If your investments average a modest 7-percent return, you will have saved an astounding $57,341 for retirement in just 10 years. And you only had to put away $2,000 a year of your own money. Without your employer's match, you would have saved just half that — $28,670.50.

Save thousands in retirement taxes

Your employer has just announced the company will offer a Roth 401k in addition to the regular 401k, and you're wondering which one you should contribute to. You can actually add to both, and contributing to a Roth 401k will mean less in taxes — and more in your pocket — during retirement.

Compare the plans. When you put money into a standard 401k, it's pre-tax — meaning you pay no taxes on it now. Instead, when you withdraw that money in retirement, you pay taxes on both your contributions and the dollars those contributions have earned. With a Roth 401k, you pay the taxes now but pay no taxes on your contributions — or their earnings — when you withdraw the money during retirement.

Which 401k to choose depends on whether you expect your retirement tax bracket to be higher or lower than your current tax bracket. This may be tough to predict, so some experts suggest you contribute part of your money to a standard 401K and part to a Roth 401k.

Figure your tax advantage. If you put the current maximum amount of $15,500 in a traditional 401k for 15 years and get a 6-percent return, you will earn $382,424. You'll build the same nest egg if you put $7,750 in your Roth 401k and $7,750 in your regular 401k for 15 years with a 6-percent return. But you will pay half as much in taxes when you withdraw it because you're only taxed on monies from the traditional 401k. If you're still in a 25-percent tax bracket, that would amount to a savings of $47,803.

Consider other benefits. Another plus is that Roth income doesn't count when determining whether your Social Security benefits are taxable. And some experts warn that increasing medical costs will boost your retirement expenses, while others say tax rates will rise in the future. If they're right, you could benefit greatly from a Roth 401k.

To learn whether the Roth 401k is right for you, consult with a tax or financial professional, or run the numbers to determine how it will affect your current taxes, retirement taxes, and potential nest-egg size. You'll find helpful financial calculators online at *www.dinkytown.net*.

> **ALERT!**
>
> If your employer matches your Roth 401k contribution, the company's contributions will still be taxable in retirement, just as in a traditional 401k. Plan accordingly.

Keep fees from eating away savings

The tax man isn't the only one out to get you. The brokers and mutual fund managers charged with growing your retirement fund could be the same ones whittling it away into nothing. That's because everyone with a hand in managing your 401k charges a fee for their services. And those fees can take a serious bite out of your savings over time.

Fortunately, you have a lot of control over how much you pay these people. No firm or mutual fund charges the same amount. If you decide one of your 401k investments is too costly, you can simply switch to another.

First, though, you have to figure out what you're paying. Call each mutual fund company you own in your 401k account and request a copy of their prospectus. Look inside for the fund's expense ratio, then total up the ratios for all the funds you hold in your 401k. The total should be less than 1 percent. If not, look for ways to start cutting.

Switch funds. Fill your 401k with mutual funds that boast low expense ratios, such as low-cost index funds, institutional funds, and no-load mutual funds. Search *www.fundgrades.com* for those that earn an "A" in expenses, and ask your employer to offer more low-cost choices if necessary.

Avoid "actively managed" funds. These pay an investment advisor to constantly research and trade fund holdings, like stocks. Actively managed funds typically charge higher fees than passively managed funds, like index funds, but they don't necessarily perform better.

Beware the dreaded 12b-1. Funds charge 12b-1 fees to pay for advertising, commissions, and other services. Unfortunately, these can eat away at your savings. 12b-1 fees usually range from 0.25 to 1.0 percent of the total money in the plan each year. Never pay more. Experts suggest looking for funds that don't charge any 12b-1 fees. Look for these fees in the fund's prospectus under the heading "Annual Fund Operating Expenses."

Have a heart-to-heart with the boss. Talk to your employer if you notice big fees in your 401k plan. The company may be able to switch to a 401k management firm with lower fees or offer lower-cost funds.

Don't get caught with company stock

You worked 33 years for your company, and they rewarded your loyalty with loads of company stock in your retirement account. What seems like a great gift could turn around and bite you.

Pegging too much of your nest egg on a single stock is dangerous. They're riskier than mutual funds, which own lots of different stocks, and you need stability in your nest egg when you reach retirement. Investments like 401ks that are loaded with one stock are vulnerable to the wild swings that characterize the stock market.

Avoid sinking more than 5 to 10 percent of your 401k savings in any one stock, even your own company's. Too late? Slowly sell your company stock and put the money in other 401k options. Ask the benefits department where you work if there are any restrictions on selling company stock.

Some employers match your 401k contributions not with cash but with company stock. If that's your case, at least avoid using your own contributions to buy more. Invest your share of money in mutual funds or other diversified options, but be careful not to invest in mutual funds that hold lots of your company's stock. Check out funds at *www.morningstar.com*, or read the prospectus of each before buying into it.

---

4 assets safe from bankruptcy

Rest easy knowing your retirement funds are safe during bankruptcy. Creditors can't touch:

- qualified corporate retirement plans such as pensions and 401ks.

- qualified self-employed retirement plans, such as SEP and SIMPLE IRAs.

- IRA assets that were rolled over from any of those qualified plans.

- up to $1 million contributed directly to an IRA rather than rolled over.

Double your nest egg in no time

Starting a small home business can supercharge your retirement savings. Take advantage of retirement accounts for the self-employed, and you could save up to $49,000 toward retirement, while lowering the taxes you and your business owe Uncle Sam.

SEPs make sense. If you work two jobs, choose a SEP (Simplified Employee Pension) IRA. You can open one even if you have another retirement account with another employer, such as a 401k at your day job. A SEP lets you tuck roughly 20 percent of your business's net income into it annually, up to $49,000 in 2009.

There are no minimum contributions, so in lean years you don't have to contribute any money. Plus, they're easy to set up and require less paperwork than other retirement plans.

Simple plan for savings. SIMPLE (Savings Incentive Match Plan for Employees) IRAs make a good choice for part-time, self-employed people. You can contribute up to $11,500 of your income in 2009 each year, plus an extra $2,500 if you're over age 50. In fact, if your business only makes that much one year, you can stash all of it in a SIMPLE plan.

A 401k just for you. Business owners who earn a little more money and have no employees other than a spouse should look into an Individual 401k. It has higher contribution limits — up to $49,000 a year in 2009, or $54,500 if you're over age 50. To reach this amount, you can withhold up to $16,500 from your own paycheck ($22,000 if you're over 50), then kick in up to 25 percent of your business's income as your own employer.

Get advice from a Certified Public Accountant about which plan is right for you. Lots of well-known financial services firms, such as Fidelity, Vanguard, and T. Rowe Price, will manage these plans for you, saving you the paperwork and headaches. Shop around for a firm with low fees, since these can eat into your investment earnings.

Rollover tips keep nest egg growing

You face a major choice about what to do with your 401k when you retire — leave it where it is or roll it into an IRA. Most plans let you leave your money in them, even if you retire or change jobs. That's a good option if:

- it's a generous 401k plan with investment choices you like.

- you think you may want to go back to work for the old boss later.

- the old employer will pay your 401k investment fees.

- the investments in your 401k charge lower fees than those in an IRA.

- you plan to retire early, before you turn 59 1/2. 401k plans let you begin withdrawals, penalty-free, at age 55.

On the other hand, rolling your savings into an IRA makes sense if:

- the IRA charges lower fees than your old 401k plan or the new one, if you changed jobs.

- you don't like the investment choices in the 401k.

If you do decide to roll over those 401k funds, do it as a direct rollover. Otherwise, you could face stiff tax penalties. Set up the new IRA account first with whatever investment firm you choose, then have the funds transferred directly from your 401k into the IRA account.

ALERT!

Don't roll employer stock into your IRA. Leave it in the old 401k plan, if possible. You'll pay higher taxes when you cash it out down the road if you move it to an IRA.

Social Security simplified

Jump-start your retirement

Ernest Ackerman, a motorman from Cleveland, didn't wait long to claim his Social Security benefits. Just one day after the program went into effect, Ackerman retired. A nickel was withheld from his pay for his last day of work, and he received a lump-sum payment of 17 cents. Of course, 17 cents went much further back then — but it's clear his lump-sum payment did not fund his retirement.

Ida May Fuller, who received the first monthly retirement check, got a little more out of Social Security. A legal secretary who retired in 1939, Fuller started collecting Social Security in 1940 at age 65. Her first check totaled $22.54. She lived to be 100 years old, collecting $22,888.92 in Social Security benefits during her lifetime.

You may not live to be 100, but Social Security will still play an important role in your retirement plan. In fact, the average retiree will receive the equivalent of about $250,000 in retirement savings. That's a lot more than 17 cents.

Here's a quick look at the history of Social Security, the many changes through the years, and details about how the program works.

Why it was created. As its name implies, Social Security was designed to provide some economic security for older people. In the past, extended families took care of older family members when they could no longer work. But, during the early part of the 20th century, several factors changed family dynamics.

The Industrial Revolution turned many self-employed agricultural workers into wage earners for big companies. Fewer people lived on farms or in rural communities, as more people moved to cities for work. This led to the decline of the extended family. Instead of several generations living together, families were pared down to parents and children. With advances in health care and sanitation, people were also living longer than ever before. Add the stock market crash of 1929 and the following Great Depression to the mix, and you get a perfect storm.

How it works. As part of his response to the Great Depression, Franklin D. Roosevelt introduced the Social Security Act in 1935. Several changes have taken place since. For instance, benefits for workers' spouses, minor children, and survivors were added in 1939. In 1950, cost-of-living allowances were included to offset the effects of inflation on a fixed income. And in 1956, benefits for disabled workers were added. But the basic idea remains the same. You pay into the program through payroll taxes during your working years, then collect benefits when you retire.

Why you should plan ahead. Social Security provides a steady income in your later years, but you should not rely exclusively on it to fund your retirement. Even with the cost-of-living increases, your monthly payments will probably not be enough to keep up with your living expenses. Think of Social Security as an important part of your retirement plan — but not the only part. At the same time, it's important to get the most from Social Security. That means knowing the ins and outs of the program. Read on to discover how to maximize your Social Security benefits.

Unravel the secrets of qualifying for benefits

You may have heard Social Security referred to as an "entitlement program." That's because you're entitled to it. After all, you worked for it. You've earned it.

As you start unraveling the secrets of Social Security, keep in mind everything is based on your work record. That includes not only your retirement benefits, but also disability benefits and benefits for your dependents and survivors.

Stow away work credits. To qualify for Social Security, you must accumulate work credits. You can earn a maximum of four work credits a year, depending on how much you earn. If you were born after 1929, you'll need a total of 40 work credits. These credits are relatively easy to earn. For example, in 2008, you got one work credit for every $1,050 you earned.

So if you're only a few work credits short of qualifying for Social Security benefits, strongly consider getting a job. Even a low-paying, part-time job can put you over the top. That could mean the difference between a lifetime of benefits and nothing at all.

Beef up your benefits. How big those benefits will be depends on your earnings record. To determine your benefits, Social Security uses complex calculations based on the 35 years in which you earned the most money. If you worked fewer than 35 years, the formula factors in zeroes for those years. Once again, a little more work can go a long way. Every extra year you work wipes out a zero. This can boost your payment significantly.

Remember, only employment-related income on which you've paid Social Security taxes counts toward these calculations. All other sources of income, including interest, dividends, capital gains, or rent does not factor into your benefits.

Know your full retirement age

Year of birth	Full retirement age
1937 or earlier	65
1938	65 and 2 months
1939	65 and 4 months
1940	65 and 6 months
1941	65 and 8 months
1942	65 and 10 months
1943–1954	66
1955	66 and 2 months
1956	66 and 4 months
1957	66 and 6 months
1958	66 and 8 months
1959	66 and 10 months
1960 or later	67

Note: Persons born on January 1 of any year should refer to the full retirement age for the previous year.

Sneak a peek at your benefits

How much money will you get from Social Security? There's no one-size-fits-all answer. Fortunately, you can find tools to help you estimate your future benefits and plan accordingly.

In 2008, the average monthly payment for someone who reaches full retirement age came to about $1,100. The maximum monthly payment for someone first claiming benefits was about $2,200. Once you claim benefits, the amount gradually climbs each year to account for cost-of-living increases.

While there is a maximum, there is no minimum. It all depends on your earnings record. If you earned very little money during your working years, you'll get a very small monthly benefit. However, the lower your average earnings, the higher a percentage of them you get. For example, if you earned an average of around $20,000, you'll receive about 50 percent of what you earned in the years just before you claimed benefits. If your average earnings were a little higher, such as $30,000, you'd get about 40 percent. And if you ranked among the higher average earners, you'll get only about 20 percent.

You can get a general idea of what your benefits will be from these numbers, but for the most accurate peek at your future benefits, check out the Retirement Estimator tool at the official Social Security Administration Web site. Just go to *www.ssa.gov*, and click on "Estimate Your Retirement Benefits." You can also go to *www.ssa.gov/estimator*. Here are three good reasons to give it a try:

- Private. Only you can gain access to your personal information. You'll have to provide some information, including your name, Social Security number, date and place of birth, and mother's maiden name.

- Accurate. Because this tool is linked to your actual Social Security earnings record, it's the most accurate way to estimate your benefits.

- Flexible. You can compare retirement options by changing your retirement age or expected annual earnings.

That's not the only benefit calculator available on the Web site. Others, which do not require you to log in or provide personal information, give more general estimates. Go to *www.ssa.gov/planners/benefitcalculators.htm* for more options.

You'll find a Quick Calculator, Online Calculator, and a Detailed Calculator, which you'll have to download to your computer to access. These calculators help you estimate not only retirement benefits, but also disability and survivors benefits if you become disabled or die. Just plug in your numbers and see where you stand. It never hurts to get a glimpse of your future while you can still do something to change it.

Catch mistakes before it's too late

Mistakes happen — especially in a big bureaucracy like the Social Security Administration. But don't let errors cheat you out of the benefits you deserve. Make sure you check your Social Security statement carefully.

According to Social Security estimates, employers make mistakes in wage reports about 4 percent of the time. And about $1 for every $100 reported fails to be credited to the right worker's account.

You're more likely to encounter mistakes if you change jobs frequently or have more than one employer. Your name could also cause confusion. Women who have reported earnings under different names — after being married or divorced, for instance — may run into problems. Hyphenated names, names with spaces in them like "de la Hoya," and names where the family designation does not come at the end, such as "Yao Ming," may also stump the computers.

To guard against any potential errors, you should check your earnings record at least once every three years. You'll need to submit a form called SSA-7004, Request for Social Security Statement. There are several ways to submit the form.

- Fill out a form online at *www.ssa.gov/mystatement*.

- Download the form online and mail it to:

  Social Security Administration
  Wilkes Barre Data Operations Center
  P.O. Box 7004
  Wilkes Barre, PA 18767–7004

- Call 800-772-1213 to request a form by mail.

- Stop by your local Social Security office and pick up the form.

Once you receive your statement by mail, make sure everything is accurate, including your name and Social Security number. You also want to match your earnings record with your own records from tax forms and pay stubs. You may need to get this information from your employer or previous employers.

If you spot any mistakes, you should request a correction right away. Call 800-772-1213 to report the error. Or make an appointment at your local Social Security office so you can talk to someone in person. Either way, you'll need to provide your name, Social Security number, the year or years that are not correct, and the business name and address of your employer during those years. Make sure you have your benefits statement and any supporting documents — such as W-2 forms or tax returns — handy. This can be a long process, but be patient and persistent. It's important to set the record straight so you get what you deserve.

For more information, visit the official Web site of the Social Security Administration at *www.ssa.gov*. Here you can learn more about the details of Social Security, download forms, use helpful tools to plan your retirement, apply for benefits, find a local office, and even get a replacement Social Security card.

Consider life expectancy before claiming benefits

You know you're going to die at some point. You just don't know when. If you did, it would be much easier to decide when to start claiming Social Security benefits.

In theory, it shouldn't matter when you claim benefits. Social Security is designed so you should collect the same total amount of benefits no matter when you claim. You either receive a lesser amount every month for a longer period or a larger amount every month for a shorter period. Either way, it should even out in the long run based on the average life expectancy.

Of course, that's just in theory. You are not a statistic. You may live much longer than expected or die earlier. That's why the decision of when to claim is a tough one.

On one hand, you don't want to claim early, then be stuck taking a smaller amount of money for a long time if you live well into your 90s. On the other hand, you don't want to postpone retirement only to die without collecting a dime. Recent statistics show that men who reach age 65 live, on average, until age 82. Meanwhile, women who make it to age 65 live an average of three extra years, to age 85. Consider your personal and family medical history, as well as your financial situation, when making your decision. But, ideally, you'll see that Mr. Spock of *Star Trek* summed it up best: "Live long and prosper."

Assuming you'd receive $1,000 a month at full retirement age, here's a comparison of your total benefits if you claim early, at full retirement age, or at age 70.

Claiming age	Monthly benefit	Age 70	Age 75	Age 80	Age 85	Age 90
62	$750	$72,000	$117,000	$162,000	$207,000	$252,000
66	$1,000	$48,000	$108,000	$168,000	$228,000	$288,000
70	$1,320	$0	$79,200	$158,400	$237,600	$316,800

Good things come to those who wait

You can start collecting Social Security benefits at age 62 — but that doesn't mean you should. In fact, you could be making a big mistake. In a survey by the Employee Benefit Research Institute, 65 percent of current workers planned to retire before age 65, while only 32 percent plan to wait until full retirement age before claiming Social Security benefits. Maybe they should rethink that.

People are living longer than ever. That's why Social Security has gradually raised the age of full retirement, from 65 to 67, in increments. Retirement may last longer than you think. If you reach age 62 and decide to take the money and run, you may run out of money.

Social Security provides monetary incentives to postpone retirement. Benefits increase by 7 percent each year from age 62 until full retirement age. If you can hold out until age 70, the increase is even more dramatic — 8 percent each year from full retirement age. Once you reach age 70, there's no reason to wait any longer, since that's the maximum you'll get.

For example, assuming you'd get $1,000 a month if you claim benefits at full retirement age, you would get only $750 if you claimed at age 62. That means, for the rest of your life, you'd be stuck with 25 percent less money each month.

On the other hand, if you wait until age 70, you would get $1,320 each month. If you start collecting benefits at age 62, you'll get about 76 percent less each month than you would if you waited until age 70. As an added bonus, postponing retirement will also help your spouse and children. As your retirement benefits increase, so do their dependents and survivors benefits.

Remember, waiting to retire may not always be the right move. It's a personal decision. Maybe you're in poor health and don't expect to live long. Or maybe you really need the money now. Claiming early could also let you do things like fund your grandkids' college education, buy a vacation home, travel, or otherwise enjoy your retirement years with a little extra money. But, in most cases, if you can afford to wait until full retirement age — or later — before claiming benefits, it makes sense to do so.

Postponing retirement pays off

Monthly benefit amounts differ based on the age you decide to start receiving benefits. This table is based on the assumption that your full retirement age is 66, and your benefit starting at age 66 is $1,000 a month.

Age	Monthly benefit
62	$750
63	$800
64	$866
65	$933
66	$1,000
67	$1,080
68	$1,160
69	$1,240
70	$1,320

The truth about earnings limits

Just because you started collecting Social Security benefits doesn't mean you have to stop working. But make sure you pay attention to the earnings limits. Here's how these limits work. Once you reach full retirement age, there is no limit on how much you can earn, so you have nothing to worry about. However, if you claim retirement benefits before full retirement age, some benefits may be withheld if you earn more than a low, yearly limit. In 2008, that limit was $13,560.

For every $2 you earn above that limit, you lose $1 in Social Security benefits. Sounds like a pretty steep price to pay for continuing to work. But the Social Security Administration stresses that these "lost" benefits are not lost permanently. Rather, you should think of them as being delayed. That's because as you continue to work your monthly benefits may increase based on your annual earnings.

When you reach full retirement age, Social Security recalculates your benefits to compensate for any months in which you did not receive some of your benefits because of your earnings. Those extra years of work could pay off with higher monthly payments later.

Remember, the formula for calculating benefits considers the 35 years in which you earned the most. So if you're earning less now than you did during your lowest earning years, working won't help boost your future benefits. But if you're still at the peak of your earning years, working a few more years can wipe out some of your lowest years — and boost your future benefits. The key word is "future." In the short term, you will take a hit because of the withheld benefits. And your ability to recoup these lost benefits depends on how long you live.

Besides the chance for higher future benefits, working after claiming Social Security has other payoffs. Obviously, it gives you extra money to help make ends meet. Perhaps most importantly, your job likely provides health insurance for you and your spouse. If you don't yet qualify for Medicare, it's much easier and cheaper to get health insurance through your employer than on your own. As long as you keep working, you can also keep stashing money in your 401k, IRA, and other savings accounts.

Here's more good news. In the year you reach full retirement age, the earnings limit relaxes. From January 1 of that year until your birthday, the penalty shrinks to $1 withheld for every $3 you earn above a higher limit. In 2008, that limit was $36,120, or $3,010 a month.

Avoid paying taxes on benefits

The U.S. government giveth — and the U.S. government taketh away. If you're not careful, taxes can wipe out a good chunk of your Social Security benefits. Discover important information on how to avoid paying taxes on 50 percent — even up to 85 percent — of your benefits.

According to the Social Security Administration, less than one-third of current beneficiaries pay taxes on their benefits, but that doesn't mean you won't have to. Here's a quick look at the rules.

- If your income from all sources is lower than $25,000 — or $32,000 for a married couple — your benefits are not taxable at all.

- If it is between $25,000 and $34,000 — or between $32,000 and $44,000 for a married couple — up to 50 percent of your benefits are taxable.

- If it exceeds $34,000 — or $44,000 for a married couple — up to 85 percent of your benefits are taxable.

Luckily, you can tiptoe around the tax issue. First, check the rules for your state. Only 15 of the 41 states with personal income taxes tax Social Security benefits. You may be able to enjoy lower tax rates by first disposing of non-retirement assets, like stocks and mutual funds, while postponing Social Security. A similar tactic involves spending down your IRA before claiming Social Security benefits. You may pay higher taxes in the short term, known as the "bridge period" between when you retire and when you claim Social Security, but you'll save thousands each year in taxes for years to come.

Upgrade your monthly benefit to a higher amount

You aren't necessarily stuck with lower monthly payments the rest of your life if you've claimed your retirement benefits early. You can upgrade your monthly Social Security check to a higher amount, thanks to a little-known provision you've got to read to believe.

This provision lets you withdraw your application for benefits using Social Security Form 521. The catch is you have to repay the benefits you've already received. That could be tough — and costly. But once you repay those benefits, Social Security treats you as if you never had filed. Your benefits get recalculated based on your current filing age, and you end up with higher monthly payments the rest of your life.

Keep in mind this strategy comes with some risks. For instance, you could die before you get back what you repaid. And you may have to go without Social Security benefits for a few months while the agency figures out how much you have to repay and you reapply for benefits. Congress could also change the rule at any time if it tackles Social Security reform. It's not wise to plan on this option ahead of time. Yet, it's nice to know if you regret claiming your Social Security benefits early — and have the means to repay them — you can get a chance to start over.

MAKING IT **WORK**

Johnny Eager started collecting Social Security benefits as soon as possible — at age 62. Now, instead of getting $1,000 a month, he only gets $750. Four years later, he realizes his mistake. Here's how he can get a "do-over."

First, Johnny must withdraw his application for benefits. He also has to repay the benefits he's received so far. At $750 a month, that comes to $9,000 a year, or a total of $36,000. After reapplying at full retirement age, Johnny restarts his benefits at a higher rate. Now, he gets $1,000 a month, or $12,000 a year. In three years, he'll recoup what he paid back. And he'll enjoy an extra $250 a month, or $3,000 a year, for life.

Play it safe instead of playing the market

It may be tempting to claim Social Security benefits early and invest them. After all, it's like getting an interest-free loan from Social Security. But the risks may outweigh the rewards. In theory, you can start receiving benefits at age 62 and invest them. Later, you can repay whatever benefits you've received — without interest — and restart your benefits at a higher rate. Meanwhile, you get to keep whatever profit you made on your investments. It's a sneaky, but perfectly legal way to make more from Social Security. However, what sounds great in theory may not happen in practice. Namely, you're not guaranteed to make money through your investments. In fact, you could lose money in the stock market.

On the other hand, unlike investments, Social Security benefits are guaranteed. They also include automatic cost-of-living increases, and come with incentives to delay claiming. Every year you delay claiming from full retirement age to age 70, your benefits increase 8 percent. You would need a very good return on your investment to match or exceed what you'd get from Social Security — especially once you factor in taxes. That means making much riskier investments.

The safer — and likely more profitable — approach would be to think of Social Security as a lifetime annuity. If you don't need the money, simply waiting to claim your Social Security benefits is a smarter option than claiming early and gambling your future income in the stock market.

Dynamite tips for dependents

You most likely think of retirement benefits when you think of Social Security. But Social Security also provides for a worker's family in the form of dependents benefits. Spouses, minor children, and even ex-spouses are among those eligible for these benefits. In states that recognize common-law marriages, longtime partners may also qualify.

Like all Social Security benefits, dependents benefits are based on the worker's retirement benefits. When your spouse files also matters. At full retirement age, your spouse can receive monthly payments equal to 50 percent of your retirement benefits. If your spouse claims dependents benefits early, at age 62, the monthly payment drops to 35 percent of your retirement benefits.

Here's a more detailed look at how when you claim affects the amount of your benefit.

Dependent spouse's age	Percent of worker's benefit
62	35
63	37.5
64	41.7
65	45.8
Full retirement age	50

Remember, when you file for retirement benefits not only affects your monthly retirement benefits, but also your spouse's dependents benefits. If you claim early, you permanently lower both types of benefits.

Here's something every woman needs to know. Dependents benefits are gender-neutral. Both men and women can collect them. But it's usually women, who tend to earn less than men, that claim them. Not only do women have a tendency to earn less, they also tend to live longer. So it's especially important for them to make the right decisions regarding their Social Security benefits. Remember, you can only collect one type of benefit at a time. Here's how to get more from your Social Security payout.

Different situations call for different strategies. For example, because women tend to live longer than men, a single woman should probably wait longer to claim her retirement benefits. That way, she'll get larger monthly payments for the rest of her life. Single men, on the other hand, may not live long enough to reap the benefits of delayed retirement. So they should probably claim early.

Things get much more complicated for married couples. You have a few tactics to choose from.

- Depend on your spouse's record. You may opt to collect spousal benefits rather than your own retirement benefits. Depending on your spouse's earnings record, you might get a higher monthly payment that way.

- Claim and switch. If both you and your spouse have reached full retirement age, you can claim spousal benefits now while you keep working to build up your own retirement benefits. Then switch to those at age 70.

- Work together. Coordinate your Social Security strategy with your spouse. While every couple should consider their own situation, in general, the system encourages women to claim retirement benefits early, while men should delay retirement to maximize spousal and survivors benefits.

If your marriage is on the rocks after nearly a decade, try to stretch the marriage to 10 years. That way, you qualify for dependents benefits even after a divorce.

Super strategy for spousal benefits

To get the most enjoyment from many movies and TV shows, you have to suspend disbelief. In other words, don't nitpick about how the Professor can build a robot but can't figure out how to get Gilligan and his pals off the island. Just sit back and enjoy the show.

Married couples may enjoy retirement more by adopting a similar tactic. Only instead of suspending disbelief, the higher earning spouse suspends retirement benefits after filing. Here's how it works. A wife or husband can't claim spousal benefits until their spouse signs up for Social Security. However, it's easy to get around that rule once you reach full retirement age.

Simply apply for your retirement benefits, then immediately suspend payment of your benefits. This allows your wife or husband to start collecting spousal benefits now, while you keep working to build up a higher monthly payment later. As an added benefit, waiting to claim your own retirement benefits also increases your spouse's survivors benefits after your death.

MAKING IT WORK

Looking to maximize Social Security benefits, Ma and Pa Kettle decide to use the "claim and suspend" strategy. When he reaches full retirement age at 66, the higher-earning Pa files for Social Security, then immediately suspends payment of his benefits. He plans to delay retirement until age 70, boosting his monthly payment from $1,000 to $1,320.

Meanwhile, Ma can now claim spousal benefits and receive 50 percent of Pa's retirement benefits, or $500 a month. That extra $6,000 each year comes in handy in the Kettle household until Pa's bigger monthly checks arrive in four years.

Tips to speed up a disability claim

Injuries, accidents, and illnesses can rob you of your livelihood. Social Security disability benefits help people who can no longer work because of a physical or mental disability. Unfortunately, qualifying for these benefits can be tricky. You need to be organized, patient, and persistent.

The key is to prove your disability prevents you from doing any gainful work. This can be tough. Your disability must also be expected to last at least one year or result in death. However, you won't be penalized for making a quicker recovery. It must also be a medical condition, one that can be discovered and verified by doctors. Some acceptable conditions include but are not limited to:

- diseases of the heart, lungs, or blood vessels

- severe arthritis

- mental illness

- brain damage

- cancer

- AIDS

- diseases of the digestive system

- loss of a leg

- loss of major function of both arms, both legs, or an arm and a leg

- serious loss of kidney function

- total inability to speak

As with retirement benefits, you must also meet work credit requirements. Younger workers need fewer work credits, and those disabled by blindness also have less-strict rules.

When to file a claim. Applying for disability benefits can be a slow, difficult process. In fact, a recent report by the U.S. Government Accountability Office found that a whopping 576,000 of the 1.5 million disability claims awaiting a decision were backlogged. You need to be organized, patient, and persistent.

While the process may be slow, you shouldn't be. File your claim right away, as soon as you must stop working and your doctor determines your disability will keep you out a year or more. You won't start receiving benefits until you've been disabled for six months. But, since the process may take from two to six months, there's no time to waste.

Besides your Social Security number and work history, you'll need the names, addresses, and phone numbers of your doctors, hospitals, or clinics. You could even bring your medical records to speed up the process.

What to expect. Once you complete your claim, it will be forwarded to a Disability Determination Services office. Using your medical records and employment history, the DDS office determines whether you're eligible for benefits. You may need to provide more medical records or even undergo further medical examinations. You may also be referred to a vocational rehabilitation agency for job counseling, training, and placement so you can continue working despite your disability.

Social Security will notify you in writing whether your claim was approved, how much you get, and when your benefits start. Even if you receive disability benefits, these benefits are not necessarily permanent. You may be called for periodic eligibility reviews. If your condition improves, you may also return to work on a trial basis with rules that make it easy to restart benefits if your condition worsens again.

Applying for Social Security disability benefits can be a long, tough journey, especially if you're on your own. Luckily, a private company called Allsup can help. Started in 1984 by former Social Security field representative Jim Allsup, this company helps speed up the process — and gets results. In fact, Allsup boasts that 97 percent of people who complete the process with the company are awarded disability benefits. If you're not, you don't pay a fee. Otherwise, you may be charged up to 25 percent of retroactive benefits awarded — but not more than $5,300. For more information and resources, visit the Allsup Web site at *www.allsup.com* or call 800-854-1418.

Best way to appeal a decision

Don't take "no" for an answer. Seventy-five percent of all Social Security disability applications are denied. But 53 percent of those applicants who appeal will receive their benefits. If your claim is denied or you get less money than you expected, here's some easy-to-understand information that will get you the money you deserve. Remember, it's almost always worth the effort to appeal. Why just accept a negative decision that can have a major impact on your life when you can take a few simple steps to fight it? Each step requires new forms and deadlines, but don't get discouraged. Be persistent and fight for what you deserve.

First, you'll need to fill out a Request for Reconsideration form, or SSA-561-U2. You can download the form at *www.ssa.gov* or call 800-772-1213 to request one. Your local Social Security office will also have any forms you need. Make sure to review your file, too. It could be missing something essential to your case or it could contain a mistake. Call your local Social Security office to make an appointment to look at your file. If you find anything out of order, write a letter explaining the situation and ask that the letter be included in your file.

Your appeal may be short and sweet, but be prepared for a long and tedious process, with several possible stages.

- **Reconsideration.** The necessary first step, the reconsideration process may involve an informal interview, but you probably won't need to appear at all. Someone other than the person who made the original decision will consider your file and any new information you've provided.

- **Administrative hearing.** If your claim is denied again, you may request a formal hearing before an independent administrative law judge.

- **Appeals Council review.** If the judge rules against you, your next step is a written appeal to the Social Security Administration Appeals Council. You'll need to explain why you think the judge was wrong and include any supporting documents. You'll also want to hire a lawyer, if you haven't already.

- **Civil suit in federal court.** This is obviously the last resort. It's a lengthy, complex, and costly process — but it may be worth it if your claim is approved.

DON'T FORGET

There is a time limit for filing appeals. From the date on the written notice of Social Security's decision, you have 60 days to file a written notice that you are appealing that decision. The same 60-day time limit applies to each stage of the appeal process.

Survival strategies for survivors benefits

Losing a spouse is always difficult. While the emotional pain may never go away, you can ease the financial burden by making the most of Social Security survivors benefits. Designed to help the surviving spouse and minor children of a worker who dies, survivors benefits may also go to a divorced spouse or a common-law spouse. In most cases, you must be at least 60 years old to claim survivors benefits. But there are exceptions for spouses caring for disabled children or children under age 16.

While you can claim survivors benefits at age 60, it pays to wait. You can collect monthly payments equal to 100 percent of your deceased spouse's retirement benefits at your full retirement age. Claim earlier, and you'll get between 71 and 99 percent, depending on your age when you file. Minor and disabled children get 75 percent, but the total for a family cannot exceed 180 percent.

The good news is that claiming survivors benefits before you reach full retirement age does not reduce your own retirement benefits — and vice versa. For instance, you can claim reduced survivors benefits at age 60, then switch to your retirement benefits when you reach full retirement age or later. Or you can claim reduced retirement benefits at age 62, then switch to full survivors benefits later. Your strategy depends on your earnings record — and your spouse's.

However, claiming retirement benefits while your spouse is still living will have an effect on your spouse's future survivors benefits. That's because they are calculated based on what your retirement benefits would have been. So if you're already receiving lower monthly payments because you claimed early, your spouse will also receive reduced survivors benefits. Working longer may help your spouse after your death.

Besides monthly survivors benefits, your family may also qualify for a one-time payment of $255 to defray funeral or burial expenses.

At age 62, Mary Widow will be eligible for two types of Social Security benefits. She can claim either her own retirement benefits or survivors benefits based on the work record of her late husband. Because she would be claiming before full retirement age, either benefit would be reduced.

If she waits until her full retirement age of 66, she would get $800 a month in retirement benefits or $1,000 each month in survivors benefits. Claiming at age 62 lowers her retirement benefits to $600 and her survivors benefits to $775. Since claiming early for one type of benefit does not reduce the amount of the other, she can switch to a full benefit in four years.

So she can claim the $775 reduced survivors benefit now, then switch to her $800 full retirement benefits later, which keeps her income relatively stable. A better move would probably be to claim her reduced retirement benefits of $600 now and make ends meet with the lower monthly payment for a few years until the much bigger survivors benefit kicks in.

Untangle the rules when retying the knot

Life goes on. After your spouse's death, you may eventually find someone else to share your life with. But how does remarrying affect your survivors benefits? It depends on your timing. If you remarry before age 60, you lose your survivors benefits, even if you are caring for your former spouse's children. However, the children are still eligible for benefits. If you remarry after age 60, you do not lose your survivors benefits. But, at age 62 or older, you may opt to switch to dependents benefits, based on your current spouse's earnings record, if that would mean more money.

Not all marriages last until death. If your second marriage ends in divorce, you will again be eligible for your deceased spouse's survivors benefits once you reach age 60 — as long as your first marriage lasted at least 10 years. Even if you were divorced from your former spouse at the time of his death, you can collect survivors benefits as long as your marriage lasted at least 10 years. That's the case even if you remarried before age 60 and then became divorced or widowed.

Extra help for needy people

Social Security provides retirement income for older Americans, but some people need a little extra help. That's where Supplemental Security Income (SSI) comes in. SSI, a program jointly operated by federal and state governments and administered by the Social Security Administration, helps financially burdened older, blind, or disabled people. Unlike other Social Security programs, you can receive SSI benefits in addition to other benefits. To qualify for this program, you need to meet very strict income and asset limits.

For example, the federal limits for income stand at about $500 to $700 a month for one person or $750 a month for a couple. Asset limits are usually $2,000 for one person and $3,000 for a couple. Limits vary from state to state, and some things, like your home, don't count toward these limits.

In 2008, the basic federal benefit was $637 a month for one person and $956 a month for a couple. But your exact monthly payment depends on where you live and your income. Not many people qualify for SSI benefits, but if you think you might, it could be worth applying for. If you're age 65 or older, blind, or disabled and living on a small or fixed income with relatively few assets, give it a try.

Clever advice to smooth the application process

Can't wait to start collecting Social Security retirement benefits? Apply three months before your 62nd birthday. That way, you give

Social Security time to process your claim so you can start collecting your benefits as soon as you're eligible.

You can apply in person at your local Social Security office or file an application online at *www.ssa.gov*. You can also get help and advice over the phone by calling 800-772-1213. Even if you start the application process online or by phone, you will probably need to stop by your local office to complete the process. This can take a while, but you can save time by being prepared. Bring the proper documents to the office, and always keep copies of all forms and documents. Include your name and Social Security number with all your papers so they can easily be traced to you.

You'll need the following documents or information when you apply for retirement benefits.

- Social Security number

- birth certificate

- military discharge papers, if you served in the military

- most recent W-2 tax form or federal self-employment tax return

- account number at your bank, credit union, or other financial institution, so your benefits go right to your account

Other types of benefits require additional documents. For instance, if you're applying for dependents benefits, you'll need your marriage certificate or birth certificates for any children claiming benefits.

Make sure to note the name of the caseworker you speak to at the Social Security office. Get her direct phone line, too. It's easier to deal with the same person throughout the application process.

To find out more about the ins and outs of Social Security, visit the Web site of the National Committee to Preserve Social Security and Medicare. This organization's in-house expert, senior policy analyst Mary Jane Yarrington, answers questions in a column called "Ask Mary Jane." You can view the "Ask Mary Jane" archives, which include helpful questions and answers from the past 20 years, at *www.ncpssm.org/contact/ask*. Or ask your own question at *www.ncpssm.org/maryjane*.

5 confusing rules explained

You paid into it for years — are you getting everything you can from Social Security? Here are five common provisions many people miss, according to *The Wall Street Journal*.

Double bonus. If you qualify for both retirement and survivors benefits, you can take one of the benefits initially and switch to the other, without a reduction, at full retirement age. Consider your options and do the math before filing.

Marital bliss. Your spouse and multiple ex-spouses may qualify for spousal benefits based on your work record, without payments to one reducing the benefits for the others or for you. That's why you don't need to worry about your ex-spouse shortchanging your new spouse.

Perfect 10. Get divorced before 10 years of marriage, and you lose the chance to qualify for spousal benefits based on your ex-spouse's record. If you've been married just shy of a decade, consider delaying your divorce until you reach the magic 10-year mark.

Widow wisdom. If you are under age 60 and qualify for a survivor's benefit, you give up that benefit if you remarry and remain married.

If you're nearing age 60, consider waiting until after your birthday to remarry.

Early bird warning. Start collecting retirement or spousal benefits early, and your retirement benefits at full retirement age will be smaller than if you had waited until that age to begin. Wait until full retirement age if you don't need the money now.

Fast way to locate your local office

It's easy to find your local Social Security office. Just go to *www.ssa.gov* and click on "Find a Social Security Office." Enter your ZIP code, and you'll see the address and phone number of the nearest location, along with their business hours. You can also use your trusty phone book. Look under the "United States Government" listings in the white pages. You may want to call the toll-free number, 800-772-1213. You're less likely to get a busy signal than with your local office number.

Once you find the right office, pick the best time to visit. The busiest times tend to be early in the week and early in the month, so try to avoid those. The best day to go is the day after Thanksgiving, when local offices are open but quiet. To speed up the process, make an appointment. Otherwise, you should expect a long wait. If you have a computer, you may not need to go to the office at all. You may be able to conduct your business online.

SuperSaver

Even if you don't have a bank account, you can skip the hassle and cost of paper checks. With a Direct Express debit card, you can have your Social Security money deposited directly onto a pre-paid debit card every month. You can use this card to withdraw cash from an ATM or make purchases anywhere that accepts MasterCard debit cards. To sign up for the card or get more information, call 877-212-9991 or go to *www.usdirectexpress.com*.

Foil fraud and abuse

Not everyone uses Social Security in good faith. Unfortunately, fraud and abuse take a toll on the program. Make sure you play by the rules and stop others from cheating the system.

Blow the whistle. Fraud ranges from making false statements on claims to bribing a Social Security Administration employee to receiving benefits belonging to someone who is deceased. Other possible abuses that can get you in trouble include:

- concealing facts or events that affect eligibility for benefits

- misusing benefits by a representative payee, someone appointed by Social Security to handle money for those unable to take care of their own financial affairs

- buying or selling Social Security cards or information

- impersonating Social Security employees

- participating in workers compensation fraud

- receiving benefits for a child not under your care

- concealing marriage or assets from Social Security while receiving disability benefits

- residing overseas and receiving disability benefits

You can report these types of illegal activities at the Social Security Administration Web site at *www.ssa.gov*. Click on "Report Fraud, Waste, or Abuse" and follow the instructions. You can also call the Fraud Hotline at 800-269-0271. Be prepared to provide information regarding the suspect, victim, and details of the potential crime.

Safeguard your SSN. One growing type of fraud is identity theft. In this scam, thieves steal some of your personal information to get loans, credit, and other goods and services. Your Social Security number obviously comes in handy for this — so guard it carefully.

Keep your Social Security card in a safe place with your other important papers, and avoid giving out your Social Security number when you don't need to. If someone requests it, ask the following questions.

- Why do you need my number?

- How will it be used?

- What happens if I refuse?

- What law requires me to give you the number?

Do not give out your number if you're not satisfied by the answers you get. To report identity theft, contact the Federal Trade Commission at 877-438-4338, or 877-IDTHEFT.

Most misused number sold in stores

In 1938, the E.H. Ferree company, a wallet manufacturer, promoted its product by showing how a Social Security card could fit inside. Each wallet came with a sample card inserted for display purposes. The number on the card — 078-05-1120 — was the actual Social Security number of Hilda Schrader Whitcher, the secretary of the company's vice president and treasurer.

Because the wallets with the sample card were sold in Woolworth's and other department stores, thousands of people had access to the number and adopted it as their own. The Social Security Administration eventually voided the number and issued the secretary a new one. But over the years, more than 40,000 people reported it as their Social Security number — and 12 people were still using it as late as 1977.

Protect yourself against an uncertain future

Payroll taxes will cover only 78 percent of promised Social Security benefits by 2041. That's because, as the large Baby Boomer generation retires, far more people will be claiming benefits, while not many more will be paying taxes. Eventually, something must be done to keep the system working.

Solutions to the problem. Fixes might include raising taxes or the cap on taxable earnings, reducing benefits or the cost-of-living adjustment, delaying the age at which retirees become eligible for benefits, or some combination of those measures. Another way to raise revenue would be to use other taxes, like the estate tax, to fund Social Security.

A controversial proposal involves privatizing Social Security by diverting funds from the Social Security trust funds to private investment accounts. But as the current economic crisis shows, that could have disastrous results if the stock market takes a nose dive.

One thing is certain about the future of Social Security. Even if the government does not address this problem now or in the near future, it will have to deal with it by 2040.

What this means for you. According to the experts, if you're nearing retirement age, don't worry too much about it. There's no reason to panic and claim your benefits early. It's extremely unlikely that anyone in their late 50s or early 60s now will have their benefits cut.

However, if you're still far from retirement age, reconsider your plans to account for the possibility of lower benefits in the future. You may want to save and invest more aggressively or plan to work longer if you can.

Ins and outs
of IRAs

Roth or regular: Pick the right IRA for you

Individual retirement accounts (IRAs) can supercharge your retirement savings. With two types to choose from — a traditional IRA and a Roth IRA — one is sure to suit your needs.

You can fill both types with stocks, bonds, mutual funds, and other investments. The money you earn from those investments grows tax-free, just as with a 401k plan. The big difference between the two IRAs comes in how the IRS takes its slice of your pie.

Traditional IRA. You put money in before paying taxes on it, let the money grow tax-free, then pay income tax as you withdraw it in retirement. With any luck, you are in a lower tax bracket during retirement than you were while working, which cuts your tax burden.

Roth IRA. These plans, named after their congressional backer Senator William Roth, offer a new way to save for retirement. Here, you pay taxes on your money before putting it in the IRA. When you withdraw it in retirement, you pay no taxes — not even on the interest it earned — as long as you follow certain rules.

Pros and cons. Both types have limits on how much cash you can stash in them each year, and both cap how much income you can earn and still contribute to an IRA. There are no limits on how many IRAs you can have, but there are limits on how much money you can tuck in them, total, every year. Ask yourself these questions to decide which kind is right for you.

- Are you older than 70 1/2? Stick with a Roth. You cannot contribute money to a traditional IRA after you turn 70 1/2. Roths, however, have no age limit, so you can keep contributing for as long as you live.

- Do you hope to leave the money in the account to your spouse or children? Choose a Roth IRA. Your heirs will inherit the money tax-free with a Roth account, whereas they will owe taxes on a traditional IRA.

- Do you have other retirement income lined up? Choose a Roth IRA. You must start withdrawing money from a traditional IRA by age 70 1/2 or pay stiff fines. You never have to withdraw the money in a Roth if you don't need it.

- Are you in a higher tax bracket now than you will be in retirement? Go with a traditional IRA. You'll save money by postponing the income taxes until you're in retirement.

- Do you earn more than $105,000 a year if single or $166,000 a year if married and filing jointly in 2009? Choose the traditional IRA. Unlike the Roth, it has no limits on how much money you can earn, as long as you got that money from working and not from another source like a pension.

- Are you older than 59 1/2 and plan to withdraw your IRA money in the next five years? Open a traditional IRA. You can withdraw as much money from it as you want after you turn 59 1/2. With a Roth, you can take out your money at any time, but you must own the Roth account for at least five years before you can withdraw the interest earned on that money.

DON'T FORGET

If you have more than one traditional IRA, you have two choices when it's time to withdraw. You can take the minimum withdrawal from each IRA. Or you can combine the minimum distributions you're required to take and withdraw the total amount from just one IRA.

Switch to Roth for tax-free savings

That traditional IRA has served you well, but consider converting it to a Roth as you enter retirement. Roths aren't right for everyone, but they do have some advantages for seniors. Plus, some experts think income taxes will rise in the coming years, even for retirees. If they're right, then converting now could save money down the road.

To convert, simply set up a Roth account through a bank, brokerage firm, credit union, or other entity. Then start moving the money from your traditional IRA directly into the Roth account.

Convert gradually. You didn't pay taxes on the money that went into your traditional IRA, and you won't owe taxes when you take it out of the Roth. The IRS wants its share, so you'll have to pay up when you convert.

You must pay the income tax the year you convert the money, so take the sting out by converting gradually. Spread it over a number of years, moving a portion of the regular IRA to the Roth each year. This way, you won't get hit with taxes all at once.

Take advantage of 2010. Thanks to a special tax provision, you can convert to a Roth IRA in the year 2010 and owe no taxes until 2011. Even then, you can pay those taxes over the course of two years, half in 2011 and half in 2012. It's like getting an interest-free loan to grow your savings.

Until 2010, only people who make less than $100,000 a year can convert their regular account to a Roth. Starting in 2010, there are no income limits. If you are married, you can only convert if you and your spouse file taxes jointly. You can't convert if you are married but file separately. Talk to a financial advisor before you start moving funds. You'll need to set up a Roth IRA first, and an expert can help you avoid any pitfalls and penalties.

ALERT!

Be careful when you convert a traditional IRA to a Roth IRA, because the early distribution penalty can catch you here, too. As you know, you will owe taxes on the money you move. Don't pay them with money from the IRA if you are younger than 59 1/2, or you will trigger the early distribution penalty.

5 tips to maximize growth

A few simple tips can protect your nest egg from hefty penalties and maximize your money's growth in retirement.

- Don't contribute more than the maximum amount each year. People over age 50 can stick up to $6,000 in either a traditional or a Roth IRA, as long as that money comes from a job, not a source such as a pension or annuity. Put in more, and you get slapped with a 6-percent penalty tax.

- Contribute to your IRA early in the year to earn the most interest on it. If you send the custodian a deposit between January and April, it can count for the previous year as well, so be sure to write a note explaining which year the contribution is for.

- Open an IRA for your stay-at-home spouse. You can sock money from your job in it, up to $6,000 a year if you are over age 50. Remember, though, the IRS limits how much money total you can put in all your IRAs combined. If both you and your spouse are over age 50, that limit is $12,000. If only one of you is over 50, the limit is $11,000.

- Keep all your IRA accounts with the same bank, credit union, or brokerage firm. This keeps fees to a minimum and makes the accounts easier to track.

- Don't buy "tax-advantaged" investments like municipal bonds with a traditional IRA. There's no point, since their earnings are tax free, anyway. Besides that, they don't typically earn as much as other investments you could put in your IRA.

DON'T FORGET

You can't touch the funds in a Roth account for five years from the date you deposit them, regardless of how long you had them in the traditional IRA. And if you have a lot of cash saved up in the regular IRA, converting could briefly push you into a higher tax bracket.

Don't leave loved ones in the lurch

If you own IRAs, you should name your spouse as your beneficiary. The IRA may outlive you, and, even if you leave it to your spouse in a will, it may not go to the right person.

Some IRAs will name the spouse your beneficiary by default, but not all do. If yours doesn't, and you die without naming one, then the IRA is declared to have no designated beneficiary — no matter if your will names one or state laws dictate who should receive it. Without a designated beneficiary, the IRA distributions could speed up after your death, creating big tax problems for whomever ends up with it.

While you can leave your IRA to other people, tax law definitely favors the spouse. Spousal beneficiaries get a wider range of rollover options and more choices about how to take the distributions than others who might inherit.

Reclaim your money without paying penalties

Putting your money into an IRA is pretty easy. Getting it out is the tricky part. Traditional and Roth IRAs have slightly different rules, and it pays to understand them. Mess up, by either withdrawing money at the wrong times or not withdrawing at the right times, and you'll pay dearly in IRS penalties.

Dodge early distribution taxes. With a Roth IRA, you can withdraw the money you put in at any time, but you can't touch the interest it earns until you turn 59 1/2. With a traditional IRA, on the other hand, you can't touch any of the funds until you turn 59 1/2. Otherwise, you'll get slapped with a 10 percent "early distribution" penalty on the amount you withdraw.

The IRS isn't totally heartless, though. It will waive the penalty under certain circumstances, for instance, if you become disabled. Talk to a tax advisor if you need early access to your IRA to make sure the money is penalty-free.

Take your money when it's time. You can withdraw your funds from a Roth IRA at any age, as long as the money has been in the account at least five years. However, you can't withdraw the interest it earned until you turn 59 1/2. In truth, though, you never have to withdraw money from a Roth. You can leave it there to grow tax-free for as long as you like.

Traditional IRAs aren't as generous. You can withdraw as much or as little cash as you want between ages 59 1/2 and 70 1/2, but you absolutely must start making withdrawals after you turn 70 1/2. The IRS wants a shot at taxing those funds before you die, but it can only tax them when you withdraw them.

You can cash out as much money as you want, but at the very least you must take "required minimum distributions" (RMD) after you turn 70 1/2. The IRS bases this "minimum" amount on your (and sometimes your spouse's) life expectancy. The calculations can be complicated, so talk to a financial advisor or Certified Public Accountant for help figuring out your RMD.

Get tips on paying the least amount of taxes when you take your withdrawals in *Take tax-savvy distributions* in the chapter *Outsmart the IRS*.

MAKING IT WORK

According to economist Burton Malkiel, the "miracle of compound interest" is why it's best to start saving sooner rather than later. Here's a good example.

Joan and Jane are 65-year-old twin sisters. Joan set up an Individual Retirement Account (IRA) when she was 20 years old and contributed $2,000 a year until she was 40. Jane didn't start her IRA until she was 40 but has continued to put in $2,000 every year. Both sisters earn 10 percent interest per year. Who do you think has more money today?

Do the math, and you'll find that Joan has almost $1.25 million in her IRA account, and Jane, who contributed five years longer, has less than $200,000. That's the miracle of compounding.

Mutual funds:

low-risk

moneymakers

Make more money with fewer risks

Traditionally, mutual funds have offered one of the safest ways to invest and still earn a healthy return on your money. These funds pool the money of thousands of people just like you, hire experts to research stocks, bonds, and other investments, then invest that cash on your behalf.

Buying into a mutual fund brings instant diversity to your retirement savings, more than you could get on your own. And when it comes to investing, diversification tends to insulate you against roller-coaster market rides. Mutual funds also save you the time and trouble of researching hundreds of individual stocks on your own.

A mutual fund manager can't buy just any stock, bond, or investment they want. They must follow the guidelines laid out in the fund's prospectus, the document that outlines the fees, risks, terms, and conditions. Take a look at some of the funds you can choose from, and talk to a trustworthy financial advisor about which ones meet your needs.

- Money market funds give you a short-term place to stash cash with low risk but also low earnings. Be careful. Fees charged by these funds can eat into your savings.

- Bond funds come in short-, mid-, and long-term varieties, as well as taxable and tax-free. They may invest in a mix of corporate, municipal, and U.S. Treasury bonds. Most pay you the interest you have earned once a month.

- Growth funds aim to buy stock in companies with lots of potential for growth, but they offer few dividend payments and can be risky.

- Value funds try to invest in companies with underpriced stocks in the hopes the stock price will rise, making you money.

- Income funds invest in bonds and stocks that pay nice dividends to shareholders like you. These are best for investors who need regular monthly income.

- International funds specialize in foreign stocks and bonds. They offer the safest way to invest in foreign markets, safer than buying stock in individual foreign companies.

- Sector funds buy stocks in a specific industry, like technology. They invest in a range of companies within that industry, which reduces the risk, but they can still be riskier than other types of funds and may charge higher fees.

- Index funds buy stock in the companies that make up the major and minor stock or bond market indexes, such as the S&P 500. Their goal is to match the performance of their chosen index.

ALERT!

Buying different types of mutual funds helps reduce your risk of loss, but not if you end up owning funds that invest in the same companies. You can double-check your fund diversity for free at the Web site *www.morningstar.com*. Click on Tools, then on Instant X-Ray. Type in the ticker abbreviations of your mutual funds to see how much their holdings overlap.

Slash fees to save big bucks

Mutual fund fees can take a huge bite out of any money you make investing. Pad your nest egg with thousands more dollars by keeping a lid on these expenses.

Walk away from loaded funds. Loads are sales fees or commissions that you pay the mutual fund company or broker who sold you the shares. Paying extra for expert help may sound reasonable, but loads can cost you a bundle.

Shop around for no-load mutual funds, instead, and save yourself more than 5 percent a year in sales charges. Skip the stock broker and buy no-load funds directly from the mutual fund company by calling its toll-free phone number.

Dodge 12b-1 fees. Mutual funds slip these fees in to pay for marketing and advertising. Unfortunately, they can eat up to 1 percent of your investment each year. Some funds are particularly sneaky, calling themselves "no-load funds" while charging up to 0.25 percent in 12b-1 fees annually. To get the real scoop on what a fund charges, request a copy of its prospectus and look under "Annual Fund Operating Expenses" for 12b-1 fees.

Look for low expense ratios. This number sums up the cost of all the management and 12b-1 fees, including the fund's paperwork and advertising. Check the prospectus and look for funds with an expense ratio of less than 1 percent per year. The lower, the better.

Invest in index funds. These typically charge lower fees than other types of mutual funds because they don't require a team of experts to constantly research and trade shares. They virtually run themselves. Simply look for a fund with the word "index" in its name.

Meet the minimum account balance. Some fund companies hit you with fees if your portfolio balance drops below a certain amount, much the way banks charge if your savings account balance drops too low.

Unfortunately, you have less control over your portfolio balance than your bank balance. If the stock market tanks, the value of your portfolio drops, too, and that can bring you below the minimum balance. If you get caught in this pinch, call your fund company and ask if they will waive the fee.

Go high tech. Ask your fund company or brokerage firm if they will cut their fees if you:

- switch from paper to electronic statements.

- manage your account online, moving money via the Internet instead of through a broker.

- sign up for automatic investing, and have money automatically deducted from your paycheck or bank account and invested in your mutual funds on a regular basis.

Secrets to spotting the best mutual funds

Figuring out which funds to buy may feel overwhelming, but a few simple guidelines can put the power and knowledge in the palm of your hand.

Don't buy based on hot tips. Mutual funds are a lot like fashion trends. Some styles are classic and timeless, but many are popular for one season, then out the next. Fill your portfolio with those classic mutual funds, and resist chasing the hot trends. You are more likely to overpay if you buy based on hot tips, and you could lose money when the market moves on to the next big thing.

Look at long-term performance. When researching funds, look at how they performed over the last five to 10 years, not just in the last year or two. Compare several, then choose those that consistently outperformed other funds. The financial research firm Morningstar rates fund performance with a star system. See how your picks stand at *www.morningstar.com*.

Compare apples to apples. Don't put small-cap funds up against large-cap ones when comparing their long-term performance. Different types of funds do well during different market cycles. Only compare small-cap stock funds to other small-cap stock funds, or large-cap bond funds to other large-cap bond funds to get a true picture of their performance.

See how fees stack up. The most successful mutual fund won't earn you much money if it charges ridiculously high fees. Look for funds with low expense ratios and loads. Low-fee funds can make more money for you in the long run than high-performing funds with outrageous fees.

Keep an eye on management. Once you find a few funds you like, make sure the managers who made them so successful over the last five or 10 years are still in charge of them. Digging up this info is easy.

- Check out Morningstar's fund interpreter, a free service that tells you how a fund's fees and performance compare with others in its category, how long the managers have been there, and more. Head to *www.morningstar.com* and type your fund's ticker symbol into the Quotes box.

- See how mutual funds rank in terms of their diversification, risk, performance, and fees at *www.fundgrades.com*.

- Once you have narrowed down your list of mutual funds, call each one and order a copy of its prospectus to learn details about the fund's fees, risks, investing philosophy, and other information.

Easy way to pick a winning fund

You don't need a crystal ball to tell which mutual funds will do well. You just need to know who runs it and whether they invest their own money in it. Those are the findings from a recent study by international experts.

About half of all mutual fund managers invest their own money in the funds they run. But this study found the more they invest, the better the fund performs. Funds with significant manager investment also tend to charge lower fees and have less management turnover, other factors important to success.

Finding out whether or how much a manager invests in his own fund can take a little digging, but the returns make it worthwhile when your earnings statement arrives in the mail. The Securities and

Exchange Commission now requires mutual funds to disclose whether the fund manager has put his own cash on the line. Here are two ways to find out.

- Call the mutual fund company and request a copy of its Statement of Additional Information, or download it directly from the fund company's Web site.

- Go to *www.morningstar.com* and type the fund's abbreviation, or ticker symbol, into the Quotes box. Check the Stewardship Grade under the Fund Snapshot that appears.

Manager investment isn't the only bellwether of success, although it is an important one. When making decisions, also keep in mind fund expenses, such as fees and loads, as well as investment strategy and long-term performance.

Know your stock funds

Stocks and the mutual funds that buy them come in three sizes — small, medium, and large, just like t-shirts.

- Large-cap funds invest in only the biggest, most valuable companies, like Coca-Cola. These should make up the bulk of your portfolio, because big companies are less likely to go bankrupt.

- Small-cap funds buy stock in companies worth less than $1 billion. They can sweeten your portfolio in small amounts, but too much and the risk could give you a stomachache.

- Mid-cap funds invest in companies of medium worth, between $1 and $8 billion. They're generally more stable than small-cap but less than large-cap, putting their risk somewhere in between.

Worry-free fund for easy investing

A new type of mutual fund is perfect for people who want to invest but don't know how. Simply buy a target-date fund and forget it.

As you age, experts say you should start moving from risky investments into safer bets, guarding your savings more closely in the retirement years. Target-date mutual funds, sometimes called retirement-date or life-cycle funds, do this for you automatically.

You choose your target date — the date you plan to retire. Find a fund with that date in its title and start investing. You can even purchase it through an IRA or 401k plan. The fund manager will change the types of stocks, bonds, and other products your money is in as the fund gets closer to the target date. You don't have to research lots of different funds or move your money around every few years.

What's more, if you invest in a target-date fund, you don't need any other funds in your portfolio. In fact, experts warn against it. Not only could you throw off the careful balance of your stock, bond, and cash holdings, you'll also end up overpaying in fees.

Since you will only own one fund, do your homework and choose it carefully.

- Pick a fund with a target date closest to the year you plan to retire.

- Review the funds' strategies. Not each target-date fund invests the same way. Some stay more heavily in stocks, even in your retirement years, while others play it safe and move into bonds or money market funds early. Research them carefully and pick the one you are comfortable with.

- Find one with expense ratios that total less than 1 percent.

- Save on brokerage fees by buying the target-date fund directly from a firm like Fidelity, Vanguard, or T. Rowe Price.

Highs and lows of stocks and bonds

An outstanding investor's secrets to picking winning stocks

What would you give for a chance to pick the brains of a very successful private investor who survived the 2008 – 2009 stock market crash with a higher portfolio value a few months after the crash than before? "Mr. Smith" has used the ideas of great investors like Warren Buffett, Benjamin Graham, and Maynard Keynes very successfully for many years. While he prefers not to be identified, he did agree to share his secrets, starting with this one.

"The most important thing is, don't think of owning shares in a company as owning a stock. Think of it as a partial ownership of a business," he advises. "Would you like to own a piece of a great company at an attractive price — even if there was no stock price quoted? This is the ultimate question. If the answer is clearly yes, the stock market becomes your friend. When the price of those shares drops, be happy! You can then buy them at a bargain price, if you have funds," says Smith with a big smile on his face.

Here are the questions Smith asks when zooming in on a select few businesses.

Is the business in an industry where it's not difficult to make a good profit? Particularly a profit the business could return to shareholders without lowering its competitive standing? Almost all airlines, retail merchants, restaurants, or other industries where it's easy for a newcomer to start a competitive business will fail this test. Declining industries such as newspapers, magazines, and TV stations are also out. Smith says he also usually avoids technology companies because only a handful of these have an enduring competitive advantage that can withstand the latest technological breakthrough by a potential competitor.

What's the profit margin? Do they have a good profit margin with profits being more than just a tiny percentage of sales? If not, the company may lack advantages over their competitors, and price competition may limit their profitability.

What's the long-term earnings history? How much money has the business made each year for the last 12 years? Look at the company's record of annual earnings, Smith says, and make sure that the 12-year period includes at least one general economic upswing and downswing. "Look for a track record demonstrating that a company has done relatively well in the last big downturn. With allowance for the ups and downs of the business cycle, look for fairly consistent and generally rising earnings without unpleasant surprises. This crosses many businesses off your list right away. Companies with a history of strong and increasing earnings, with acceptable earnings even in a downturn, are likely to survive and come out on top. However, a recent poor earnings report that triggers a decline in the stock price could present a buying opportunity if the rest of the long-term record is good and future prospects a year or two in the future are bright."

What's the CEO's record? Is he a substantial owner? "Start-up" companies don't have an earnings history to go by, and almost all start-ups should be avoided unless the CEO has had an outstanding long-term record in that industry. Find out who runs the business, what other companies or partnerships the CEO headed, and how much money those companies have earned and returned to shareholders. Smith says an ideal CEO would be a founder who has his own fortune invested in a proven, successful company, a leader who doesn't take advantage of minority shareholders through excessive pay, options, or sweetheart deals.

Smith strongly prefers to invest in companies controlled by founder owners with outstanding track records in good industries. "Owner operators usually try to put shareholders at the head of the line for claims on the company," Smith says. "They will usually fight tenaciously if the company gets in trouble, when many 'hired hand' CEOs might give up. Leadership is crucial for any company in the financial area, because the tested skill and proven judgment of a CEO owner is the most important indicator of success for companies that have large amounts of money to invest." However, Smith says that companies with extraordinary entrenched "moats" that protect them from competition, such as companies with great brand names that dominate their markets, may be good investments that are more forgiving of mediocre management than companies without moats would be.

"When Warren Buffett took control of Berkshire Hathaway, an investor might have hesitated to buy its stock because it didn't meet the 12-year rule of having good, consistent earnings. Had that investor, however, looked at Buffett's outstanding 12-year record with his previous investment partnership, a very profitable exception to the 12-year rule might have been made," Smith conjectures.

Smith made an exception to his 12-year rule when he bought shares in Lancashire Holdings, a Bermuda property casualty insurance company, not long after its start-up in early 2006 when insurance rates were very high and profitable after the industry had large losses in 2005 from hurricane Katrina. Lancashire's CEO, Richard Brindle, had a very substantial interest in the new company. Brindle had a 20-year track record as a highly successful underwriter for insurance syndicates at Lloyd's of London. Smith did a little research and found out that his record was the best in the industry in returning "underwriting profit" to the "names" who owned shares in those Lloyds syndicates. Underwriting profit is a measure of how much the value of insurance premiums received exceeds the cost of claims and related expenses.

Brindle's syndicates returned over 20 percent per annum to their investors over many years when most Lloyd's syndicates struggled to make any profit. Therefore, it was no surprise to Smith that Brindle's new company, Lancashire, not only had a relatively good underwriting profit in 2008, a bad year for hurricane losses, but also survived the 2008 – 2009 financial meltdown with the value of its financial assets intact. Lancashire actually increased value for shareholders during a period when almost all other financial companies lost enormous real value that was reflected in a steep decline in the market price of their shares.

Prem Watsa, the CEO of Canadian property casualty insurer, Fairfax Financial Holdings, another one of Smith's favorite companies, is also an outstanding CEO owner. Smith says that Watsa showed great fortitude a few years ago as he turned the company around after it experienced unexpected underwriting losses. All in all, Fairfax has returned over 20 percent per year in value to shareholders over the two decades it's been in business.

Watsa's strength is in financial management, a different skill than Brindle's. Watsa, in Smith's opinion, is in Buffett's league in managing financial assets, although Buffett has no equal in picking stocks. They both follow principles established by Benjamin Graham, Buffett's early mentor. Watsa, who is about a generation younger than Buffett, even named his son, Benjamin, after Graham.

"Fairfax's underwriting results have not been exceptional, but Fairfax had its most profitable year ever in 2008, despite large underwriting losses from hurricanes, because of Watsa's amazing skill in reducing risk in managing financial assets. This occurred while most financial companies lost their shirts in 2008," says Smith.

Does the business pay you back? It was surprising to learn from Smith that earnings alone don't make for a good investment. "There are many industries where businesses have to reinvest all their earnings just to keep up with the Jones'," Smith says, citing the airline industry as a horrible example. This means that most or all of the money a company manages to make in good years must be plowed back into its business just to stay competitive — not a strategy for long-term success.

"You want a company that, at the end of the year, has money left over that it can deliver to its shareholders in the form of dividends, share buybacks or by investing in its own business very profitably. Most of the value of owning stocks over the last 100 years has been from dividends. The inflation-adjusted value of capital gains from rising stock prices has been far less. You're looking for consistent earnings and the ability and willingness to return them to shareholders or to grow earnings nicely through reinvestment," Smith advises.

"Don't buy a company unless it has the ability to pay a nice dividend," Smith cautions. "If a company has good earnings but doesn't pay substantial dividends or buy back shares and, instead, reinvests its retained earnings, check to see if the long-term growth trend of earnings is strongly up over the complete business cycle. This will reveal how well they have reinvested their profits."

How much debt do they have? You wouldn't throw your money into a bottomless pit, so why plow your savings into deeply indebted companies? "It's usually better to stick with companies that have either no debt or very low debt, compared to the value of their shares," he says. Make sure that any substantial debt doesn't have to be repaid in the near future. "If they don't have debt coming due, they won't have to make short-sighted decisions based on that," Smith points out. A company not burdened by debt is likely to survive an economic downturn, and may even have extra funds available, like Buffett usually does, to buy other great businesses at a bargain price when the stock market goes down.

Where's the green? How much cash a company generates is one of the most important measures of its health. Smith recommends investing in businesses that produce cash earnings every year. "You want to see companies that are consistent, cash-flow generators, above the normal depreciation schedules for hard assets. Look for companies that might even generate extra cash in a downturn. Be skeptical of companies that report large amounts of non-cash income like Enron did before it collapsed a few years ago. Use the many resources now available to spot and avoid companies that don't take their reported earnings to the bank."

What's the business environment? You can't evaluate a business in a vacuum. Check how it compares to other companies in its industry, and how the strength of that industry compares to others. See how well a company has done, and how well that industry has done in the past. Do they have something that makes them better than most other companies in the same industry, something that gives them a long-term competitive advantage? Once again, don't rely on the stock price to tell you. Compare the company's earnings history with that of the industry and the industry with the broad economy.

"Here's a good exercise," Smith says. "Look up the last 20 years of Nucor's earnings history, for example, and compare it to other steel companies. Their outstanding long-term earnings growth and high return on capital is no accident. Their 'mini mills' have great cost advantages over most steel mills." Smith says to stick to businesses that have something that makes them better than most companies.

What's the company's return on its capital? Imagine that you bought a run-down Dairy Burger franchise for a fair appraisal of $200,000, managed it well, and made a $50,000 profit. Your return on capital would be 25 percent. However, if you paid $2,000,000 for a brand new super Dairy Burger and made twice the profit, $100,000, your return on capital would be only 5 percent, not a very good return.

Likewise, a company that doesn't consistently make significantly more on the total capital employed in the business than the historical risk-free rate of about 5 percent, is likely to be a poor long-term investment no matter how high their earnings are or how cheap their stock is. Smith likes to buy companies that have an edge that enables them to make a long-term average return on total capital of at least 15 percent. Smith says that companies with consistently high returns on capital may be able to keep some of their earnings and use them in a way that increases their profits nicely in future years. However, companies with low returns on capital will usually stagnate. These poor businesses are forced to use their profits to make improvements, merely to keep from losing ground to the competition. See the *Making It Work* box on page 199 for an example.

What's an attractive price to pay for a stock? If a company meets all the tests for being a great business, Smith still won't buy shares if the price isn't attractive. How attractive should the price be? He looks for an earnings yield (average annual earnings per share divided by the current stock price) of at least 10 percent, with a much higher threshold after a market crash when bargains are easy to find. Smith cautions to stick to companies with mostly consistent earnings over several years while avoiding companies that have made foolish investments that caused substantial losses in past years. Smith normalizes earnings before he determines an earnings yield. For his calculation, he averages the earnings of the latest three years and disregards unusual contributions to earnings that can't be sustained. He likes to see that the average earnings of the latest three years is substantially higher than the three-year average for a comparable period during the previous business cycle. Smith avoids owning stocks of highly cyclical companies when business is booming near the top of their cycle. Smith says that the prices of shares in cyclical companies often go down a lot as the cycle rolls over.

Snap up shares in good companies when there is an overreaction to a problem that a company can survive. Smith says that academic theorists have taught a whole generation of mutual fund managers that the stock market is rational and efficient. He says that a private investor with common sense can profit handsomely when most of the other market participants are in the grip of this delusion. In Smith's opinion, the market really is rational most of the time. Then unexpectedly, the market goes bonkers! There are periodic bubbles and busts not only in the whole stock market, but also with specific stocks. This gives an intelligent investor an opportunity to make a large profit.

Buying at a depressed price can give you what Warren Buffett and Benjamin Graham have called a "margin of safety." "Buy shares in a good business at an attractive price," Smith advises. "If you think a share is worth $100 and you can buy it for $50, then there's your margin of safety in case you've made a miscalculation." Smith has bought shares of great companies for even less than half of what he thinks they're worth. He says that's hard to do in a bull market, but surprisingly easy in a bear market when amazing bargains may suddenly appear.

A little research can help you decide what a company is really worth, as opposed to its stock price, a hypothetical number called its "intrinsic value." See *The Next Step* box on page 204 for books Smith recommends to help you in this search.

When all is said and done, even doing your homework doesn't guarantee good results. "If you really want to do well, you'll have to kiss a lot of frogs before you find your prince," Smith jokes. "Be sure you think you really have a prince before you buy shares in what could be a frog kingdom. If you make a mistake, don't hesitate to sell your shares at a loss and then put the remaining funds in a better business. Never continue to hold shares of a poor business whose stock price has gone down, trying to break even after you know you've made a mistake. Admit your mistake and move on. However, if the stock of a company that is a good business with a competitive advantage goes down — don't sell automatically. Instead, consider buying more shares with available funds. If you're cash poor, sit tight. Time is the friend of the better business — and the patient investor."

MAKING IT WORK

Remember the tale of two Dairy Burger franchises? Here's the rest of the story. The owner of the low-priced DB used his excellent 25-percent return on capital and $50,000 first-year's profit to invest in another cheap DB, planning to pay it off in three years. Four years after his first purchase, he owned two downscale DBs that produced $100,000 annual profit on a total investment of $400,000. Not bad! After four years, he now made as much on his $200,000 initial investment as the other man who invested $2,000,000.

The owner of the expensive Dairy Burger, with the poor 5-percent return on capital, took the $100,000 annual profit he expected to make over 20 years and invested in another $2,000,000 Super DB that also earned him $100,000 each year. After he finally paid it off, could he enjoy his $200,000 annual profit? Not really. He then owned two 20-year-old DBs that needed equipment updates and remodeling every few years to keep them looking new.

Whereas the first owner paid off his loan in three years and could then use some of his profits toward improvements, the second owner had to spend 19 years paying off his loan before he could replace outdated equipment and remodel his stores. At that point, it was difficult for him to take more than a third of his profits out of the business each year to live on. To add insult to injury, the now somewhat shabby DBs had a market value that was less than he paid for them.

This parable illustrates the problems every large company faces when the return on capital in their business sector is poor.

How to follow the leader and beat Warren Buffett at his own game

Warren Buffett's stock picking record is legendary. A recent long-term study reveals that his average gain was 31 percent per year during the three years after his initial purchase of a stock. Remarkably, anyone could have done slightly better than Buffett, according to Mr. Smith, if she had bought the same stocks a few months after Berkshire Hathaway, Buffett's company, reported its purchases to the Securities & Exchange Commission (SEC) as required by law.

Look for a low price. Buffett won't buy a stock unless the price is attractive. His purchases often occur after the price has gone down sharply. At this point, most investors will shun that stock in fear that the price will continue to decline. When Buffett buys a falling stock, the mindless herd selling the stock is usually right about the short-term trend continuing to be down. The price tends to be weak for a few months after Buffett's first purchase. This is why individuals who can tolerate a possible short-term paper loss can equal Buffett's performance just by buying what Buffett had bought a few months earlier! Most fund managers won't follow this common-sense strategy because they are afraid of being criticized for underperforming if they buy a stock that continues to go down.

Copy Buffet's strategies. When Berkshire Hathaway buys a stock, you can't always be sure that Buffett himself made the decision to buy it. If the dollar amount purchased was large, a billion dollars or so, or if the company was in an industry that Buffett favors, Buffett himself almost certainly made the decision to buy it. Buffett likes to choose stocks from certain industries that he understands very well. Insurance and other financial companies, railroads, manufacturing companies, consumer products companies with strong brand names and electric utilities are some of his current favorite categories. However, smaller stock purchases, particularly in industries that Buffett doesn't favor, could have been made by an associate of Buffett who manages a relatively small portfolio within Berkshire Hathaway.

You can see what stocks Berkshire recently bought by going online to the SEC's Edgar Filing Information and compare Berkshire Hathaway's Form 13F-HR Quarterly report quarter to quarter to see the latest changes in their holdings. When Buffett buys more than 5 percent of a stock outstanding, this purchase will show up within 10 days on Schedule 13D or 13G.

Be patient. Smith takes this Buffett copycat strategy one step farther, simply by waiting patiently to see what happens to the prices of stocks after Buffett makes his initial purchase. Smith will sometimes invest 40 percent or more of his portfolio value in one stock if he fully understands why the purchase is likely to have a high reward with low risk. Smith, like Buffett, regards risk by how durable the value of the business is, not by the up and down volatility of the stock's price.

Smith points out that Buffett and Keynes had very concentrated holdings in only a few companies during their best years when they didn't manage huge funds. Smith believes that this strategy, if well executed, is much better than investing in widely diversified mutual or index funds. "Diversified funds that are supposed to reduce risk actually have hidden risk because they inevitably follow the market when it crashes," Smith says.

Does Smith think he's better than Buffett? "That's absurd," Smith replies. "Buffett's a top bridge player, and I'm not. However, I could partner with another average player, and we could beat Buffett paired with the world bridge champion if we could see their cards." Smith is able to trump Buffett in investing only because Buffett has to show his hand through his SEC filings.

Follow Smith's example. Buffett bought USG in the fourth quarter of 2000 for an average price of about $15 a share. In June of 2001, USG filed for Chapter 11 bankruptcy protection after being overwhelmed by mostly fraudulent asbestos claims. Buying the stock of a company in Chapter 11 is a recipe for disaster, says Smith. Shareholders are usually wiped out during bankruptcy. Smith says he wouldn't have touched USG with a 10-foot pole if Buffett hadn't bought it.

Buffett's purchase piqued Smith's curiosity. Close examination revealed that USG had the best competitive position and highest return on capital in its industry. It was a great company with an able, highly respected "straight shooter" CEO, Bill Foote. The asbestos claims were legally walled off from the rest of the company in one of USG's subsidiaries. The value of USG's other subsidiaries was worth about double the $15 per share that Buffett paid. However, this value would never have been realized, Smith says, if USG's leadership had capitulated to the payment demands of the lawyers who pressed mostly fraudulent claims against the company.

Smith bought substantial amounts of USG's stock for less than $6 per share, but only after he determined that USG's highly principled CEO was very attentive to Buffett, his largest shareholder, and was determined to fight for value for shareholders during Chapter 11.

Reap the rewards. Five years later, after a long legal battle, both Buffett and Smith were rewarded handsomely when USG paid a sum that was equivalent to about half the value of the whole company to settle the asbestos claims. USG emerged from Chapter 11 into a bullish market in 2006 with its stock still in the hands of its share-holders. Buffett's financial backing was key to USG's ability to secure the funds needed to pay off the asbestos claims and exit Chapter 11. Smith sold most of his USG shares when they rose above his esti-mate of their intrinsic value, about $60 per share, before USG's stock peaked at $120 per share in mid 2006.

"Don't be greedy and try to get the highest price," says Smith. "You should always anticipate that you will hold on to shares in good com-panies for many years as they continue to build value. However, if the price of a stock goes substantially above a conservative valuation of the portion of the business that you own, sell it! That way you'll have money to buy a different stock when you find another great company at a bargain price."

When the stock market crashed in late 2008, USG's stock tumbled down again to nearly $5 a share as their business experienced losses. This was another great buying opportunity as Buffett once again invested money in USG to help it weather that financial storm. Guess who was buying USG the very day before Buffett announced his latest rescue of the company? Smith just smiles like the cat who swallowed the canary! He says that Buffett has a history of helping save the companies he invests in if they get in trouble.

Smith continues to pay close attention to what Buffett does. In the spring of 2008, Buffett bought the stock of NRG, a very well-managed electric utility company for about $40 a share. When the stock market crashed in late 2008, an investor could have bought NRG for as low as $17 per share. Smith is sure Buffett knew that NRG's electric generating plants were worth about $65 a share when he bought the stock.

Does Smith think that buying a stock for about half what Buffett paid was a sure thing? "There's no such thing as a sure thing in the stock market," says Smith. "There's always a certain amount of risk. However, buying pieces of various outstanding companies for half what Buffett paid has less risk than any other method of investing I know. Buffett's batting average is about 980 in stock picking. This means he's right about 49 times for every time he's wrong," Smith says. Buffett's amazing batting average is why Smith is very happy to tag along like a batboy following after the world's greatest investor–hitter, to paraphrase an analogy Buffett himself has used.

Expect to weather some losses. Smith cautions that the stock market can be irrational. An investor should always be prepared to experience a paper loss before an investment that is ultimately successful, pans out. "Be philosophical about paper losses," Smith says.

"It's unreasonable to think that you can always sell a stock at its peak price. Why then should you think that you can always buy a stock at its lowest price?"

The inevitability of fluctuations in share prices means that stocks should never be bought with margin loans that will be called for repayment if the prices of stocks used as collateral declines. Smith also cautions never to buy stocks with funds that might be needed in the near future. "You'll sleep well if you follow this advice," Smith concludes. Now that sounds like the best advice of all!

THE NEXT STEP

Smith recommends these books to help you research your investments.

The Snowball: Warren Buffett and the Business of Life
by Alice Schroeder

The Essays of Warren Buffett: Lessons for Corporate America, Second Edition
by Warren E. Buffett and Lawrence A. Cunningham

The Intelligent Investor: The Definitive Book on Value Investing. A Book of Practical Counsel (Revised Edition)
by Benjamin Graham, Jason Zweig, and
Warren E. Buffett

The Little Book That Beats the Market
by Joel Greenblatt

Keynes and the Market: How the World's Greatest Economist Overturned Conventional Wisdom and Made a Fortune on the Stock Market
by Justyn Walsh

Guard against dishonest brokers

A dishonest stock broker or investment adviser can steal your life's savings. By law, brokers, investments advisers, and their firms must be either licensed or registered. If you give your nest egg to one who isn't — only to watch them disappear or go out of business — you may never get your money back, even if a court rules in your favor. Don't give them the chance. Find out who to trust before handing over your dough.

Dig up the dirt on brokers. The Central Registration Depository (CRD) is a computer database with information on brokers and the firms they work for. It can give you the broker's educational background and work history as well as whether:

- they are licensed in your state.

- they have had any run-ins with regulators.

- other investors like you have lodged complaints against them.

You can't peek at the CRD yourself, but your state's securities regulator can. Call and ask for information about the broker or brokerage firm's CRD. The Financial Industry Regulatory Authority (FINRA) also provides CRD information through its BrokerCheck hotline at 800-289-9999. Try your state securities regulator first, though, as they have more information, especially regarding investor complaints.

While you're at it, find out if the brokerage firm is a member of the Securities Investor Protection Corporation (SIPC). This group protects your money if a member-brokerage goes out of business, similar to how the FDIC insures your money with member banks. SIPC won't guard your money against stock market losses, though.

Investigate investment advisers. They must register with either the federal or state government. Even the people who work for them, the investment adviser representatives, must be licensed or registered in your state.

Have the investment adviser or representative show you his "Form ADV," or get it from your state's securities regulator or online from the Investment Adviser Public Disclosure (IAPD) Web site at *www.adviserinfo.sec.gov*. Part 1 of Form ADV tells you whether regulators or other clients like you have filed complaints against them. Part 2 outlines the adviser's fees, services, and investment strategies. Read both parts carefully. Some advisers are also brokers, so check both Form ADV and the CRD, if available.

Grill new prospects. Ask some basic questions before you hire anyone to handle your money. Find out what products and services they offer and how they charge for their services — by the hour, flat fee, or commission.

Cheap, easy way to invest

Exchange-traded funds (ETFs) are a cross between stocks and mutual funds. With funny names like Spiders and Cubes, ETFs invest in a basket of stocks or bonds. Most track an index, such as the S&P 500.

ETFs boast super-low expenses, even lower than index mutual funds, and are tax efficient. Consider them if you have a lump sum to invest, but not if you contribute a little at a time to your nest egg, since you'll pay a brokerage fee each time you buy or sell ETF shares.

Free help shopping for stocks

Picking stocks just got simpler with free, Internet stock screeners. Simply tell these computer programs what kind of stock you are looking for — the industry, company size, price-to-earnings ratio, and more. You'll get an instant list of ones that meet your criteria.

Lots of good screeners are free, so don't pay for the privilege of using one. These can get you started.

MSN Money	*moneycentral.msn.com*	Click on Stock Research and then on Stock Screener.
Yahoo! Finance	*biz.yahoo.com/r/*	Click on Stock Screener.
Morningstar	*www.morningstar.com*	Click on Tools, then click on Stocks under Basic Screener.

THE NEXT STEP

Get easy-to-read investing advice from the greats. Settle in with Benjamin Graham's classic book *The Intelligent Investor*. Or get tips from Warren Buffet online at *www.berkshirehathaway.com*. Read his Letters to Berkshire Shareholders and the Owner's Manual.

Turn old stock certificates into cash

Old stock certificates gathering dust in the attic could be worth their weight in gold. Finding out is easy with the click of a mouse or one quick phone call.

Find out for free. Visit the Web site *www.google.com*, and type the name of the company that issued the certificate into the search field.

With any luck, the search results will tell you if the company is still in business and what the stock now trades for.

Dig a little deeper. If Google doesn't give you what you need, hire a pro. These for-fee financial sleuths will find out what happened to the old business and what your shares are worth today. Even if the shares themselves are worthless, the certificate may have value as a collectable. These contacts can help you get started.

- Financial Information Inc's Custom Research department at 800-367-3441

- OldCompany.com at 888-STOCKS6 or *www.oldcompany.com*

- Stock Search International at 800-537-4523 or *www.stocksearchintl.com*

Replace a lost certificate. Looking for a missing certificate? Don't panic. Ask your broker to look up the transfer agent, then call the agent and place a "stop transfer" against the shares. This works the way a "stop payment" does on a check. It keeps a thief from transferring the stocks from your name into theirs. The transfer agent or broker will also report the missing certificates to the Security and Exchange Commission's lost and stolen securities program.

Next, get a replacement certificate. Contact the company that issued the shares to request a new one. You will need to:

- file an affidavit explaining what you think happened to the old certificate.

- buy an indemnity bond worth 1 to 2 percent of the lost shares, to protect the company and transfer agent in case someone else tries to cash in the lost certificate down the road.

- request a new certificate before someone shows up with your old one.

If you do happen to find it, call the transfer agent to remove the "stop transfer" order. Otherwise, you may have trouble selling your shares.

Guard nest egg from uncertainty

Bonds provide a safe haven for some of your precious retirement savings, while earning you income and sometimes avoiding taxes. They're an essential part of any retirement portfolio, especially as you age.

Bond prices usually rise when the stock market declines, which helps cushion wild market swings. Holding bonds also helps diversify your investments, exposing you to less risk. Plus, they produce steady income you can live off of or reinvest, as needed.

All bonds are not created equal, however. Some are safe, while others are risky, just like stocks. Stick with these high-quality bonds.

U.S. Treasury issues. These come in many flavors, from Treasury Bonds and Notes to Treasury Bills and I Savings Bonds. They're as close as you can get to no-risk investments. After all, the federal government can print its own money. Plus, you don't pay state or local income tax on bonds issued by the U.S. Treasury. Learn about all the types of Treasury securities at *www.savingsbonds.gov*.

Municipal. Safer than most but not as safe as U.S. Treasury issues, these bonds are issued by state and local governments to pay for

roads, schools, and other projects. Most are also exempt from federal —
and sometimes state and local — income tax.

Corporate. Corporations issue these investment-grade bonds, while
independent firms such as Moody's Investors Service rate them. Only
triple-A and double-A bonds qualify as investment-grade. Just like in
school, the more A's the better. While highly rated bonds may not pay
as much interest, the companies behind them are less likely to default.

Check the two major rating systems before buying a bond —
Moody's Investors Service and Standard & Poor's Corp. Different
grades on the same bond usually mean uncertainty about a company's
future. Never buy unrated bonds. They are simply too risky.

Buy bonds at deep discounts

Zero-coupon bonds offer a way to buy solid, secure bonds at a steep
discount, perfect when you only have a little money to invest and
want to stretch it as far as possible.

- Pay less than half their face value. The longer the bond term,
  the bigger the discount. When they mature, you redeem
  them for their full-face value and pocket the difference.

- Unlike regular bonds, zeros don't pay any interest until the
  bond matures. Then you get it all in one lump sum. The
  interest at the end accounts for the difference between the
  discounted price you pay for the bond and the full-face value
  you redeem it for.

- Even though you don't receive interest payments while you
  hold the bond, you pay income tax on it as if you did. But
  since you pay these taxes "up front," you won't owe any when
  the bond matures.

Lots of different entities issue these bonds, from the U.S. Treasury to local governments and corporations. Here's how to make the most of this investment.

Dodge the tax hit. Buy municipal zero-coupon bonds. You pay no federal, and in some cases no state or local tax, on the interest. If muni's aren't an option, buy regular zero-coupon bonds through a tax-deferred retirement account, such as an IRA. The interest will accrue tax free until you withdraw it.

Earn bigger rewards. Look into investment-grade, corporate zeros. They carry a higher risk than the government issues but offer bigger potential payouts. If the company defaults, however, you may never get the interest you are owed.

Aim for stability. If taking risks makes you sweat, buy U.S. Treasury zeros, also known as STRIPS. They have virtually no risk of default. You cannot get them directly from the government, only through qualified financial institutions and brokers.

Build a 'ladder' to savings success

Climbing a bond ladder is a lot less risky than climbing a house ladder and a lot less stressful than climbing the corporate ladder. But the rewards can really pay off.

"Laddering" your bonds simply means buying several with different maturities, say a one-year, three-year, five- and 10-year bond. This staggers the interest payments you receive, so that you're always getting some income, and protects you against inflation and fluctuations in bond interest rates. If the rates being offered rise, you'll always have a bond about to mature which you can roll into a new, higher-paying one.

As a result, you get better-than average returns, because you end up with short-, mid-, and long-term bonds of various yields. Each bond represents one rung in your ladder. The more "rungs," the more diversification you have. To get the best returns, you need to own one bond with at least five more years left on it.

Build your ladder with stable bonds that have little to no chance of defaulting, such as U.S. Treasury bonds. You don't have to stick with just one type, though. You can choose from a variety of Treasury securities, as well as investment-grade corporate or municipal bonds. You can even ladder bank Certificates of Deposit. Just don't try laddering bond mutual funds because you have no control over their timing and maturity.

SuperSaver

Cut out the middle man, and get government bonds and securities directly from the U.S. Treasury. You'll save yourself the typical $50 transaction fee charged by brokers, banks, and dealers. Contact the Treasury at 800-722-2678, or buy online at *www.treasurydirect.gov*.

Municipal and corporate bonds, however, can be complicated. Look for an experienced broker to help you purchase them.

Know the best time to sell

A change in the economy may prompt you to sell your bonds before they mature. However, you probably won't trade them for their face amount. A bond may sell for a premium — more than its value — or at a discount, depending on several factors.

Credit worthiness. If the credit rating drops, you may want to sell for less rather than risk losing it all if the company goes bankrupt.

Maturity. You may want your money right away and give a discount in order to cash out the bond before maturity.

Interest rates. When overall interest rates rise, bond prices fall. When rates are down, bonds are up. Interest rates are the biggest factor in bond pricing and may dramatically affect your decision on when to sell. For example:

- A $10,000 bond at a 7-percent rate will pay $700 per year.

- A $10,000 bond at 10 percent will pay $1,000 per year.

- At 10 percent, it only takes $7,000 to get $700 per year.

In simple terms, you lose $3,000 when rates go from 7 percent to 10 percent because a buyer can get a higher return on $10,000 with a new bond. If you want to sell yours, you must discount it to $7,000 so it earns at the same rate as a new one. Fortunately, falling interest rates work in reverse. Your bond is worth more, since it will pay better than a new one.

Despite the relative safety of bonds, the risk of losing money is just as real as with the stock market. As with all investments, you need to review your bond holdings each year to be sure they're keeping pace with your goals.

Beware scam of historic proportion

Old bonds are being given new life, this time as the tool of scam artists. Historical bonds were once valid bonds issued by private companies, such as Chicago, Saginaw, and Canada Railroad; the East Alabama and Cincinnati Railroad Co.; the Noonday Mining Co.; and many others. Some of these bonds were issued more than 100 years ago. Today, they're only valuable as collector's items and have no value as bonds. But con men want to convince you otherwise.

Scam artists try to sell these virtually worthless historic documents to unsuspecting investors, often for far more money than their face value. Be immediately suspicious if someone selling you a bond claims:

- the bond is payable in gold. United States courts have said otherwise, ruling that the antiquated terms of these bonds cannot be enforced.

- a bond issued by a private company is backed by the U.S. Treasury. The Treasury does not back bonds from private issuers.

- a historic bond is part of a high-yield investment. The scammer may call the investment "trading programs," "debentures," or "medium-term notices" from "Prime Banks." None of these programs exist.

- a third-party evaluator guarantees the historic bond is worth a bundle. Often, these appraisers are really in league with the con artist.

Skip out on this "historic opportunity," and stick with real, recently issued bonds, instead.

Scam-proof your savings

Don't get slapped with hefty penalties

Retirement accounts carry strict rules about when you can withdraw your own money. Slip up, and fines will take a big bite out of your savings.

The biggest rule to remember — don't withdraw money from a retirement account before you turn 59 1/2. This includes 401k plans, IRAs, and even annuities. The government wants you to keep your hands off that cash for as long as possible so it has time to grow large enough to sustain you in retirement.

To discourage you from touching it, Uncle Sam hangs hefty penalties over your head — withdraw it early, and you'll owe not only immediate income tax but also a 10-percent "early distribution" tax on it. Luckily, there are a few loopholes. You may be able to dodge the penalty if you:

- become disabled.

- need the money for medical expenses.

- receive it as dividends from an ESOP (Employee Sponsored Ownership Plan).

There are a few other instances as well. In some cases, you must take the money as a loan and pay it back within a certain time frame. Some, but not all, 401k plans allow early withdrawals if you are 55 or older the year you retire. Ask your human resources department if yours does.

You may be able to get money out of an IRA early by taking what the IRS calls substantially equal periodic payments. The size of these payments depends upon your life expectancy, and they can be figured three ways. The free online calculators at *www.72t.net* can help. It pays to have a Certified Public Accountant or financial planner check the math, though. If you stray from the payout schedule or miscalculate the payments, the IRS slaps you with a 10-percent retroactive penalty, plus interest.

Make your money last a lifetime

Don't let fears about running out of money in retirement keep you awake at night. Rest easy. You can stretch your nest egg into your 90s by following the simple 4-percent rule.

Experts generally say you can withdraw 4 percent of your retirement savings each year once you reach your 60s. You would withdraw 4 percent the first year, then slightly more in following years to keep up with inflation.

You can also adjust your withdrawals depending on how much interest your investments earn. Take out more in years when they do well and earn more than 4 percent plus inflation. Trim living expenses and take out less in years your investments do poorly.

Experts recommend waiting as long as possible to tap your IRA, 401k, and other tax-deferred retirement accounts, though. Waiting lets the interest compound as much as possible, further padding your retirement funds.

MAKING IT WORK

Figuring out how much money you need in your retirement account is a snap. Add up all sources of income, not counting retirement accounts, then subtract all expected expenses. If you get a negative number, you will need to tap your retirement savings to make up the difference. Divide this difference by 4 percent, or the percent you plan to withdraw each year.

For example, if you need an extra $12,000 a year to make ends meet, then divide $12,000 by 0.04. The answer, $300,000, is the amount of money you need in your retirement account in order to withdraw $12,000 a year for life.

Sidestep this sneaky tax trap

You get penalized not only for withdrawing money too early but also for withdrawing it too late. It's an honest mistake lots of people make, but it can cost you half your retirement savings.

The year you turn 70 1/2, you must start taking money from most retirement accounts, including workplace saving plans and traditional, rollover, and SEP IRAs. The IRS even has a fancy name for these forced withdrawals — required minimum distributions (RMDs). Of course, there is always an exception. You do not have to:

- take RMDs from a Roth IRA you opened.

- make withdrawals from a tax-deferred annuity until you turn 90, as long as you bought it outside of your workplace.

- take RMDs from a company retirement plan if you still work there, no matter your age or how many hours you work. However, you must start withdrawing money by April 1 the year after quitting.

If you miss your RMD deadline, you'll get more than a slap on the wrist. The IRS will take half the remaining money you should have withdrawn that year and keep it for itself.

Find your start date. Pull out your calendar and find your birthday. Now look for the date six months after that, when you turn 70 1/2. Flip to April 1 of the next year. This is your "required beginning date" (RBD), the deadline for taking your first required distribution. This date only counts for the first year you take an RBD. For every year after, the deadline is Dec. 31.

Add up your savings. Find April 1 again, then move backward four months to December. Find out how much money you had in all your retirement accounts as of that Dec. 31. You'll need to figure the amounts of each traditional, SEP, and SIMPLE IRA that you own. Set up a column for each one.

Figure your life expectancy. The RMD is based on how long you are likely to live. Call the IRS at 800-829-3676 and request Publication 590, or get it from the IRS Web site *www.irs.gov*. How old were you on that Dec. 31? Look up your life expectancy in the Uniform Lifetime Table based on that age.

Calculate your RMD. Divide the total money in each column by your life expectancy to get the RMD for each group of accounts. RMDs change every year because your life expectancy changes. You'll have to recalculate new RMDs every year.

You can withdraw the entire RMD amount all at once or in smaller payments throughout the year. And remember, the RMD is simply the minimum amount you must withdraw. You can always take out more.

Whatever you decide, don't wait until the last minute. You must withdraw the money by Dec. 31 each year, but experts recommend doing it by Thanksgiving to give yourself plenty of buffer against the 50-percent penalty.

DON'T FORGET

Start withdrawing money from most retirement accounts the year after you turn 70 1/2, or face stiff IRS penalties.

Avoid penalty with full disclosure

So you took the wrong Required Minimum Distribution (RMD), or none at all. Don't stick your head in the sand and hope the IRS doesn't notice. They will. You need to make amends and beg forgiveness.

The best thing to do is to ask for a waiver when you file your tax return for that year. You'll have to pay taxes on it so report the amount you forgot to withdraw on Form 5329, and attach this to your Form

1040. Then attach a short letter explaining why you didn't take the right RMD. Maybe you didn't know about it, or maybe you did the math wrong. Whatever happened, tell the truth. In many cases, the IRS will waive the penalty. But it won't be automatic, so be sure to ask.

Simple trick to building your nest egg

People who retire with a million dollars in the bank aren't money-making geniuses — they just know the secrets of asset allocation and rebalancing.

Asset allocation is how you invest your retirement savings. You might put half your money in stocks, a third of it in bonds, and the rest in money market funds or Treasury securities, for instance. How you divvy up your hard-earned cash depends on your age and risk tolerance. Generally, as you age, you should move into safer investments. A good financial planner can help you strike the right balance.

Once you decide where to put the money, keep track of it so it doesn't get out of balance. Say you start with 50 percent in stocks, 35 percent in bonds, and 15 percent in a money market fund. The stock market does well one year, and soon the stocks are worth 70 percent of your portfolio, with bonds only 20 percent and money market funds just 10 percent. Now you have too much cash in stocks. You need to rebalance. Get back to your original goal of 50-35-15 by selling some of those stocks and putting the money back into bonds and money market funds.

The Schwab Center for Financial Research found that rebalancing your retirement portfolio annually actually reduces risks and makes more money for you in the long run. Schwab suggests rebalancing at least once a year or whenever your asset allocation gets out of whack by more than 5 percent.

5 biggest investing mistakes

The riskiest moves you can make with your money aren't what you think. These five mistakes can derail your retirement.

Playing it too safe. Generally, the safer an investment, the less interest it earns. Savings accounts and money market funds may be safe, but they may not earn enough interest to keep up with inflation.

Higher-yield investments make the most of compounding, what Albert Einstein declared the world's greatest math discovery. When you put $2,000 into a savings account at 3 percent interest compounded annually, you earn $60 of interest after one year. The next year, you'll earn interest on $2,060, generating interest of $61.80.

Every year, your pile of money grows by itself. The bigger it gets, the more interest you earn, and the more interest you earn, the bigger it gets. Compounding interest helps grow your money like crazy. It's the easy way to enjoy a carefree retirement, knowing you don't have to run out of savings.

That's not likely to happen, though, if you keep all your cash in a savings account, because it earns so little interest. Stocks in the form of mutual funds and index funds give you a much better chance of not just meeting your retirement savings goals, but of making your money last a lifetime.

Failing to diversify. Putting all your eggs in one basket, like stocks, is a recipe for disaster. If that basket falls off a cliff, your nest eggs are scrambled. That's why financial advisers suggest spreading the wealth among different types of stock mutual funds, index funds, bonds, Treasuries, and other investments.

Borrowing to invest. Don't give into the temptation of borrowing against your house, credit cards, or future to invest in stocks or bonds. Investments may not earn more interest than you pay for borrowing the money, and stock market cycles are not stable enough to guarantee a good return.

Betting against the future. Along the same lines, don't raid your 401k, IRA, or other retirement account to pay for stuff. Not only do you lose out on all that compounding interest, but you may face hefty penalties and taxes.

Bailing when things get bad. Everything that goes up must come down, and the stock market is no exception. By pulling all your money out during bad times, you do the opposite of what wise investors preach — you sell when prices are low and miss your chance to buy stocks on the cheap.

Not even experts can time the market. Don't try. Talk to a financial adviser now about your asset allocation. Choose a mixture of investments that suits your age and risk tolerance, and rebalance your portfolio at least once a year.

Secure your future with a good adviser

Think of them as doctors for your bank account. A good financial adviser can pave the path for a long, happy retirement and help you weather any financial storms that appear on the horizon.

Anyone can call themselves a financial planner, but certain professional designations set planners apart in their education and experience. Certified Financial Planners (CFPs) have the most training, but Chartered Financial Consultants (ChFCs) are close behind. CPA and PFS are Certified Public Accountants who have taken extra courses in financial planning to become Personal Financial Specialists. Before you hire anyone:

- ask how they get paid and how much they typically charge, and get it in writing. Fee-only experts can be expensive, but you may prefer them over someone who earns a commission off the products they recommend.

- find out how long they have been a financial planner and which companies they have worked for. Do they specialize in certain areas, like taxes or estate planning? Find one who can address your needs.

- grill them on their investment style, and make sure it's a good match with yours. If you tend to be cautious, you won't want someone who loves to take risks handling your money.

- get a copy of their disciplinary history, called the IARD, from your state's securities regulator.

- ask the planner which professional organizations or government agencies regulate them, then contact those groups for a background check. For CFPs, call 888-CFP-MARK or visit the Web site *www.cfp.net*.

- find out if customers or regulators have had problems with a planner at the Securities and Exchange Commission Web site *www.sec.gov/investor/brokers.htm*.

THE NEXT STEP

Professional organizations can help you find trustworthy, well-trained experts. The Financial Planning Association will steer you mostly toward CFPs via its Web site *www.fpanet.org*, or by phone at 800-282-7526. The National Association of Personal Financial Advisors can find one near you on its Web site *www.napfa.org*, or by calling 888-333-6659.

Free help managing your money

Financial planners around the country offer free help to people just like you. You just have to know where to find them.

Climb aboard the money bus. Free seminars and financial planning help are the basis of the "Your Money Bus" tour sponsored by the National Association of Personal Financial Advisors, the Consumer Education Foundation, TD Ameritrade, and Kiplinger's Personal Finance magazine. See when the Money Bus is coming to your town at the Web site *www.yourmoneybus.com/tour.html*.

Get a financial checkup. CFPs give free educational workshops and personalized help with your retirement, estate, insurance, and investment planning during clinics offered by the Certified Financial Planner (CFP) Board of Standards. To learn about upcoming clinics near you, call the CFP Board at 800-487-1497.

Call for help. You can get free financial advice through telephone and Internet chats with NAPFA members several times a year thanks to the National Association of Personal Financial Advisors and Kiplinger's Personal Finance magazine. Visit NAPFA's Web site, *www.napfa.org*, to find out about the next "Jump-Start Your Retirement Plan" Day.

Turn to Uncle Sam. Request a free copy of the "My Money" Tool Kit from the federal government by calling 888-MY-MONEY between 8 a.m. and 8 p.m. Eastern time. You'll get publications about Social Security, investing, budgeting, and general consumer tips.

THE NEXT STEP

Many trusted financial-planning organizations and companies offer free self-help articles on their Web sites.

- *www.napfa.org/consumer/index.asp*
- *www.kiplinger.com*
- *www.fpaforfinancialplanning.org*
- *www.cfp.net/learn*
- *www.mymoney.gov*
- *personal.vanguard.com/us/planningeducation*

Give financial frauds the boot

Scam artists come in all stripes. Some wear nice suits and call themselves brokers or financial experts. They claim they can produce incredible returns on your money and maybe even guarantee your income for life. Before you sign over your savings, learn to spot the scams and separate the real experts from the frauds.

Don't buy "free lunch" seminars. Even if they occur at work, they may not be backed by your employer. These seminars are rife with unscrupulous so-called financial experts. Beware any speaker who claims:

- everyone can retire early.

- you can make as much money in retirement as working.

- your investments can earn returns of 12 percent.

- you can withdraw 7 percent or more yearly from your retirement account and not run out of money.

Promises like these suggest your money will be put in high-risk investments.

Guard your nest egg. Think twice before cashing in your pension, 401k account, or other company plan. A shady broker or adviser may pressure you to retire early, cash out, and invest your money with them. Talk to a tax expert first to learn what kind of tax hit you would take. Seek sound advice from a Certified Financial Planner or other expert about whether you would have enough money to live on.

Stay in charge. Never do business with someone who pressures you to give them total control over your investments.

Seek a second opinion. Have someone you trust — preferably an attorney or financial planner — look over any contract before you sign it.

Walk away. Say "no thanks" if a broker or financial planner is unwilling to give you time to think things over, check their background, or get outside advice.

File a complaint. Contact the Financial Industry Regulatory Authority (FINRA) with questions or complaints about early retirement pitches you received or lunch seminars you attended. Visit them online at *www.finra.org/complaint* or write to FINRA Complaints and Tips, 9509 Key West Avenue, Rockville, Maryland 20850-3329.

Put the brakes on pre-approved offers

All those offers giving you thousands of dollars in easy credit not only junk up your mailbox, they're also easy pickings for crooks bent on stealing your identity. Cut off thieves before you become a victim by opting out of pre-approved offers.

This action stops the credit offers at their source — the credit bureaus. To opt out of mailing lists, call 888-567-8688. You will need to give details such as your name, telephone number, and social security number, but the information is kept confidential and only used to process your request.

You can also opt out in writing. Send a letter to each major credit bureau, stating your full name, social security number, date of birth, current mailing address, and any past addresses you want removed.

While you're at it, cut back on other junk mail. Send the same letter to the Direct Mail Association's (DMA) Mail Preference Service at P.O. Box 643, Carmel, New York, 10512. You will still receive some junk mail, but you should get less of it for the next five years.

Guard your credit for free

You are now entitled to a free copy of your credit report every year, thanks to the federal government's Fair Credit Reporting Act. Now you can check for mistakes before applying for a loan, insurance, or even a job without paying for a copy of your report.

Removing wrong, negative information can boost your chances of getting good interest rates on loans and getting hired. Checking your credit report also helps guard against identity thieves by catching them early in the act if they open accounts or take out loans in your name.

Order your copy by calling 877-322-8228 or visiting the Web site *www.annualcreditreport.com*. You'll need to provide your name, address, social security number, and date of birth. The Web site delivers your report immediately, but it may take up to 15 days to arrive if ordered by phone.

Only one free report a year may seem stingy, but the law also guarantees you a free copy if you:

- are on welfare.

- are unemployed and plan to look for a job within 60 days.

- discover the report is wrong because of fraudulent activity, such as identity theft.

- are denied credit, insurance, or a job based on your credit report.

You can still order a copy of your credit report from each of the three reporting agencies, even if you have already used your free copy for the year, but you may have to pay up to $10.50 per copy.

ALERT!

Beware of fake "free" credit reports from other Web sites. Only *www.annualcreditreport.com* is authorized to fill your free credit report order. Anyone else who claims to offer free reports or monitoring may, in truth, be signing you up for a paid service or simply trying to collect your personal information.

Take your time typing in the address *www.annualcreditreport.com*. Some imposter Web sites use misspelled versions of this address.

Defend yourself from identity thieves

A crook who breaks into your house may steal your television, but a thief who steals your identity can cause a lot more damage. In 2008, nearly 10 million Americans had their identities stolen — and it cost them an average of $4,849 a pop, according to a study by Javelin Strategy & Research. Some lost much more.

Surprisingly, the number 1 source of identity theft is still the old-fashioned kind. Lost or stolen wallets, checkbooks, and credit cards accounted for almost half of all ID theft cases where the cause was known. The Internet, on the other hand, only accounted for one in 10 cases.

All too often, the thief is someone you know. One out of every 10 victims knew the person who stole their identity. What's worse, these thieves stole twice as much money as thieves who were strangers because the theft went unnoticed longer. Locks and alarm systems won't stop these crooks, but this advice can.

Go digital. Paper bills and the checks mailed with them are big targets for ID thieves. It may go against common sense, but paying your bills online can actually be safer. Get the latest antivirus and anti-spyware programs for your computer, and set your operating system, programs, and Internet browser to update themselves automatically to make bill-paying more secure.

Get off junk lists. Opt out of pre-approved credit card offers and remove your name from junk mailing lists to give thieves fewer ways to steal from you.

Shred everything. Invest in a good crosscut shredder that turns paper into confetti. Shred all your junk mail, old bills, financial statements, canceled checks, and anything else with personal information a crook could use.

Keep privacy private. Don't give out your social security number, Personal Identification Numbers (PINs), passwords, or sensitive financial information over the phone or Internet. The exception — give them out only if you dialed the number or surfed to the Web address listed on the back of a bank, credit card, or other official statement.

While you're at it, ask to get a driver's license or state-issued ID without your social security number on it, and don't carry your social security card in your purse or wallet.

Read the fine print. Only shop with credit and debit cards from companies that guarantee you will not be held liable for fraudulent purchases. Make sure your bank and credit card company have zero-liability rules on lost and stolen cards. Cancel any unused cards and credit accounts to give thieves one less thing to steal.

Mind the mail. Send your bills, tax returns, and other important mail directly from the post office, not your house mailbox. Have new checks sent to the bank instead of the post office, or have them delivered to your home via registered mail.

Catch ID theft early

Unlike regular robberies, there are no broken windows to let you know when your identity has been stolen. In fact, you may not notice for months, unless you're on the lookout for these four sure-fire clues that someone has stolen your identity.

- Inaccurate information on your credit report, such as accounts you didn't open, addresses you never lived at, and employers you never worked for.

- Calls or letters from businesses or debt collection services, telling you to pay for items and services you did not buy.

- Being denied credit or loans, or being offered only bad terms like high interest rates, when you know you have good credit. Crooks may have trashed your credit score.

- Failing to receive bills or other mail you normally get. Call the companies to find out what happened. Thieves may have stolen the mail, taken over the account, and changed your billing address to cover their tracks.

Be wary, as well, if you get credit cards in the mail you never applied for, or if you receive bills and statements for accounts you don't remember opening.

Javelin Research & Strategy found that catching identity theft early can limit the damage and save your good name. The sooner you notice the theft, the less money you lose.

The best way to spot this fraud is to monitor your accounts and bank statements, according to the Federal Trade Commission. Read through all financial statements carefully each month, looking for charges or withdrawals you didn't make. Doing your banking online can make this simpler, because you can check your accounts any time of day and as often as you like, for free, instead of reviewing them just once a month when your statement comes out.

Review your credit report at least once a year, more often if possible. Check it for accounts you didn't open; credit checks from companies you didn't contact; unexpected debts on existing accounts; and incorrect addresses, employers, social security number, and name or initials.

ALERT!

Costly credit monitoring services will alert you to suspicious activity in your accounts, but the Federal Trade Commission cautions that many of these services only monitor one credit bureau, not all three.

Before you sign up, be clear about how much protection you are really getting. And investigate the service with your local Better Business Bureau, consumer protection agency, and state Attorney General's office for any complaints.

First steps when ID theft strikes

Having your identity stolen doesn't have to mean the end of the world. Take these steps to save your credit.

Get the word out. Place a fraud alert on your credit reports to keep the thief from opening more accounts in your name. Call one of the credit reporting agencies toll-free. They will alert the other two agencies on your behalf.

- Equifax at 800-525-6285

- Experian at 888-EXPERIAN

- TransUnion at 800-680-7289

Check your file. Once you place a fraud alert, you are entitled to a free copy of your credit report from each agency. Order yours and review them carefully. Figure out which accounts have been affected, and make sure your social security number, address, name, initials, and employers are all correct.

Close bad accounts. Call the banks and businesses that hold the affected accounts and ask to speak with their fraud or security department. Explain what happened, and always follow up in writing. In your letter, include copies — not originals — of any supporting documents they request. Send these letters via certified mail, return receipt requested. Keep a copy of each, and note when the company received it.

Get the government involved. File a complaint with the Federal Trade Commission (FTC). Visit the Web site *www.ftccomplaintassistant.gov*, and click on the FTC Complaint Assistant button. Fill out the form, then print a final copy.

If you don't have Internet access, call the FTC's Identity Theft Hotline at 877-ID-THEFT. File a complaint with the ID theft counselor, and ask for a copy of the ID Theft Affidavit.

Notify the police. Contact either your local police department or the one in the town where the theft occurred. If they refuse to take a police report, call your county or state police, or the state's Attorney General's office. You can also ask to file a "Miscellaneous Incidents" report with police if they won't file an identity theft report.

Give the officer a copy of the ID Theft Complaint form you filled out with the FTC, if you have one. Get a copy of the police report or the report number.

Dispute fraudulent debts. For charges made to one of your existing accounts, call the company involved and ask them to send you their fraud dispute forms. For new accounts fraudulently opened in your name:

- ask the business if they accept the Identity Theft Report.

- if they refuse, or if you don't have a report, ask if they accept the FTC's ID Theft Affidavit.

- if they again refuse, ask for their fraud dispute forms, fill them out, and mail them to the company's billing address.

Once you settle the dispute, ask the business for a letter stating that the disputed accounts are closed and all fraudulent debts are canceled. Then file this letter. It's your proof if the company ever tries to collect money or report the debt to the credit reporting agencies.

Set the record straight. Next, get the info removed from your credit reports. Write to each of the three credit reporting agencies and tell them what information you think is inaccurate and why. Ask them to remove or correct the information. You can even enclose a copy of your credit report with the faulty items circled. Also enclose copies of any documents that support your claim. Be sure to send it certified mail, return receipt requested.

Reestablish your privacy. Create new passwords and Personal Identification Numbers (PINs) for all your accounts, both existing and new. Order copies of your credit reports periodically the first year after the theft, and check for new fraudulent activity.

You're never alone when fighting identity theft. In addition to the FTC, these groups can help you get back your good name.

Identity Theft Resource Center
888-400-5530
www.idtheftcenter.org

National Consumer League's Fraud Center
202-835-3323
www.fraud.org

Call for Action
301-657-8260
www.callforaction.org

Freeze out credit fraud

Stolen identity can destroy your life. A security freeze is a great way to block criminals from ruining your good credit. In fact, it's so good, most states have laws to assure it's available.

It's the number one way to put the freeze on ID thieves before they strike. This move prevents creditors and other third-parties from accessing your credit file, which blocks thieves from opening accounts in your name. This move isn't a cure-all, though. A security freeze won't:

- protect against thieves using existing credit cards and accounts.

- prevent them from opening new accounts that do not require a credit check, such as some telephone, cell phone, and bank accounts.

- block companies you already do business with from accessing your credit report.

- put an end to pre-approved credit offers.

- affect your credit score.

In some states, anyone can freeze their file; in others, only identity theft victims can. Most people must pay up to $10 to each credit reporting agency. However, ID theft victims can freeze free of charge in many states.

To protect yourself, you'll need to contact each credit reporting agency. Equifax requires written notice, but TransUnion and Experian let you place a freeze by either phone or mail. If you write, include your full name, date of birth, social security number, current address, previous addresses for the last two years, photocopy of your driver's license or state-issued ID, proof of current address such as a copy of a recent utility bill, and payment for any fee.

To place a freeze by phone, call Experian at 866-580-2347 and TransUnion at 888-909-8872. Or mail your request, documents, and payment to:

> **Equifax Security Freeze**
> P.O. Box 105788
> Atlanta, GA 30348
>
> **Experian Security Freeze**
> P.O. Box 9554
> Allen, TX 75013
>
> **TransUnion**
> Fraud Victim Assistance Department
> P.O. Box 6790
> Fullerton, CA 92834

Keep in mind, if you apply for a loan or credit card, you will need to lift the freeze temporarily, often for a charge. Use the Personal Identification Number (PIN) each credit agency gives you to lift it.

Outsmart
the IRS

Work off your property taxes

A small investment of your time could eliminate your property taxes. And surprise — it's courtesy of your government.

Towns, cities, and counties across the country have begun offering a new program to older adults. Instead of paying property taxes, people just like you are lowering or erasing their property tax bill by working part time for their local government. For example, Boulder, Colorado residents eased their tax bill by landscaping, gathering climate data, clipping newspapers, and manning the courthouse information booth. Program participants in Massachusetts worked off taxes by doing research, data entry, and groundskeeping. What's more, some people need only work for a few weeks out of the year to shrivel their tax bill.

To find out whether your local government offers a similar program, contact its Human Resources department, Senior Citizen or Elder department, or Taxpayer Assistance office.

DON'T FORGET

Once you get your tax bill, you only have a certain number of days to file your appeal with the tax authority board. Call your tax assessor's office to find out the deadline, or you might have to wait at least a year before you can appeal. Also ask what forms are required and what other deadlines you must meet.

'Appeal'ing way to cut your property taxes

Property taxes depend on your local government's estimate of your home's value. But figures from the National Taxpayers Union suggest those values are often too high. You can stop them from charging more property tax than you owe. File an appeal and your tax bill may shrink.

Learn how the taxable value is figured. It may be based on cost to rebuild, percentage of your home's estimated value, recent sales of similar homes, or something else entirely. Call the assessor's office and ask what methods or percentages they use. Also, ask how to file an appeal if one is needed.

Find out whether you have a case. Visit the tax assessor's office and ask for the documents used to value your home. When you get them, find the copy of your property card. This card describes characteristics of your home that affect its taxable value, such as square footage and number of bathrooms. Check for mistakes. Tight deadlines, drive-by inspections, and high workloads can lead to errors on these cards.

If you see no mistakes on the property card, perhaps they still got your home's value wrong. If you can find homes similar to yours that have been sold or assessed for at least 10 percent less value, you may have a case. "Similar" means a similar-size home and lot that's roughly the same age, preferably with the same number of bedrooms and baths. If your neighbors' homes qualify as similar, look up their valuations at the assessor's office. Otherwise, try to find five to 10 similar homes that sold either recently or around the time your home was assessed. A realtor can help you get this information, but some may charge a fee.

Call on your inner Perry Mason. If you found a mistake on your property card or learned that similar homes are valued at least 10 percent lower for tax purposes, gather supporting evidence. Take pictures to show how your property card is wrong, or use blueprints, surveys, maps, floor plans, or a home inspection report — or make a chart showing how other home values differ from yours. In other words, plan to make your case as if you were Perry Mason presenting to a jury.

File your appeal. Find out where to file your appeal forms. Deliver them yourself or send them by certified mail. When you get your appeal date, prepare a five-minute "Perry Mason" presentation to explain why you should pay lower property taxes.

If you win your case, you'll be rewarded with lower property taxes.

SuperSaver

Ask your local tax assessor's office about special homestead exemptions or tax reductions for senior citizens, veterans, the disabled, and low-income homeowners. Make sure you get all the property tax breaks you deserve.

Soften the blow of medical bills

The medical expenses that insurance won't reimburse can be pretty painful. Especially if you've already used up the money in your flexible spending account. Fortunately, you may have one last recourse — a tax deduction.

If you have unreimbursed expenses for yourself and family members for things like eyeglasses, prescription medicines, dental services, doctor visits, and diagnostic tests, add them up. You may get a deduction if the total is more than 7.5 percent of your adjusted gross income (AGI). To check your AGI, see lines 37 and 38 on your 1040 tax form.

Here's how the deduction works. If you have an adjusted gross income of $40,000, then 7.5 percent of your AGI is $3,000. Your unreimbursed medical expenses must be higher than that amount to qualify for the deduction. If those expenses total $4,200, for example, that's $1,200 over the $3,000 mark. So your medical expense deduction will be $1,200.

To take advantage of this deduction, remember these points.

- You must itemize.

- The payments must be specifically for diagnosis, cure, treatment, or prevention of disease or for any treatment that affects a part or function of your body. Over-the-counter medicines and payments covered by an employer or government program are not eligible.

- You're more likely to qualify if you can time your medical expenses so they fall during a single tax year.

THE NEXT STEP

To find out exactly which expenses qualify for medical deductions and which ones don't, see IRS Publication 502 available online at www.irs.gov or by calling 800-829-3676.

Surprising medical costs you can deduct

You may have a higher number of deductible medical costs than you think. Make sure you include these when tallying up your list.

- **Travel expenses.** Count your mileage to and from medical treatments if you drive. In the past, people could claim up to 27 cents per mile. If you make long trips or a lot of trips, this can add up quickly. If you take a taxi, train, or bus to medical treatments, you can deduct the fares. "One thing that people forget is they are allowed to deduct any parking fees and tolls they may have paid on their way to the medical visit," says Angie Grillo, Certified Financial Planner and Accredited Investment Fiduciary of South County Financial Planning in Orange County, California. "Also, don't forget to count mileage to and from the drug store for picking up prescriptions."

- **Medically prescribed supplements.** "Many people have certain deficiencies that cause medical conditions that are helped by supplements. Usually vitamins and supplements are considered general health and, therefore, are not deductible. However, if it has been recommended by a medical practitioner for a specific medical condition diagnosed by a physician, it is a deductible expense," says Grillo. "Chiropractors can diagnose these types of conditions. Just make sure to obtain a letter from the doctor with the diagnosis and the supplement name for your audit records."

- **Premiums.** Private supplemental Medicare premiums or Medicare part B (supplemental coverage) and part D (pharmacy coverage) premiums are deductible, Grillo adds. But this comes with a restriction. "Any insurance premium is not deductible if it is being reimbursed. If an employer is reimbursing, it is considered tax-free income."

- **Special health professionals.** Don't forget costs from visiting your chiropractor or osteopath.

- **Hearing and chewing aids.** Include costs for hearing aids or false teeth.

- **Glasses and more.** "You can also deduct the costs of glasses, contact lenses, and eye surgery, including laser eye surgery," says Teri Tornroos, Enrolled Agent and Financial Planner with Evergreen Financial Planning LLC in Marietta, Georgia. Nursing care and nursing home expenses are also deductible, she adds.

- **Stop-smoking prescriptions.** Include expenses from doctor-prescribed programs or prescription medications to stop smoking.

- **Doctor-prescribed weight loss.** If your doctor has recommended weight loss for a specific medical condition such as heart disease, you can deduct weight-loss program expenses.

"Certain permanent improvements made to your home for a disabled condition are deductible," Grillo says. These include ramps, railings or support bars, widening doorways, lowering kitchen cabinets, moving electrical outlets, landscape grading for access to the home, and lifts for stairs (but usually not elevators). "There are so many; the key is if you feel you need to modify something in your home due to a disability, contact your tax preparer to see if it would be a medical deduction," she says. Keep all of your receipts for any work done."

Secret to deducting long-term-care premiums

Here is a bonus deduction you may not know about. "A portion of qualified long-term-care insurance premiums are deductible," says Angie Grillo, Certified Financial Planner and Accredited Investment Fiduciary of South County Financial Planning in Orange County, California. "The key here is to make sure you are purchasing a qualified policy. If you aren't sure, contact your insurance company and ask that they direct you to the language in your policy stating that it is a qualified policy. If it is not qualified, consider replacing your policy to allow for the deduction. This is one area where it gets better with age. As the policy holder grows older, the maximum deduction allowed increases."

For 2008, the maximum amount of the premium that is deductible was as follows:

- Age 40 or under – $310

- 41 to 50 – $580

- 51 to 60 – $1,150

- 61 to 70 – $3,080

- 71 and older – $3,850

"Keep in mind these maximum amounts are per person," Grillo adds.

Beware Social Security's early retirement 'tax'

You've probably heard your Social Security benefit is lower if you retire early, but a little-known penalty can make your check even smaller.

You won't find this penalty in any IRS document, but experts say it slashes your income just like a tax. This "tax" only affects people who have not yet reached the exact retirement age set for them by the Social Security Administration. People who experience this penalty get fewer Social Security checks — and less money — during the years and months leading up to retirement age. But the precise penalty for retiring early depends on your total income and how far you are from that retirement age. (See the table *Know your full retirement age* in the *Social Security simplified* chapter to check your retirement age.)

If you have not reached retirement age. This is the toughest time to get the full amount of your Social Security benefit. Here's why.

"You are allowed to earn a maximum of $13,560 in 2008 and $14,160 in 2009 before your benefits would be reduced," says Certified Financial Planner Angie Grillo. "If you earn more than the maximum allowed, your benefits will be reduced $1 for every $2 earned over the maximum." It's as if you're charged a 50-percent tax on every dollar above the maximum.

"For example, if you earned $15,000, that is $1,440 over the maximum allowed of $13,560. Your Social Security benefit would be reduced by $720," says Grillo. You would divide $1,440 by two to get that amount. (See graph on the next page.)

If you have reached retirement age. "You are allowed to earn a maximum of $36,120 in the months before your full retirement birthday in 2008 and $37,680 in 2009 before your benefits would be reduced," says Grillo. That's an improvement over the earlier income limit. What's more, the penalty isn't nearly as painful.

"If you earn more than the maximum allowed, your benefits will be reduced $1 for every $3 earned over the maximum," Grillo says. That's just one-third of every dollar over the maximum "taxed" away — instead of one-half.

For example, if your full retirement birthday is in November, and you earn $38,000 during the months leading up to it, you'll be $1,880 over the maximum allowed of $36,120. Divide that by three and you'll get $626.66 — the amount your Social Security benefit will be reduced.

However, if you only earned $36,000 by your full retirement birthday, your Social Security benefit would not be reduced, Grillo points out.

After your first full year of retirement. "Once you have reached full retirement, your Social Security benefits will not be reduced no matter how much you earn in subsequent years," Grillo says.

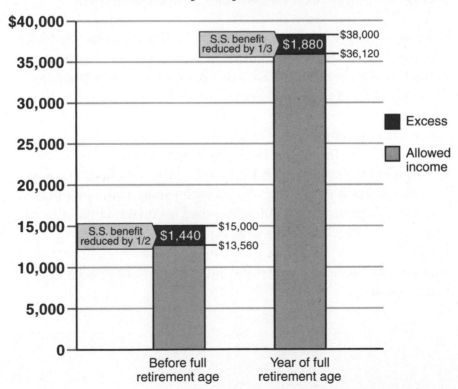

Social Security Early Retirement "Tax"

Save yourself from Social Security taxes

"About one-third of people who get Social Security have to pay income taxes on their benefits," says Teri Tornroos, Enrolled Agent and Financial Planner of Evergreen Financial Planning, LLC in Marietta, Georgia. "If you work while receiving Social Security benefits, it will increase your adjusted gross income and more than likely put you into the 85-percent level of taxation on your benefits," adds Financial Planner Angie Grillo of Orange County, California. "The thing to look at here is whether your benefits will be reduced because of your working."

Be aware that the following rules can affect anyone taking Social Security regardless of whether you've reached retirement age or not.

"Social Security benefits fall into one of three levels of taxation. Either they are nontaxable, 50 percent of the benefits received are taxed, or 85 percent of the benefits are taxed," says Grillo.

The level of taxation is based on "total combined income," which is determined by taking your adjusted gross income plus tax-exempt interest earned (like Muni Bonds or tax-exempt Money Market funds) plus half of the Social Security benefits you receive.

This may sound confusing, but it's really not. Adjusted gross income is the number on line 37 or 38 on your Form 1040 or line 22 on 1040A. It's made up of all taxable income minus above-the-line tax deductions. Taxable income includes such things as wages, salaries, tips, taxable interest and dividends earned on investments, state or local income tax refunds, alimony, capital gains, and IRA and pension distributions. Above-the-line deductions are the ones subtracted from your gross income to get the amount of your adjusted gross income.

Once you know your combined income, you can get a rough idea of what tax category you might fall into. See examples in the table below.

Single, head of household or qualifying widow(er) with combined income of:	Married filing jointly with combined income of:	Taxes paid on Social Security benefits:
less than $25,000	less than $32,000	none
$25,000 to $34,000	$32,000 to $44,000	50 percent of the benefits received
more than $34,000	more than $44,000	85 percent of the benefits received

Tips to trim taxable income

Choices you make can reduce either your taxable income or incoming money so you can avoid paying taxes on Social Security. Consider how these tactics may affect your overall long-term financial picture as well as your taxes.

- Avoid investments that generate taxable income such as dividend-paying stocks. Instead, consider stocks that pay little or no dividends — or tax-managed mutual funds that promise little or no taxable distributions.

- Put off taking money out of taxable retirement accounts such as traditional IRAs and 401ks until you reach the age of 70 1/2.

- Draw some income from Roth IRA distributions, which are tax-free. Before you try this, consider carefully how this may affect your long-term financial picture. You may decide that your overall finances will fare better if you let your Roth earnings continue to grow untouched.

Surefire way to trim taxes

Imagine cutting your taxes and pumping up your monthly Social Security benefit. You can do it if you haven't begun taking Social Security yet. Here's how.

During retirement, distributions from your traditional IRAs and 401ks are 100 percent taxable. If you add Social Security to that, up to 85 percent of your Social Security benefits could be taxable. That could cause a painfully high tax bill. So, instead of taking Social Security when you reach retirement age, live off distributions from your taxable accounts such as IRAs and 401ks for awhile. After all, if you wait until age 70 to start taking Social Security, you'll get a bigger monthly Social Security check.

If you get a higher percentage of your income from IRAs and 401ks before age 70 but then reduce distributions from those retirement accounts when you start taking Social Security, your total tax bill may drop during your Social Security years. Why? Because your total taxable income will be lower even if your total income in dollars is the same as before. Remember, Social Security only becomes taxable when you have high amounts of other income coming in with it.

This strategy may not be right for everyone and may actually be a poor financial choice for some. So before making a decision, calculate what your after-tax income would be before 70 and after — or talk to a financial advisor.

How to get thousands tax free

You could put thousands — even hundreds of thousands — of dollars into your pocket tax free. If you own a home, this much could be yours.

Here's how. If your home has appreciated in value or you've paid off part of your mortgage, you may be able to refinance your home for more than you owe. If so, you can pay off the "old" mortgage and pocket the remaining money tax-free.

For example, Jack bought his home for $150,000 with a mortgage of $120,000. While he paid that mortgage down to $108,000, his home value rose to $337,500. If he refinances for $200,000, he can pay off the remaining $108,000 on his old mortgage. Because $200,000 - $108,000 = $92,000, he can pocket $92,000 tax-free.

Of course, it's money you have to pay back. But if you have a sound reason for needing a loan, refinancing might be a beneficial way to get it. Just remember this:

- Your lender must agree to this type of refinance loan.

- Ask whether the terms of the new loan will restart the clock so that you'll be paying the mortgage for the next 30 years.

- Check for pre-payment penalties on the old loan before applying for a new one.

- How you use the pocketed money may determine whether your loan interest is deductible on your tax return. If you use it to improve your home, the interest is probably fully deductible. But if you use that money for anything else, the amount you can deduct will likely dwindle. See IRS Publication 936 for a worksheet to help you figure whether your interest is deductible.

To learn more, consult a financial or tax professional.

Enjoy a windfall from company stock

If your 401k plan includes company stock, you could cut your taxes during retirement with a little-known tax secret.

Beware this tax pitfall. If you are 59 1/2 or older and you leave your employer, you might roll your entire 401k — company stock and all — into an IRA. But if you do, you'll pay your regular income tax rate when you take that stock out of the IRA as a retirement distribution. If, at that time, your income tax rate is higher than your capital gains tax rate, you could miss out on hundreds or thousands in tax savings.

Take a tax cut instead. If shares of your employer's stock were purchased through your Employee Stock Purchase Plan and put into your 401k, part of that 401k distribution at retirement may be in stock shares. That may qualify you for a tax break called Net Unrealized Appreciation (NUA). "NUA occurs when the value of employer stock increases when in a qualified plan," says Financial Planner Teri Tornroos of Marietta, Georgia. "To take advantage of NUA, the distribution must be as employer stock, not as cash."

> Net unrealized appreciation is a tax break for retirees whose 401k contains employer stock bought via an employee stock purchase plan.

"Do not roll over your entire 401k plan to an IRA," says Certified Financial Planner Angie Grillo of Orange County, California. "To take advantage of Net Unrealized Appreciation on employer stock that is held in your 401k plan, it is important that the employer stock be separated from the rest of your 401k holdings."

So tell your retirement administrator to roll part or all of your company shares into a taxable brokerage account while rolling the rest of your 401k into an IRA. When you do, you must pay income tax, but only on each share's original purchase price. If company shares are more expensive today than when yours were purchased, you won't pay taxes on those gains yet. The NUA is taxed only when the stocks are sold, explains Tornroos. That's why those gains are call "unrealized" appreciation because they haven't become "real" spendable dollars for you yet.

If you hadn't rolled the shares into the brokerage account, you'd have paid income taxes on those gains. But now you'll only pay capital gains tax when you sell the stock. If the capital gains tax rate is lower than your income tax rate, you may save big. See the *Making it work* box for details.

MAKING IT WORK

While Joe Retiree worked for Company Y, 1000 shares of Company Y stock at $10 per share were purchased for Joe's Employee Stock Purchase Plan (ESPP). These shares, totaling $10,000, went into Joe's 401k.

When Joe is ready to retire, he finds his company stock has gone up to $30 per share and his stock portfolio is now worth $30,000. Joe tells his retirement administrator to roll his company shares into a taxable brokerage account while rolling the rest of his 401k into an IRA. As a result, he must pay income tax on each share's original price of $10. That leaves $20 of each share untouched by taxes. So his net unrealized appreciation (NUA) is $20,000 ($30,000 - $10,000).

Joe waits to sell his stock until its value is $50,000. He pays tax on the $40,000 gain at the long-term capital-gains rate instead of his ordinary income rate. If Joe's income tax rate is 25 percent and the capital gains rate is 15 percent, he will enjoy a $4,000 tax savings.

Know the requirements. NUA isn't for everyone and here is why.

- You can only use NUA if you withdraw the entire balance from all your employer's qualified plans, including profit-sharing, pension, stock bonus, and 401k, within a single year.

- Only company stock purchased via a combination of employer contribution and employee pre-tax dollars qualify for this tax break.

- NUA is best for those in higher tax brackets whose company stock has appreciated a lot.

"There are also potential estate planning issues," says Grillo. "It is important to have a liquidation plan for this stock to prevent passing on a large capital gains tax burden to your heirs."

Consider talking with a tax professional or financial planner to ensure that everything related to NUA is done correctly.

ALERT!

If you sell your "NUA" stock less than one year after rolling it into a taxable account, you may have to pay a higher short-term capital-gains tax rate on any gains made by the stock during that year. Gains made prior to the NUA rollover still fall under the often cheaper long-term capital-gains rate.

Get tax credit for retirement savings

"If you make eligible contributions to a qualified IRA, 401k, or certain other retirement plans, you may be eligible for a tax credit of up to $1,000 if you file single and $2,000 if you're a joint filer," says CPA Gina L. Gwozdz. And this isn't a secret tax loophole for the rich. In fact, you'll get the biggest benefit if you're just an average Joe.

To qualify for the saver's credit:

- You must have contributed to a 401k, traditional IRA, Roth IRA, SEP, SIMPLE, 403b, or other qualified retirement plan during this tax year.

- "In 2008, this credit phases out for taxpayers with incomes greater than $26,500 if you are married and file separately; $53,000 if you are married and file jointly and $39,750 if you file as head of household," says Gwozdz. This means your Adjusted Gross Income — the figure on line 37 or 38 of your 1040 form — had to be less than these numbers in 2008. But these "ceiling" amounts can change and may be significantly higher by now.

- You must not be a dependent on someone else's tax return or be a full-time student.

- You must submit IRS Form 8880 available free from *www.irs.gov* or by calling toll-free 800-829-3676. This form shows the current income limits for this tax credit and will help you figure how much of the credit you should receive.

To learn about other requirements you must meet, check Form 8880.

ALERT!

Withdrawing money from a retirement plan or taking distributions can reduce or eliminate the saver's credit.

New tax break for widows

You've just lost your spouse and now a friend tells you that you must sell your house within a year or face painful tax consequences. Fortunately, that's not true anymore. As long as you haven't remarried, you can wait up to two years after the date of your spouse's death to sell your home and keep up to $500,000 in profits tax-free. This not only gives you more time to plan but also helps you build a brighter financial future with profits from your home sale. To learn about requirements you may need to meet, visit *www.irs.gov* or call the IRS Help Line toll-free at 800-829-1040.

The IRS appears to take pity on a person who has lost a spouse during the year. When preparing your tax return for the year your spouse passed away, you may still file as "married filing jointly" as long as you haven't remarried and no executor or administrator has been appointed by the time you file your taxes.

Bump up your standard deduction

Strange but true — the IRS will give you a "senior discount" if you don't itemize.

If you were 65 or older during the tax year, you can claim both the regular standard deduction and an additional standard deduction. For example, in 2008, you could deduct $1,350 (single) or $1,050 (married). But you must use Form 1040 or 1040A to get this deduction. For more information, see IRS Publication 501 available free from *www.irs.gov* or by calling toll-free 800-829-3676.

Play it smart and come out ahead

Don't throw out those old investment statements. They might help keep you out of a higher tax bracket during retirement.

Be a record holder. If you squirrel away money in a taxable investment account as well as your IRA or 401k accounts, you have an opportunity. Resist the temptation to toss your investment statements after 10 years or so. Instead, keep copies of all the statements and reports you get from your investments including confirmation statements and 1099 forms. They'll help you track the purchase price and date and the selling price and date of your individual shares. Here's how that could pay off.

Control taxes in retirement. If you buy shares of your favorite stock or mutual fund every year to add to your retirement savings, you'll pay a different price each year. When retirement arrives, you can take a distribution by selling some of those shares. But if you just tell your broker to sell x number of shares, he'll follow the IRS's first-in first-out rule and sell your earliest-bought shares first. If those shares are your cheapest, you'll end up with higher capital-gains taxes.

But if you kept good records, you'd know whether you had bought later shares for a higher price. Then you could use the "specific identification" method. That means you give your broker written instructions to sell shares you bought at a higher price. Your written instructions must include the purchase price and date the shares were bought, and you must receive written acknowledgment of your instructions. Selling the more expensive shares reduces your capital gain and capital-gains taxes.

Take a big picture view. Of course, you'll sell your lower-priced shares sooner or later, so can this strategy really help you? Yes. Sell lower-priced shares with their higher capital gains in years where your expected tax burden is lower. Then sell higher-priced shares (with their lower capital gains) in years where you expect to pay high taxes. This may keep you from accidentally slipping into a higher tax bracket.

> Capital gains tax is a tax paid on any profit you make from selling stocks, bonds, or similar investments. A long-term capital-gains rate applies if you sell investments you've owned for more than a year. You pay short-term capital gains taxes — at your normal income tax rate — on those you've owned for less than a year.

Remember, the key to this tax secret is to keep careful track of when you bought each share of stock, what you paid for it, and whether you have already sold it or not. It may require extra time and effort, but it won't cost you a penny. And it could end up saving you a bundle.

You buy 100 shares of your favorite stock every year, and lucky you, it keeps going up. The first year it costs $10 per share; the second, $20; and the third year, $30. When retirement arrives, the shares are selling at $50. You tell your broker to sell 100 shares, so he follows the IRS's first-in, first-out rule and sells your $10 shares. That gives you a capital gain of $40 per share. If your capital-gains tax rate is 15 percent, you'll be taxed $6 per share.

But if you use the specific identification method to sell the shares you bought for $30, selling at the current $50 price would give you a $20 capital gain. So you'll pay only $3 per share in capital-gains tax instead of $6.

You will earn $50 per share regardless of which shares you choose to sell, but your tax burden will be lighter with the $30 shares.

Beware this careless tax mistake

Your goal is to pay the least amount of taxes on your investments. So when you notice you get the smallest capital gains by selling shares you bought within the last year, you jump on it. But watch out. This can be a quick way to reduce — or even eliminate — the tax savings you're aiming for.

If you've owned the shares for 366 days or less, your gains are considered short-term capital gains. Short-term capital gains are taxed at regular income-tax rates. If your income-tax rate is higher than the long-term capital gains tax rate, that difference could wipe out part or all of your tax savings. See the *Making it work* box on the next page for details.

Of course, your tax rate and the prices of your shares could be different from the ones in this example. And in some cases, it might still pay to sell shares bought more recently. So before you sell, run the numbers to figure out which shares will truly allow you to pay the lowest taxes.

MAKING IT WORK

Your shares are currently selling at $10 per share. Just under a year ago, you bought 400 shares for $7. Two years ago, you bought the same number of shares for $6. Your income tax rate is 25 percent and the capital gains rate is 15 percent.

If you choose to sell the $7 shares:

- you'll earn short-term capital gains of $3 per share ($10 - $7 = $3)

- $3 x 25% income tax rate = 75 cents tax per share

- 400 shares x 75 cents = $300 total taxes

If you sell the $6 shares instead:

- $10 - $6 = $4 in long-term capital gains per share

- $4 x 15% capital-gains tax rate = 60 cents tax per share

- 400 x 60 cents = $240 total taxes

By selling the older shares and accepting the higher per-share capital gains, you actually pay $60 less in taxes.

Don't get caught in a mutual-fund tax trap

Buy mutual fund shares at the wrong time of year and you could pay extra taxes. Here's what you need to know to save money.

Occasionally investments inside mutual funds generate capital gains and even dividends. By law, mutual funds are required to pass these along to their investors once a year. This distribution happens during the last few months of the year. If you buy right before the distribution, you must pay taxes on that distribution even though you didn't own the mutual fund for most of the year. In other words, you'll be paying capital-gains taxes for gains you never got.

Fortunately, if your mutual funds are already tucked up inside a traditional IRA, Roth IRA, or 401k, you won't have to pay tax on fund distributions as long as you keep the fund shares in your account. You'll just pay ordinary income tax rates on your earnings when you take withdrawals in retirement. But if you're considering buying shares of a particular mutual fund for a taxable account, ask the mutual fund company when the fund's distribution date is. Buy shortly after that date instead of a few days before, and you'll save on your tax bill.

SuperSaver

Invest in tax-efficient or tax-managed mutual funds, and you'll avoid the tax hazards of mutual fund distributions. Just remember, taxes should never be your sole reason for choosing a mutual fund.

Give yourself a Christmas present

It's December and you're already dreading the high tax bill you'll pay for this year's successful investments. But don't fret. It may not be too late to cut your tax bill.

If you have losing investments you were already planning to dump, go ahead and sell them before the year ends. If they sell for less than their purchase price, this will give you a capital loss. You may be able to use capital losses to offset some of your capital gains — the profit you made from successful investments. And if your capital losses exceed your capital gains, you can use those losses to offset up to $3,000 of your regular income — or $1,500 if you're married filing separately.

This doesn't mean you should sell investments you expect to eventually recover and earn profits. But if you had already planned to cut your losses on a losing investment, do it during the year where it can do the most good. If this is the year, you'll enjoy Christmas more knowing you'll pay lower taxes in April.

Shrink your 'golden years' taxes

Some experts say you should put your money in regular 401ks and traditional IRAs while others recommend Roth IRAs and (when available) Roth 401ks. What should you do?

Get the lowdown. If you expect to be in a lower tax bracket during retirement than during your working years, tax-deferred accounts like traditional IRAs and 401ks offer an advantage. Instead of paying today's higher tax rate on your retirement contributions, you'll pay a lower tax rate on the money when you withdraw it during retirement.

But if you expect to be in a higher tax bracket during retirement, contributing to a Roth IRA may be better. You'd pay today's "low" tax rate on your Roth contribution while working, but you'd withdraw the money tax-free during retirement when your tax rate would be higher.

The problem is that it's tough to predict which tax bracket you'll be in during retirement.

Hedge your bets. Consider including both tax-deferred accounts (traditional IRA and 401k) and tax-free accounts (Roth IRA and Roth 401k) in your retirement plans. This effectively splits your tax burden between your working years and retirement years.

Just remember that the IRS limits the amount you can contribute to each of these retirement accounts based on your income. So be careful to avoid contributing too much to any single account or to any combination of these accounts. For more information on Roth vs. traditional plans, see the chapter *Ins and outs of IRAs*.

THE NEXT STEP

For more information on the yearly limit for retirement account contributions, visit www.irs.gov — or check IRS publication 590 available free from *www.irs.gov* or by calling toll-free 800-829-3676. You may also find helpful information at *www.vanguard.com* or *www.fidelity.com*.

Tax help for free

Tax help doesn't have to be expensive. Check out these programs that will answer your tax questions at no cost.

- The IRS's Volunteer Income Tax Assistance (VITA) program offers free tax-return help to low- to moderate-income taxpayers of all ages who can't afford professional tax preparers. If you're 60 or older, you can turn to the Tax Counseling for the Elderly (TCE) program for help with your tax return. Trained volunteers with these programs will let you know about credits and deductions you are eligible to claim. To find the nearest VITA or TCE location, call 800-829-1040.

- As part of the TCE program, AARP offers the Tax-Aide counseling program. To find the closest AARP Tax-Aide site, call toll-free 888-227-7669, or visit the AARP Web site at *www.aarp.org/money/taxaide*.

- The IRS also provides pre-recorded tax information 24 hours a day at its Teletax number. Available topics include deductions, tax credits, IRAs, 401ks, and more. Just call 800-829-4477 and have pencil and paper ready. For a directory of topics, listen to topic 123. Write down the numbers of topics that interest you. Then use option 2 and listen to as many topics as you like. Be sure to take notes.

For more details on free tax information and services, order IRS Publication 910 for free from *www.irs.gov* or by calling toll-free 800-829-3676.

Simple, smart way to convert your IRA

Taxes may not be the first thing you consider when deciding whether to convert a retirement account into a Roth IRA. But the taxes from a Roth conversion can affect today's finances as well as your retirement. Make wiser choices with these tips.

Beware Roth IRA conversion taxes. You can convert a traditional IRA, 401k, or other qualifying pension, stock bonus, or profit-sharing plan to a Roth IRA. But you must pay income tax on the amount you convert. For example, if you convert $10,000, that's like adding $10,000 to your taxable income. That might even bump you into a higher tax bracket. So before you convert, figure out how many extra tax dollars it will cost you.

Make converting affordable. If you can't afford the taxes, don't convert the entire amount all at once. Instead, consider converting a portion of the total amount each year for several years. Run the numbers to be sure you can afford the new amount — and to make certain you won't end up in a higher tax bracket during any of your conversion years.

Converting to a Roth IRA may not be right for everyone, so consult with a financial professional before you take the plunge. Also, make sure you meet the income restrictions and any other requirements for a legal conversion to a Roth IRA. For more details, see *Switch to Roth for tax-free savings* in the chapter *Ins and outs of IRAs*.

In some cases, contributions to a traditional IRA are not tax deductible, so the nondeductible contributions get taxed before you put them in. If you later convert to a Roth IRA, you should not pay taxes on any nondeductible portions of the traditional IRA that you're converting.

Take tax-savvy distributions

Withdraw too much from your traditional IRA and you could get shoved into a higher tax bracket. But with a little planning, you can avoid this ugly surprise.

The "powers that be" make sure you accumulate funds in your IRA by charging a big penalty if you withdraw any money before age 59 1/2. But if you haven't withdrawn any money by age 70 1/2, you're legally required to withdraw a government-specified amount of money every year. So you can withdraw as early as age 59 1/2 or you can wait until 70 1/2. That decision is up to you.

But whenever you decide to start withdrawals, remember these rules.

- Keep withdrawals as small as possible if you want to minimize taxes. This means you must plan ahead and budget carefully so you'll withdraw just enough money to cover both expenses and the taxes you'll pay on the withdrawal.

- Pay close attention to your expected taxes to determine whether your withdrawals can be adjusted up or down. For example, you might be able to afford a slightly larger withdrawal in years where you expect a lot of deductions — or you might skimp on withdrawals in years where you expect to have higher taxes due to extra income from other sources.

So before the 70 1/2 mark, aim to keep your distributions small enough to stay in one tax bracket. After that date, you can only limit taxes by keeping your withdrawals no bigger than the minimum required distribution.

Harvest your cash at the right time

You have planted the seeds for your retirement and will help them grow for years. But when the time comes to harvest some cash, you'll do even better if you have three kinds of "fields" to harvest from — taxable income, tax-deferred accounts, and tax-free accounts.

Harvest taxable income first. That includes pension distributions and the dividends and interest from investments. Taxable accounts — such as brokerage accounts for stocks, bonds, and mutual funds — get no protection from taxes, so take out cash from these accounts early in your retirement.

Withdraw tax-deferred money next. Tax-deferred accounts include your traditional IRA and 401k accounts. Experts suggest you leave the money here as long as possible. Investments in these accounts grow tax free until you cash them in. Plus, your money grows faster than in a taxable account because you're not paying taxes on your earnings, which reduces your investment. So take distributions from IRAs and 401ks after your taxable investments.

Reap your Roth rewards last. Although you pay taxes on contributions that go into a Roth IRA or Roth 401k, you pay no taxes on that money when it comes out. Like traditional IRAs and 401ks, investments in your Roth IRA won't be reduced by annual taxes so they grow faster. Couple that with its tax-free status upon withdrawal, and the Roth is hard to beat. Harvest this type of investment last for tax-free income when you need it most.

Keep exceptions in mind. Legal or financial issues such as mandatory withdrawal rules or investment losses may create the need for a different strategy. Or, if a distribution from a taxable or tax-deferred account would bump you into a higher tax bracket that year, you may consider withdrawing from a different account than usual. So keep an eye on your investments, taxes, regulations, and legal requirements — and plan accordingly.

Dig deep to find a tax-friendly state

Moving to reduce state taxes can be a great way to stretch your retirement dollar, but be careful. States with little or no income tax are not necessarily tax friendly. A state with a minimal or zero income tax may make up for it with high sales taxes, property taxes, gas or auto taxes, or other taxes. Before you retire to another state, do your homework.

- Find out the property tax rate for the city, county, part of the county, and state you're considering — and ask what percentage of a property's assessed value gets taxed.

- Check for property tax breaks and exemptions, especially those for seniors and veterans.

- Examine the estate tax laws of any state you consider.

- Learn how high the state, city, and county sales taxes are.

- Find out whether the state taxes Social Security benefits, IRA distributions, and pensions.

- If the state has income tax, find out how it defines income and what its tax rates and tax brackets are.

- Check whether the state offers tax breaks for retirees.

To find this information, contact the local and state tax departments of places where you would like to move — or visit their Web sites.

2 easy ways to cut estate taxes

You want to leave your money to your heirs, not Uncle Sam. Keep more of your money in the family with these helpful tips.

Give it now. "Taking full advantage of the annual gift exclusion to family members is the easiest way to reduce your estate," says Angie Grillo, a certified financial planner and accredited investment fiduciary out of Orange County, California. "In 2009, an individual may give $13,000 as tax-free income to as many people as wanted without having to pay gift taxes. A married couple may give $26,000 to each individual."

These numbers may change so check IRS Publication 950 for the latest figures. You can order it free from *www.irs.gov* or 800-829-3676.

Go beyond gifts. "You may further reduce your estate by providing more than the annual gift exclusion to family members, tax free, in any given year by the following means," adds Grillo.

- directly pay for the private school or college tuition of anyone you choose

- directly pay for the medical expenses of anyone you choose

"The key to the above two strategies is to pay the institution directly. Do not provide the funds to the person who is benefiting," Grillo says.

ALERT!

Watch out for audit-triggering tax mistakes. Tax laws change every year, so to ensure you have the most up-to-date information, talk to your tax professional, visit *www.irs.gov,* or call the IRS tax assistance line toll-free at 800-829-1040.

Take advantage of special tax credit

You may qualify for a special tax credit if you or your spouse is age 65 or older. To qualify for this credit you must meet three requirements.

- You or your spouse must meet the minimum age requirement. For example, if you were paying taxes for 2008, one of you must be age 65 or older during 2008 or turn 65 on January 1, 2009. Why January 1? Oddly enough, the IRS considers you to be 65 on the day before your 65th birthday.

- You must complete Schedule R of Form 1040 or Schedule 3 of Form 1040A.

- You must meet the income requirement.

The income rules not only determine whether you'll get the credit, but also how much of the credit you can claim. To qualify for the credit, you must meet one requirement for adjusted gross income (AGI) and a second requirement for nontaxable Social Security and pension amounts. If you qualify, you can ask the IRS to figure the amount for you.

For example, if in 2008 both you and your spouse were over 65 and filed jointly, you could have claimed the tax credit if your AGI was less than $25,000 and your nontaxable Social Security and pension totals were under $7,500. The amounts vary based on your filing status, so see IRS Publication 524 to make sure you qualify and to get advice on how to ask the IRS to calculate your credit.

Give more to charity and less to the tax man

Donations to charity deserve a good tax deduction, but the sheer number of IRS rules can make getting that deduction a little tricky. So use these tips to help.

Contribute to "deductible" charities. For your deduction to count, it must go to an organization that qualifies for tax-deductible donations. Good examples include veterans groups; nonprofit schools, churches and hospitals; and well-known charities such as the Salvation Army or Girl Scouts. To find out whether a charity qualifies, either ask the charity or check IRS Publication 78. The publication is available for free at many local libraries or from *www.irs.gov* or by calling 877-829-5500.

Include your "invisible" donations. Cash and used property donations aren't the only things that earn deductions. You can also deduct certain unreimbursed expenses required specifically for charity volunteer work. For example, if you traveled 10 miles each month in 2008 to volunteer at a charity's office, you could have deducted 14 cents per mile. You can also deduct costs of supplies, such as stamps you bought to mail out fundraising requests. Other expenses may be deductible, too.

Donate cash wisely. Instead of tossing $20 in the Salvation Army bucket at Christmas, write a check for the same amount. Otherwise, that $20 won't be deductible. To make sure your cash contributions are deductible, you need one of the following:

- a canceled check

- a bank or credit card statement showing the amount and charity

- a written acknowledgment from the charity featuring the charity's name and the date and amount of your contribution

The amount you can deduct and the evidence required by the IRS may vary depending on how much you donated and whether you received any benefit in exchange.

Follow the property rules. If your clothing or other property donation deduction is more than $500, attach Form 8283 to your tax return so the IRS won't deny your deduction. For more details on donating clothing, see Earn top dollar on your charity donations in the Build your nest egg tax chapter. The rules for property donations vary depending on whether you donate cars, clothing, boats, art, stock, real estate, household goods, furniture, or other items.

Know your limits. The amount of charity donations you can deduct may depend on your income. The rules vary widely depending on what you donate and other factors. As long as your charitable donations stay below 20 percent of your adjusted gross income, these limit rules are less likely to affect you. Play it safe and check IRS Publication 526 — just in case the tax laws have changed. This publication will also help answer your other questions relating to charitable donations.

Report and estimate wisely. The IRS has specific requirements for the documents you must send in to prove your donations. You must also keep extra documents ready at home, in case the IRS asks for more evidence. IRS publication 526 can help you nail down what to send in and what to keep at home. But it won't always help you figure out the right IRS-accepted value of your donations. For that you may need IRS publication 561. These publications are free from *www.irs.gov* or 800-829-3676.

Double your tax break with stock donation

Writing that December check to your favorite charity may ease your tax burden, but you can pay even less to the IRS if you donate stock instead. That's because you not only get the charitable deduction, you avoid paying capital gains taxes on the profits. See the *Making it work* box on the next page for details.

Check the requirements. Before you can donate, the following must apply:

- The stock must be a publicly traded stock that sees regular activity on a stock exchange.

- You must have bought the stock at least one year ago, and its value must be higher than when you bought it.

- Your gift must be less than 30 percent of your adjusted gross income and must go to a "50-percent limit" organization such as the American Red Cross, the Salvation Army, the United

Way, or nonprofit hospitals or churches. It must be less than 20 percent of your AGI if you contribute to certain charities.

- You must itemize your deductions.

- The charity must accept stock donations. Check with your charity first, and find out if it has a minimum donation requirement.

Get the biggest benefit. To get the most from your donation, keep this in mind. The stock's fair market value — which determines your deduction — is the price you could have sold it for on the day you donated it. To complete the donation, you must transfer ownership of shares. Your stockbroker or the charity can help you do this. The date when your donation takes effect will depend on how the ownership transfer is done.

Know the rules. Depending on your particular circumstances, the stock you donate, the size of your donation, and many other tax details, extra requirements or restrictions may apply. Before you donate stock, read IRS Publications 526 and 561, or consult a tax professional.

MAKING IT WORK

Say you bought 100 shares of stock for $2 each two years ago and they're worth $5 a share now. That means you have $500 worth of stock — $300 of which would count as capital gains if you sold it today. Now, you could write a $500 check to your charity and cut your taxes by $125 if your tax rate is 25 percent. But if you donated the stock, you'd not only get the $125 deduction — you'd also forego paying capital gains tax of $45 (at 15-percent rate). When you subtract your tax savings, your total cost of donation is only $330, but your charity still gets the same $500 as if you'd written a check. It's a win-win situation.

Take advantage of free help from the IRS

The Internal Revenue Service has publications that can answer all your tax questions, and they're available free of charge. Listed below are some of the topics discussed in this chapter along with a quick reference to the appropriate publication and IRS contact.

Information about:	Found in:	Contact:
charities to which you can make tax-deductible donations	IRS Publication 78	*www.irs.gov* or 877-829-5500
charitable donations	IRS Publications 526 and 561 and Form 8283	*www.irs.gov* or 800-829-3676
medical deductions	IRS Publication 502	*www.irs.gov* or 800-829-3676
paycheck withholding	IRS Publications 505 and 919	*www.irs.gov* or 800-829-3676
tax credit for the elderly	IRS Publication 524, and either Form 1040 and Schedule R or Form 1040A and Schedule 3	*www.irs.gov* or 800-829-3676
extra standard deduction for older adults	IRS Publication 501	*www.irs.gov* or 800-829-3676
IRAs	IRS Publication 590	*www.irs.gov* or 800-829-3676
free tax-related information and services	IRS Publication 910	*www.irs.gov* or 800-829-3676
deducting interest on refinanced home loan	IRS Publication 936	*www.irs.gov* or 800-829-3676
gift taxes and estate planning	IRS Publication 950	*www.irs.gov* or 800-829-3676
retirement saver's tax credit	Form 8880	*www.irs.gov* or 800-829-3676

Straight talk about health insurance

Choose health insurance that pays

PPO, HMO, FFS — negotiating the maze of health insurance
options can make your head spin. Each type of plan works differently
and the costs vary widely. How do you know what is right for you?
The answer depends on how healthy you are and what your family
situation is. Experts say a retiring couple should expect to spend
between $250,000 and $300,000 on basic medical coverage. That
makes choosing the right plan even more important, because don't
you want to spend more of your retirement dollars on having fun?

Fee-for-service (FFS) is traditional health insurance. This type
of plan — also called an indemnity plan — lets you pick your doctor
and hospital, and your health insurance pays for all or part of the
costs. It's often the most expensive type of health insurance, but you
get the most flexibility. Try to get lower group rates through your
employer or an affinity group. If you have to buy an individual policy,
you'll really pay through the nose.

A preferred-provider organization (PPO) limits your choices.
Pick a PPO, and you're dipping your toe into the managed-care
pool. In this type plan you agree to use preselected doctors and clinics that have signed on for certain cost limits. You can see doctors
outside the network, but you'll pay more. There are often no
deductibles, so you could save money by switching to a PPO. This
may be a good choice for you if you have a chronic condition.

Be sure any lab you use — for an MRI, X-ray, blood work, or whatever — is on the list of preferred providers. Then you can get the lab
to bill your insurance company just as a doctor would. Depending on
your plan, you may only have to pay a copayment or nothing at all —
free medical testing.

Health maintenance organizations (HMOs) keep the costs low.
You'll typically pay no deductible or copayment, and deal with little
paperwork if you go with an HMO. There's just one monthly premium you pay regardless of the number of doctor visits you have. But

you have to use doctors in the network, and you need a referral to see a specialist. An HMO focuses on preventive medical care, covering many services you'd have to pay for under typical health insurance.

No matter which type of plan you choose, check out all the benefit details before you sign up. You'll want to know beforehand what your copayments will be, how high a deductible to expect, and what the plan's maximum payout is.

Policy details can cost — know before you sign

You want health insurance that covers your needs, but you don't want to pay for more than you'll use. Ask these questions before you sign up for a policy.

- Are any prevention benefits included? How often can you get well checkups? What about dental or vision care?

- Exactly what emergency services are covered?

- What is considered to be a pre-existing condition? If you have a condition that qualifies, how long must you wait to be covered?

- What special services are covered? These could include things like blood transfusions, therapy after you leave the hospital, or orthodontic care.

- Are your drugs on the formulary? See the plan's list of covered medications to find out what you'll pay.

- How high is your deductible? This is the amount you have to pay for services before insurance kicks in.

- Is there coverage for nervous and mental disorders? Can you be treated by a psychiatrist or psychologist? Is inpatient or outpatient treatment included?

- What's covered when you travel? And will the plan pay to evacuate you home if you have a serious problem in another city or country?

- Is there a cap on benefits? Will you get enough coverage if you have a serious illness?

Finally, check to see if you can use online cost comparison tools to look at different plans side by side.

Fight a rejected claim

What can you do if a medical bill is turned down by your health insurance provider? Don't take "no" for an answer. Follow these steps to get what you have coming.

Check the code. First, call your insurance company and ask about the bill. Don't give up if you're told the procedure is not covered. It's possible your doctor's office used the wrong Current Procedure Terminology (CPT) code on the paperwork. That would cause the claim to be kicked out of the system as "not covered." You can call your doctor's office to see if the right CPT code was used.

Have your doctor step in. Even if coding is not the problem, you're still not done. Check to see that you didn't make an error, like seeing a specialist without the required referral. Then ask your doctor's office for help getting the procedure covered. You may need the doctor to write a letter to your insurance company stating that your health would suffer without the treatment.

File an appeal. Next, it's time to file an appeal with your insurance company.

- Work your way up the chain of command within the insurance company. You may need to appeal both by phone and in writing.

- If you don't get the results you want, move on to your state's insurance commission. This group can act as a negotiator.

- Finally, you may need to hire an attorney to challenge the insurance company. Find one with experience in health insurance matters and you may win an out-of-court settlement.

Delay retirement to thwart high premiums

Even if you believe you have enough money saved, health insurance costs may be out of reach until you're eligible for Medicare at age 65. If you retire before that, you'll pay a high price for insurance premiums — often triple the cost of what you paid on your employer's plan. And that's only if you can continue the same coverage. *The Wall Street Journal* finds the average early retiree will pay about $3,600 a year to continue coverage through a former employer. If you stay on the job, you'll only pay around $1,100 a year for the same coverage.

6 ways to survive before Medicare

You're lucky enough to retire early, but you're not old enough for Medicare. What will you do about medical bills? Even after you say sayonara to your job and the health insurance that came with it, you have other options when it comes to paying medical bills.

Conjure up COBRA. The Consolidated Omnibus Budget Reconciliation Act is a law that lets you continue with your former employer's health insurance. If your company has 20 or more employees, you can stay on the plan for up to 18 months after you leave your job. It's a nice safety net, especially if you have health problems. But COBRA can get expensive, since you're paying for it all by yourself. The average cost of premiums for COBRA coverage are about $700 a month for a family or $250 a month for an individual.

Sock away some savings. Plan ahead and put income into a tax-free health savings account (HSA). Then you can use it for medical expenses even after you leave work. You'll lower your premiums, decrease your tax bill, and build up a tax-free stash for future medical expenses.

Look for low-cost insurance. Check out an affinity organization — professional, fraternal, alumni, or religious — to see if they offer group health insurance to their members. AARP is one example, offering a Personal Health Insurance Plan. Or get help finding an inexpensive plan from an independent insurance agent who sells group plans for a variety of companies. He may be able to dig up a deal for you. If you know you'll soon be eligible for Medicare, check out an interim insurance plan. These are typically good for 60, 90, or 180 days.

Get a guarantee. A state guaranteed issue health insurance pool may not be your first choice, since it typically offers the least amount of coverage for the most money, but if you're desperate for insurance, contact your state health insurance commissioner to see if a pool is offered in your state.

Head back to work. Some retirees go back to work just for the benefits. Even if you don't need the income, you may decide it's worth working to save hundreds of dollars every month on health insurance for you and your spouse.

Find it for free. If all other options fail, you don't have to go without healthcare. The federal Hill-Burton program provides free and reduced cost healthcare to low-income people through certain hospitals, nursing homes, and clinics. To find a Hill-Burton location near you, navigate on the Internet to *www.hrsa.gov* and click on the "Find help" link. For more information on the Hill-Burton program, call 1-800-638-0742 (in Maryland call 1-800-492-0359).

Bargain your way to lower medical bills

What's the fastest way to lower your medical bills? According to a recent survey, only 31 percent of Americans have tried negotiating with their health-care providers. That's a shame, because just about everyone who did paid less. You can take your cue from insurance companies. They typically negotiate a discount of about 60 percent off hospital costs. You likely won't get that kind of deal, but you may get a 30 percent discount. Here's how to negotiate successfully to get a bill you can live with.

Ask the right person. Talk to the hospital's social worker or patient navigator to review your insurance coverage and see if you may be eligible for a lower price. Get that person on your side.

Do your homework. Find the price Medicare pays for your procedure and use that as a reasonable starting point for negotiations. Medicare prices are typically lower than what private insurance pays. To find an average Medicare payment in your area for a specific medical condition or surgical procedure, go on the Internet to *www.hospitalcompare.hhs.gov* and click on the gray button that says "find and compare hospitals."

Start early. Get a good price before you have the treatment. Sometimes you can get a deal if you pay in advance. In fact, some hospitals require a large part of the payment up front for situations not classified as medical emergencies. If you're asked for a large chunk of money beforehand, that's the time to negotiate.

Share the facts. Don't balk at handing over your financial records or credit score to the hospital billing department. Giving this information may clear the way for a better deal.

Expand your bargaining power. Don't limit your negotiating to just hospitals. Try it with your doctor, dentist, and chiropractor, as well. You may get better terms just by paying cash since the office won't have to send a bill.

Travel for treatment and save

Medical tourism, or traveling across international borders for health care, can save you money. If you can't afford treatment in the United States, consider a country where costs are low and service and quality of care are high. Note that you can't use Medicare benefits outside the U.S. except under extremely limited circumstances, but you may come out ahead anyway.

Traveling for medical care is not a new idea. People in England and Canada frequently journey to other countries instead of waiting to get treatment at home, while Europeans routinely go to a nearby country for lower-cost care. The practice is also gaining ground among Americans, with thousands seeking more affordable treatment every year. The trip may be worth considering if you can save, say, $10,000 on a knee operation by getting it across a border. Popular destinations include Mexico, India, Thailand, and Singapore.

Find the silver lining. Getting your treatment away from home offers these benefits.

- Lower cost. Travel to a country where the cost of living is much lower than at home — but the quality of care is still high — and you can easily save 80 percent on treatment.

- Great customer service. Certain destination hospitals are known for their fine accommodations tailored to Western patients.

- Shorter waits. You'll spend time on a plane, it's true, but you should be able to schedule appointments more quickly.

- Insurance perks. Some health insurance companies are including treatment overseas. WellPoint, for example, covers some elective surgeries in India. You may even get a bonus from your company if you're willing to travel.

- Vacation options. Depending on your condition, you may be able to add some sightseeing to your visit overseas. But don't forget your main job on the trip will be to heal.

Do your homework. Just like at home, you'll need to ask some questions before you schedule a procedure overseas.

- How much will you save by going abroad? Include the cost of a plane ticket and an extended stay while you recuperate over-seas — not simply the cost of the procedure.

- Is the hospital accredited by the Joint Commission International (JCI) — a non-profit that certifies the safety of hospitals?

- Are you physically able and willing to travel a great distance for treatment? A plane ride to India may take 15 hours.

- What doctor will treat you after you return home? Major procedures require follow-up care.

You can find help in planning your trip from companies like WorldMed Assist, Premier MedEscape, and Patients Without Borders — all members of the nonprofit group the Medical Tourism Association. Visit this organization's Web site at *www.medicaltouris-massociation.com.*

Overseas savings on common medical treatments

How much money can you save by going abroad for medical treatments? Here are some sample prices in the United States and two common medical tourism destinations.

Treatment	Price in hospital in Thailand	Average price in U.S. private hospital
Complete checkup	$400	$2,000
Prostate surgery	$5,000–$7,000	$35,000–$40,000
Spinal surgery	$6,000–$8,000	$50,000–$70,000
Root canal	$320	$900–$1,000
Hip replacement	$9,000	$40,000–$50,000
Treatment	Price in hospital in India	Average price in U.S. private hospital
Heart bypass surgery	$10,000	$130,000
Angioplasty	$6,200	$57,000
Hysterectomy	$3,000	$20,000
Liver transplant	$55,000	$350,000
Knee replacement	$7,400	$40,000

THE NEXT STEP

Get help from a travel agency that specializes in medical travel. They'll know all about the area you're visiting and be able to guide you through the process. Important names in the business include Med Journeys, online at *www.medjourneys.com* or call 888-633-5769, and WorldMed Assist, online at *www.worldmedassist.com* or call 866-999-3848.

Plan wisely for tax-free savings

You can sock away money tax-free into a flexible-spending account (FSA), then use it throughout the year to pay for medical expenses your health insurance doesn't cover. An FSA account — different from a health savings account (HSA) — allows you to have pretax earnings taken out of your paycheck and set aside to pay for unreimbursed health costs.

The main drawback is you have to use up the money in the year you save it. Anything left in the account at the end of the year — or the few months grace period some companies allow — is lost. That means it's best to plan conservatively to avoid leaving money on the table. If the end of the year is drawing near, it may be time to make some doctor appointments or stock up on items you'll need later on. Check out these surprising items you can pay for using your FSA money.

- teeth cleaning, if it's not covered by a dental plan

- acupuncture and chiropractic services

- nutritional supplements, including calcium and glucosamine and chondroitin, if they're related to a certain condition and recommended by your doctor

- a pre-travel checkup or vaccinations before you go overseas

- over-the-counter cold medicine, stomach aids, or pain relievers

- equipment your doctor recommends, like a whirlpool to treat a bad back

- eyeglasses or reading glasses — even nonprescription reading glasses

- first-aid kits

- lead-based paint removal

- treatments to stop smoking

- weight-loss programs when they're needed to treat obesity or an illness, like heart disease

- a hotel stay if it's necessary to get the medical treatment you need

Check with your employer to be sure the list of approved items matches what the IRS allows. Your plan's list may be more limited.

Best-kept secret about an HSA

Like an FSA, a health savings account (HSA) lets you save money tax-free. One big difference is you can only continue putting away money into your HSA until you turn age 65. Until you reach that important birthday, stash your money with Uncle Sam's blessings.

Not everyone can have an HSA. These accounts are intended for people with high-deductible health insurance to pay their routine medical bills. There are limits on how much you can contribute to your HSA every year — $3,000 for an individual or $5,950 for a family in 2009.

But here's the best thing about an HSA. Unlike a flexible-spending account, you don't lose your money if you can't use it within the year.

Instead, you can leave it in the account and let it grow from year to year. If you still have money left in your HSA when you turn age 65, it's not lost. You can take it out and use it without penalty for any purpose. However, if you use the money for something other than paying medical bills, you'll have to pay taxes on it. Even worse, if you use it for non-medical bills before age 65, you'll also pay a 10-percent penalty.

To avoid paying taxes, be sure you use your HSA money for qualified expenses — any costs incurred to diagnose, cure, treat, or prevent disease. Those are pretty broad, and they may include:

- insurance premiums

- annual doctor visits

- prescription drugs

- long-term care

Don't worry about putting too much money in your HSA. You won't lose any extra funds — even if you die with money left in your account. It'll go straight to your spouse.

The truth about discount health cards

You've seen the ads for discount cards that claim to save you money on prescription drugs, doctor visits, dental care, and more. Don't believe all the hype. These cards often don't really save you money. You pay for the card, but it may not pay for much of what you need. Even worse, your doctor and your pharmacy may not even accept the card.

Costs vary, but you can easily pay $75 to $150 every year just for the privilege of having a discount card. Advertising claims say the cards will get you low prices on doctor visits, hospital stays, drugs, dental care — everything you usually expect health insurance to cover. But some cards charge administrative fees that are higher than any discount you'll get, so you won't come out ahead. Also, no card can replace your regular insurance coverage since it won't pay for high-price items.

Here's how you can check to be sure the card you're considering is legitimate — and that it'll pay for exactly what you need.

- Be skeptical if advertising claims there's no age limit for a card or the plan accepts all pre-existing conditions.

- Look for promises like, "savings up to 70 percent." It's unlikely you'll ever see savings that high.

- Make sure the plan covers generic drugs, and check to see that it covers the specific drugs and services you need. Then call your doctor's office to verify that they accept the card.

- Find out if you can cancel later if you want. Membership fees should be refundable.

- Contact the Better Business Bureau or your state's insurance commissioner's office to find out if the company is trustworthy.

Not all cards are scams. If your employee health insurance plan offers a free discount card, take it. You may save around 20 percent on costs — no strings, no hassle.

Clever tricks to cut drug prices

A recent survey found more than half the money seniors spend on health care goes to buy medicine. That can add up to several thousand dollars every year. Keep your costs down with a tiny bit of effort with these tricks.

Split pills. You may be able to cut your prescription costs in half by splitting your pills. If this works with your medication, you can buy higher-dose pills for the same price, then cut the pills in half for cost savings. It won't work for all drugs, so talk to your doctor before you try this clever — and perfectly legal — trick.

Substitute. Your doctor may help you figure out other cost-savings methods, like switching to a lower dose or a cheaper drug, or taking a higher dose less often. Or ask about using an older drug, which may be cheaper than the fancy new models.

Go generic. Switching to a generic could save you up to 80 percent. Find out if your brand-name drug has a generic version by checking *www.fda.gov* or *www.drugstore.com*.

Recruit the mailman. Use the mail-order service offered by your health insurance plan. You'll probably get a 90-day supply of medicine for the price of a 60-day supply, with no shipping costs. This option works well for drugs that treat chronic conditions, but you'll have to plan ahead because of the delay in shipping.

Get company help. See about drug-company assistance programs, which may provide your prescriptions for free. These programs, intended for people with financial need, are usually based on your income. You probably won't qualify if you bring in more than twice the poverty level. But some programs are based on what percent of your income you spend on drugs.

Shop around — then shop some more. You may have paid $90 for your drug at one store, then found it for $6 at another. What gives? See if your drug is one of the generics selling for $4 for a month's supply at Wal-Mart, Sam's Club, Target, Neighborhood Market Pharmacies, and other stores. Club stores, like Sam's Club or Costco, may offer better deals on generics than drugstores like Walgreens and CVS. That's because the clubs lower the price from the brand-name drug's price rather than just marking up the generic price. Try club stores even if you're not a member.

Look beyond the medicine bottle. Find out about lifestyle changes — like exercise and diet — that can help improve conditions such as arthritis or high blood pressure. You may be able to take fewer drugs and feel better.

Compare drug prices online

Use your computer to find cheaper generic versions of your drugs —
and to check the going rates of your medications online. Some price-
checking Web sites are updated daily. You can find deals at online
pharmacies, but look for the VIPPS seal (Verified Internet Pharmacy
Practice Sites) to be sure it's a safe, licensed U.S. pharmacy.

Web site	How it works
www.destinationrx.com	Online search engine with price, product, and safety information. Compares prices at online and local pharmacies. Prices updated daily.
www.pharmacychecker.com	Online search engine lets you compare prices at online pharmacies. Prices updated continually.
www.pillbot.com	Online search engine lets you compare prices at online pharmacies. Prices updated daily.
www.pricescan.com	Online search engine includes a variety of shopping categories. Search in "Health and beauty" section. Prices updated daily.
www.crbestbuydrugs.org	Provides information on drugs, price ranges, and possible substitutions and comparable generics.
www.rxaminer.com	Sign in for information on drugs, sample prices, and possible substitutions and comparable generics.
www.fda.gov/cder	FDA's Center for Drug Evaluation and Research can help you find a generic equivalent for your brand-name drug.
www.drugstore.com	Online drugstore licensed to fill prescriptions in all 50 states. Check prices or find out if a brand-name drug has a generic version.

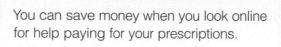

You can save money when you look online for help paying for your prescriptions.

- *www.pparx.org* — Complete a short question-naire, and you'll get information on drug-assistance programs from the Partnership for Prescription Assistance.

- *www.rxassist.org* — Search by your medication name to find assistance programs that will help you find free or low-cost medication.

- *www.needymeds.com* — Find programs that can help you get your medications free or at reduced prices. Some programs are not based on financial need.

Get wise to the Medicare 'alphabet'

With age comes wisdom — but often some expensive health problems, as well. Medicare coverage can help you pay for health care if you know how the system works. Just because one portion of Medicare won't pay for a drug, service, or treatment doesn't mean you're stuck paying for it yourself — or going without. The different parts of Medicare are intended to cover specific areas. Learn the Medicare alphabet so you can get help.

Part A provides hospital care. This will pay for expenses like inpatient care in a hospital, skilled nursing facility, or hospice. You don't have to pay premiums for Part A if you paid into the Medicare system for at least 10 years while you were working. In that case, you'll pay only an annual deductible — $1,068 in 2009 — then some of the costs after the first 60 days of care.

Part B covers outpatient care. Doctor visits, flu shots, and screening tests, like mammograms and colonoscopies, are included in this coverage. You'll pay monthly premiums and an annual deductible — $135 in 2009. Medicare Part B pays 80 percent of the cost of most covered items, while you pay the other 20 percent.

Part C includes optional supplemental "Advantage" plans.
These are HMO- and PPO-type plans, intended to fill the holes in Medicare coverage by helping pay costs regular Medicare doesn't cover. Medicare Advantage managed-care plans pay for everything traditional Medicare pays for, plus more. Yet, as with other forms of managed care, you pay less — but you have fewer choices for your care. If you choose to use an Advantage plan, remember that you're actually leaving the Medicare system and working with a private contractor. Medicare pays the contractor to take care of you.

Part D offers prescription drug coverage. The very first Medicare cardholder, Harry S. Truman, didn't have the choice to sign up for Part D coverage. These optional drug plans weren't available until 2006. With this coverage, you choose among a number of different drug plans, each with different formularies — lists of drugs covered — and prices. After you meet your Part D deductible every year, the plan pays for your drugs up to a certain limit. Then the "doughnut hole" kicks in, and you get no more help paying for drugs until your costs reach a certain higher limit. After that, Part D resumes paying the bills.

Step-by-step guide to enrollment

Your 65th birthday is drawing near, and you're eager to let Medicare pay for your health care. Getting coverage doesn't happen automatically. Follow these steps so you don't pay penalties or extra fees by not signing up at the right time.

Pick the proper plan. Your first decision is whether to enroll in traditional fee-for-service Medicare — possibly adding a Medigap policy — or a Medicare Advantage managed-care plan. These plans vary in different parts of the country, so find out what's available in your area.

Open enrollment for Medicare begins three months before you turn age 65 and ends three months after. That gives you a six-month window of opportunity. If you miss that window, you'll have to wait until January 1 of the next year. Plus, you'll pay penalties to join later.

- Miss the Part B deadline and you'll pay a penalty on your monthly premiums for the rest of your life. They'll be 10 percent higher for every year you're late.

- Miss the Part D deadline and you'll pay a 1-percent penalty on monthly premiums for every month you're late.

If you don't sign up at first because you're still covered by your job's health insurance, you won't pay penalties later if you sign up for Medicare within eight months of leaving your job.

Check your insurance. Find out if your current health insurance will continue after you hit age 65. You'll want to decide whether to use it based on costs. When you turn age 65, you may be able to retain your employer-based health insurance — whether or not you're still working. By law, insurers have to offer the same types of plans to people age 65 and older as they do to younger people. You can keep your coverage, but the price may go up when you retire. And you can keep your old insurance and use it as a supplement to Medicare. You may decide it's a better deal — and you may get better coverage — to choose Medicare and add a Medigap policy.

Don't forget about Medicaid. Look into whether you're eligible for Medicaid or other state assistance with your Medicare costs. There's help available for people with low incomes.

Decide on drug coverage. Learn about what Medicare Part D — prescription drug coverage — can do for you. Check the plan formularies — lists of drugs covered — to see if one might fit your needs.

Get your last-chance exam. Schedule an initial Medicare physical exam within six months of joining. After this one opportunity, Medicare won't pay for a regular physical. This exam can include the following tests:

- height, weight, and blood pressure checks

- heart disease and diabetes screening

- vision and hearing tests

- depression and substance abuse screening

- abdominal aortic aneurysm screening

THE NEXT STEP

There's help out there for older adults — dozens of programs in your state to help you pay for drugs, rent, food, utilities, even taxes. Get all the benefits your tax dollars paid for. The National Council on Aging can help you get your free "benefits checkup" at *www.benefitscheckup.org*. Simply log in and enter some information about yourself and where you live. You'll find out which Medicare, Medicaid, senior housing, and other programs will help you. Get what you deserve — it's all free.

3 services for free

Medicare will foot the entire bill — 100 percent — for some services. Don't skip getting these treatments because you think you'll have to pay — they're free.

- Flu shots and pneumonia shots. Check to be sure the treatment provider accepts Medicare assignment — the amount Medicare has agreed to as a fair payment. Otherwise, you may have to cover 15 percent of the bill.

- Home health-care services. These may include skilled nursing, home health aides, physical therapy, and speech therapy. Medicare pays for this type of care if you are confined to your home, if your doctor says you need the care and creates a plan, and if you use a home health-care agency that participates in Medicare.

- Clinical lab services and tests. Blood work, biopsies, urine tests, and similar items are covered.

For most doctor visits and treatments, Medicare coverage pays 80 percent of the bill after you pay your annual deductible. You pick up the other 20 percent of the cost.

Medicare help in a flash

Avoid the confusing phone tree when you need Medicare help. Call 800-MEDICARE (800-633-4227). Use these secret shortcuts to quickly bypass endless button pushing and get your problem solved fast. Speak clearly and have your Medicare card handy. You can say "agent" at any time to talk to a customer service representative.

If you are calling about ...	Say ...
Medicare prescription drug coverage	"Drug coverage"
Claim or billing issues or appeals	"Claims" or "Billing"
Preventive services	"Preventive services"
Extra help paying health or prescription drug costs	"Limited income"
Forms or handbooks	"Publications"
Telephone numbers for your state Medical Assistance (Medicaid) office	"Medicaid"
Outpatient doctor's care	"Doctor service"
Hospital visit or emergency room care	"Hospital stay"
Equipment or supplies, like oxygen, wheelchairs, walkers, or diabetic supplies	"Medical supplies"
Information about your Part B deductible	"Deductible"
Nursing home services	"Nursing home"

Before you dial your insurance company, check out *www.gethuman.com*. You'll find out exactly how to bypass the automated phone system and get live help at many companies.

Get smart about Medicare scams

There's lots of money involved in Medicare payments. That makes it a tempting arena for fraud and scams. Con artists may try to get money from you, or they may use you to get money from Medicare. Keep these warnings in mind to avoid getting scammed.

Don't be fooled by a phone call. Don't fall prey to someone calling to sell you a Medicare plan. That's not how plans are sold. Typically, you'll be the one to make a call to enroll in a plan. In addition, Medicare plan sellers can't ask you for credit card or banking information over the telephone — unless you are already a member of that plan.

Take time to consider your options. Don't let yourself be rushed into enrolling in a plan. Instead, take a few days to research and think about your options. You should never sign anything unless you are sure:

- the plan has the features you want.

- the doctors, specialists, and hospitals you prefer to use will accept the plan. Don't trust a salesperson who says the plan is "good anywhere."

If you were confused or misled when you enrolled in a Medicare Advantage plan, call the Medicare help line and ask to be enrolled again in traditional Medicare or switched to another Advantage plan.

Guard against identity theft. Keep your Medicare information safe. Identity theft happens when someone uses your personal information without your consent to commit fraud or other crimes. Personal information includes things like your full name and your Social Security, Medicare, or credit card numbers. Only give personal information to doctors, other health-care providers, representatives of plans approved by Medicare, and people in the community who work with Medicare-related programs, like Social Security.

Do a background check. Call 800-MEDICARE (800-633-4227) if you aren't sure if a provider is approved by Medicare. Or check the Medicare Web site at *www.medicare.gov* for impartial information on all your options — original Medicare, Medicare Advantage plans, prescription drug plans, and Medigap.

Earn a reward for fighting Medicare fraud

If you think you see a health-care provider taking money improperly from Medicare, report the incident. You may earn up to $1,000. First, ask your health-care provider about the problem. If you still have questions, call your Medicare contractor. The contractor's phone number is on your Medicare statement. If you think further action is needed, call the Medicare fraud hotline at 800-447-8477 (800-HHS-TIPS) to report the problem.

Winning ways to handle Medicare problems

You paid into the Medicare system for years while you worked — now they won't pay for your medical treatment. One thing you can do is catch billing errors — or downright fraud from a health-care provider — by checking your Medicare statement carefully. Compare the bill to the services you received and your bill from the medical facility. To be sure you'll remember every treatment, write down each procedure and test you have done. If you know you'll be incapacitated during a procedure, bring along a friend to keep your list.

When you catch a claim that was denied or not paid fully, see your Explanation of Medicare Benefits form or Medicare Summary Notice for details. These forms — from your Medicare carrier — explain why the claim wasn't paid and how to appeal the decision. Learn how the system works to get the coverage you deserve.

- File a request for review with the Medicare insurance carrier within six months.

- Ask for a formal hearing if the claim is still denied and the amount questioned is $100 or more.

- Arrange a hearing with an administrative law judge of the Social Security Administration if the claim is denied again and the amount is $500 or more.

- Make an appeal to a federal court if the claim is still denied and the amount is $1,000 or more.

Medicare benefits are confusing, and sometimes certain treatments are covered in one part of the country but not another. For example, new CyberKnife radiation treatment is used for prostate cancer. It's covered by Medicare in 33 states but not in the other 17 states. Regional and state decisions determine what's covered, and the states don't yet agree the CyberKnife is effective.

ALERT!

If you qualify for both Medicare and Veterans Administration (VA) benefits, you can't double-dip. For any specific medical treatment, you can get coverage under Medicare or the VA system, but not both. There are exceptions in which one program may pay for the portion not covered by the other. To find out if you qualify for VA health benefits, check out *www.va.gov/health* or call 877-222-8387.

Let Medicare pay for your colon cancer screening now, and you may protect your health and save money down the road. A study published in the Journal of the American Medical Association found that more people were diagnosed with early stage colon cancer after Medicare began covering colonoscopies. Experts say screening catches colon cancer early, when treatment works best.

Build a bridge across the Medicare gap

Medicare won't pay all your medical bills, so you may need a supplement. Medigap coverage can help plug the holes left by Medicare Part A and Part B. It's better than a PPO or HMO.

A Medigap plan is a supplemental policy you buy on top of traditional Medicare. You can choose from about a dozen standardized Medigap plans, each covering different expenses. No matter what company you buy a standard plan from, coverage should be the same. The only difference is price.

Even the most basic, least-expensive plans must cover these expenses, items Medicare doesn't pay for, which would normally fall on your shoulders:

- Medicare Part A hospital coinsurance — $267 a day in 2009 — for every day you're hospitalized more than 60 days, up to 90 days, for each benefit period.

- 365 days of hospital stays after Medicare coverage ends.

- Some or all of the cost of a blood transfusion. Regular Part A doesn't cover your first three pints of blood.

- Some or all of the Part B coinsurance. That's the 20 percent of medical expenses you normally pay yourself, and it can really add up.

Beyond that, various Medigap plans may pay for skilled nursing or hospice, preventive exams, or medical care while you're traveling overseas. Pick your plan based on what you expect you'll use.

MAKING IT WORK

Good friends Gladys and Rose share the challenges of dealing with diabetes. But the sharing ends when it comes to the cost of treating this disease. These two golden girls both paid Medicare taxes while they were working, so they don't pay a Medicare Part A premium. Instead, they both pay monthly Part B premiums of $96.40.

Unfortunately for Gladys, that's where the similarities end. Gladys has only traditional Medicare, while Rose opted to add Medigap Plan F to her coverage. This plan covers excess charges from doctors who don't accept Medicare assigned payment. Without Plan F, those fees could add an additional 15 percent to your bill.

Medigap Plan F costs Rose an extra $17.33 a month. Although she is paying a bit more for the Medigap coverage, she'll earn it back quickly. According to Medicare estimates, Gladys will pay about $600 to $650 every month in out-of-pocket costs, including treating her diabetes. Rose gets off easier. She'll pay about $550 to $600 a month. That gives Rose an extra $50 to spend every month. Maybe she'll take her good buddy out to a nice lunch.

4 tips for choosing a Medigap policy

Medicare pays for only about half the medical costs of people age 65 and older. For the rest, you may need a Medigap plan. Here's how you can select the best one for you.

Check the price tag. The federal government regulates Medigap plans, and they're not allowed to duplicate the coverage you're already getting in your regular Medicare Part A and Part B plans. You'll choose among several Medigap plans, each offering different coverage. Benefits of plans in the same category must be the same, but prices can vary. Look at premiums charged and what pre-existing conditions are excluded from a plan. For a cheaper option, consider the Medicare SELECT plan. It works like a combination of managed care and a fee-for-service program.

Look for solid ground. All else being equal, you're picking a plan based on the insurance company offering it. So be sure the company has a good reputation for financial stability and customer service. You may prefer one with good service features, like automatically trans- ferring claims electronically from Medicare to the Medigap carrier to save you paperwork.

Get help. Try these handy tools to pick the perfect plan.

- Compare policies offered by dozens of companies in your area at *www.insure.com*. Scroll down the page, and click on the "Medicare Supplement" link to get a price quote.

- Try the Medicare Web site to see what's available in your area. Navigate to *www.medicare.gov*, then click on the link titled "Compare Health Plans and Medigap Policies in Your Area." Enter your state, then click on "View Plans." You'll see a list of policies in your area.

Try it on for size. You have 30 days to try out your Medigap plan. If it doesn't fit your needs, you can get a full refund during that time.

ALERT!

Medicare doesn't typically pay for routine physical exams or preventive medicine, although there are some exceptions, like flu shots. Be sure to specify your symptoms when you make an appointment to see your doctor. That way, she can indicate you're being treated for a certain condition, and it may be covered by Medicare. If your records say you saw the doctor for a routine physical exam, it probably won't be covered.

Bonus benefits from Medicare Advantage

A "C" grade in school was average, but Part C in Medicare gives you an advantage. Called a Medicare Advantage plan, this type of managed-care plan may cost you more than traditional Medicare, but the benefits may be worth it.

A Medicare Advantage plan helps pay medical costs that traditional Medicare doesn't cover. This works best if there's a good plan in your area, and if you need the services they offer. Keep in mind, Advantage plans technically are not Medicare. They're run by private companies that are compensated by Medicare. Like other managed-care plans, you'll have to use the plan's network of doctors and services.

To be eligible for an Advantage plan, you must be enrolled in Medicare Part A and Part B and continue to pay Part B copayments. You have to live in the plan's coverage area, and you can't have end-stage kidney failure. If you decide you don't like your Advantage plan, you can switch back to regular Medicare, but your choice of plans may be limited.

Sounds complicated but many Advantage plans cover these services, which traditional Medicare won't pay for.

- Prescription drugs. If they're covered, you won't need Part D coverage.

- Short-term custodial care, or help with bathing, dressing, and other activities of daily living.

- Medical equipment, like wheelchairs and hospital beds.

- Chiropractic care.

- Routine physical exams.

- Emergency care while you're traveling overseas.

- Hearing tests and hearing aids.

- Dental exams and care.

- Advice and care after regular doctors' hours, either by phone or at an after-hours clinic.

Contact your State Health Insurance Assistance Program (SHIP) to get help selecting a locally available Medicare Advantage plan. In some places, it's called a Health Insurance Counseling and Advocacy Program (HICAP).

Save big bucks on prescription drugs

You hear horror stories about how complicated Medicare Part D drug coverage is. While it can be confusing, it can save you lots of money. A recent study found that seniors who use Part D coverage enjoy significantly lower drug costs — about 17 percent lower. Consider these tips to help you sort through the confusion.

Choose a plan wisely. Part D plans are run by private insurers and charge premiums of up to $70 a month. You may be tempted by a plan with a low premium, but it's not always the best way to go.

Experts say to check the plan's formulary, or list of specific drugs covered, before you make a choice. Also, be sure the pharmacy you like participates in the plan. Beyond that premium, the details of Part D can get a bit sticky. Here's how the benefits stack up.

- Deductible. Most plans have a yearly deductible. There's a maximum amount Part D plans can charge — $295 in 2009. A few high-premium plans waive the deductible.

- Partial coverage. Once you reach your deductible — and before you reach the "doughnut hole" — the plan pays about 75 percent of the cost, and you pay 25 percent.

- Doughnut hole. After your total yearly drug expense reaches $2,700, but before your out-of-pocket costs reach $4,350 (2009 amounts), you're in the dreaded doughnut hole. That means you pay the entire cost of your drugs.

- Catastrophic coverage. If your total out-of-pocket costs in a year reach a certain limit — $4,350 in 2009 — Part D pays 95 percent of all further costs, and you pay the remaining 5 percent.

Check for changes. The Part D enrollment period is the last six weeks of every year. Be sure to check available plans to see if your drug prices and premiums change, and switch plans if you can get a better deal. For example, in 2009 Part D premiums went up an average of 31 percent, but some plans increased by 60 percent. Copayments for some drugs went up, but prices for certain generics actually went down.

To find your best deal, make a list of drugs you take and the dosages. Go to *www.medicare.gov* and click on "Compare Medicare Prescription Drug Plans." Under "Find & Compare Plans that Cover Drugs," click on the "Find & Compare Plans" button.

Appeal the formulary. You have two ways to challenge the system if your drug is not on the plan's formulary.

- Request an exception to the rule, allowing you coverage for your drug. This usually requires your doctor to say it's medically necessary.

- Appeal the plan's decision.

3 reasons to dodge Part D

Part D coverage is great for people who spend lots of money on drugs. On the other hand, if you fall into one of these categories, you don't need it.

Low income. You may spend more on drugs using Medicare Part D than you would under state-run Medicaid programs.

Employees. If you already have employer-sponsored drug coverage that beats Part D, use it instead of signing up for Part D.

G-men. If you're covered through the Department of Veterans' Affairs (VA), the Defense Department's TRICARE program, or the Federal Employee Health Benefits Program (FEHB), you don't need to join Part D. Use your existing government program for prescription drugs. Benefits are similar, but you'll pay less. For example, you can get many prescriptions through the VA for just $8 a month.

SuperSaver

Medicare Part B doesn't pay for the shingles vaccine, but Part D does. Ask your doctor about getting it. The shingles vaccine, Zostavax, is important for your quality of life. It helps prevent the painful and long-lasting symptoms of shingles. You only need the vaccine once, and you can get it if you're age 60 or older.

Clear up Medicare and Medicaid confusion

Don't be mixed up by the similar names of these two government programs. Here's what each one does.

	Medicare	Medicaid
What is the program?	Federal program that helps pay for medical care, hospital stays, and prescription drugs.	Joint state and federal program that provides help paying medical expenses for people in certain low-income groups.
Who can use it?	Americans 65 years and older and people of all ages with certain disabilities, including kidney failure.	Requirements vary by state but are based on income, age, and whether you are disabled, blind, or pregnant
How can it help you?	Medicare Part A provides basic hospital coverage and post-hospital care. Part B pays for doctor visits, lab tests, and some other outpatient treatments. Part D covers prescription drugs.	Pays cost of medical services and long-term care. Payments are made directly to the provider.
What will it cost you?	You pay a yearly deductible for Parts A, B, and D, along with copayments for hospital stays and drugs. You also pay monthly premiums for Parts B and D.	You may be asked to pay part of your treatment costs.
What are the important limits?	Generally, Medicare won't pay for treatment outside the United States. Part D "doughnut hole" means you pay all your drug costs above a certain limit, but before you reach a specified threshold.	Not every needy person qualifies.
Where can you get more information?	Call 800-633-4227 (800-MEDICARE) or visit Medicare's Web site at www.medicare.gov	www.cms.hhs.gov

Long-term care: take charge of tomorrow

Don't overpay for living assistance

When health problems signal it's time to move from your home, pick a living community at the lowest level of care that suits your health situation. You'll save money and enjoy being with people who are in the same boat as you. Here are the main categories of communities, listed from the lowest to the highest level of care.

- Residential or communal living. You have your own home or apartment, usually within a secured area, and may enjoy activities and programs, but generally receive no medical assistance.

- Assisted living. You typically live in your own room or apartment in a shared facility, but can get help with personal care like bathing, grooming, and cooking.

- Congregate housing. This type of facility usually offers more medical care than you'd get in an assisted-living facility.

- Nursing home or skilled nursing facility. Here, 24-hour care is available if you have more serious medical issues.

A continuing-care retirement community (CCRC) is a facility with houses or apartments at all levels of care, so you can move from one level to another as your health changes.

Care services can keep you at home

If you don't want to move or can't afford to leave your home, look for services available in your own neighborhood, like a meals-on-wheels program or a senior center. Adult day-care facilities are also an increasingly popular — and affordable — option.

Green Houses are small-home alternatives to the traditional nursing home. They offer a full range of personal and health care for six to 10 seniors in an environment that feels less like a hospital and more like a real home. A grant from the Robert Wood Johnson Foundation is making possible this new style of living. Find out if there's a Green House near you by visiting *www.ncbcapitalimpact.org/default.aspx?id=150.*

Sidestep nursing home dangers

Cost of long-term care is important, since a nursing home can easily run $5,000 to $8,000 a month. But it's not the only factor to consider. Do your homework before you or a loved one enters a care facility.

Check state and federal licenses. Skilled-nursing facilities must follow rules about staff, fire, safety, and infectious diseases. Contact your state's nursing home licensing agency for a copy of its standards.

Look for doctor oversight. A physician must be on call, and the nursing home should have a medical plan created by a doctor. A committee of medical experts should regularly review the facility.

Ask about administration. There should be a governing body responsible for written policies. This governing body appoints an administrator to be sure things run properly.

Have a doctor recommendation. Medicare may cover nursing-home care only if you're admitted on a physician's recommendation.

Find out about hospital transfers, drugs, medical services, and dental care. All these services should be available as needed.

Get wise to social services, food, and activities. Meals should be appropriate for the individual, and residents should get as much help as they need in the activities of daily living.

Once you've narrowed the search to a few homes, it's time to dig in and do some comparison shopping. You can see how facilities rank in surveys by the Centers for Medicare and Medicaid Services at *www.medicare.gov*. Click on the "Compare nursing homes in your area" link. You can also get help at *www.cms.hhs.gov/CertificationandComplianc/* by clicking on "Nursing homes."

Be sure to tour the facility you're considering, and talk to visitors and employees to get a sense of how residents like it there.

Super saver

You might have to pay the higher price for nursing home care if you need tube feeding, are on a respirator, or require 24-hour skilled nursing. But if you just need assistance, say, once a day — an intermediate-care facility may be just the ticket. It offers nurses on staff, but not around the clock. You'll save money if intermediate care works for you.

Medicaid maneuvers: get help with long-term care

Don't let Medicare leave you in the lurch when it comes to paying for long-term care. Medicaid may be the financial solution you need. It's a combination state and federal program that pays for certain health services and nursing home care for people with low incomes and limited assets. If you qualify for Medicaid, it may pay for long-term care at a nursing home, in another type of facility, or even at home.

Pay while you can. Medicaid is meant to help people who don't have the resources to pay their own way. So, if you have money, you're supposed to pay for your care. Each state sets the amount of assets you can keep and still qualify for aid — it's usually about $2,000, and your income has to be lower than the cost of your care. The good news is your spouse can continue living in your home, even if Medicaid is paying for your stay in a nursing home. Other details of what you can keep while getting Medicaid benefits vary by state. Check out *www.cms.hhs.gov/MedicaidEligibility* for information about the rules in your state.

Once you're in, you're good. If you enter a nursing home you like and you are paying for it, you won't be kicked out if your money dries up. That's true for all facilities that participate in Medicaid. So even though Medicaid may pay the nursing home less than you did, you can still stay. Apply for Medicaid as soon as you become eligible, and your application should be processed within 45 days. That's the law.

ALERT!

Plan ahead for a possible future move to a care facility. Don't assume you'll be able to sell your home quickly if the need arises. Changes in home prices and buyer demand mean you may have to wait out a bad market — or take a huge loss on your home. Find out if the facility you plan to enter offers help with real estate details or financing.

Top-secret strategy keeps 'half a loaf'

Medicaid rules don't let you give away all your assets — to your children, for example — then claim immediate aid for nursing home or assisted living care. There is a "look-back period" of five years, where states check to see if you've made gifts. If you have, they calculate a penalty period during which you are not eligible for Medicaid. The number of months you must wait are based on the amount transferred divided by the average cost of nursing home care in your area. This number is added on to the date you apply for Medicaid. But your loved ones may be able to hold on to some of your assets while still following Medicaid's rules on eligibility by using the "reverse half-a-loaf" method.

Let's say you give someone you trust all your assets, then immediately apply for Medicaid. You'll be penalized a waiting period as of that date. Then your "trusted person" transfers back to you half your assets, which you will use to pay for nursing home care during the waiting period. Except now, the benefit waiting period is shortened based on the new, lower transferred amount. Note there may be a gift tax and this strategy won't work in all states. Also, some people use annuities and promissory notes instead to keep control of portions of their assets.

Get good advice from an attorney who's an expert in eldercare planning in your state. Find one near you through the National Academy of Elder Law Attorneys at *www.naela.org*.

Medicaid break for at-home care

Medicaid's five-year, look-back rule doesn't apply to home care eligibility. So, even if you've recently given away assets, you may be able to use Medicaid benefits to pay for care in your home — whether it's custodial care or medical assistance. Just be sure your caregiver or agency is Medicaid certified.

Muscle your way out of the nursing home

Loss of muscle mass and strength, called sarcopenia, is one of the most common reasons seniors need nursing home care. In fact, about 60 percent of people in long-term care facilities suffer from this debilitating condition. It can make you so weak you can't get out of a chair or do other basic activities. But losing muscle mass as you age isn't inevitable. Keep yourself strong with exercise, and you may stay independent longer.

LTC insurance: 4 critical questions

You could easily spend $70,000 for a single year in a nursing home. Prices like that — and the fear that even Medicaid won't cover you — send folks flocking to buy long-term care insurance. Just consider these issues before you spend money on a policy.

Does your spouse need your assets? Even if you have a hefty retirement nest egg, it can dwindle to nothing fast paying for a long stay in a nursing home or assisted-living facility. Long-term care insurance may keep you from spending it all on care — protecting your estate. If you have no one depending on a retirement income and no heirs, it's a different story.

Is there a skeleton in your family's health history closet? If a debilitating illness runs in your family, you may want long-term care insurance. Just make sure your policy does not exclude disorders like Alzheimer's disease.

Do you need it now? Many experts say the best time to buy long-term care insurance is when you're in your early to mid-50s. Buy a policy too early, and you'll end up paying more in premiums over the long haul. But if you wait too late, the price of coverage may be too high to afford — or you may not even qualify.

Do you meet the financial guidelines? The National Council on Aging offers four traits of a good candidate for long-term care insurance. You should:

- own at least $75,000 in assets, not counting your home and car.

- have around $25,000 to $35,000 in annual retirement income if you're single.

- be able to easily pay premiums.

- be able to absorb a premium increase.

Money-saving tips for LTC success

Get the right policy if you decide to buy long-term care insurance. You don't want to pay for a plan that doesn't provide what you need. Here are ways to get good coverage without breaking the bank.

- Buy the best policy you can afford without paying more than 7 percent of your income on premiums.

- Get a plan with a 90-day waiting period before the benefits kick in. This will keep your premiums down.

- Select a three- to five-year benefit period rather than a lifetime payout. Statistics show that's all most people need.

- Look for an inflation-adjustment clause so the benefits keep up with price increases. This feature is especially important if you're younger than 70. For instance, nowadays a reasonable daily benefit is $200, but it's almost guaranteed to go up in the future.

- Get coverage that includes home care and unlicensed caregivers. This gives you the option to pay less for an aide that doesn't have to come from a licensed healthcare agency.

- Go in with your spouse on a flexible joint long-term care policy which will cover either one or both of you.

9 smart ways to pay for care

It may be smarter — and cheaper — to not buy long-term care insurance. No doubt about it, it's expensive. Seniors spent $15 billion on premiums in 2007 alone. But if you're 65 or older, there's a 50-50 chance you're going to need some kind of extended care. So how can you pay for this care if you don't or can't get LTC insurance?

Save, save, save. Self-insuring your long-term care is possible, and you may come out ahead. For example, invest that $1,000 a year you'd otherwise pay for insurance, and you can spend it on care or leave it to your children.

Go overseas. You can find unbelievable nursing home bargains if you're willing to look outside the United States. A lower cost of living in countries like Mexico, Costa Rica, and India means you can sometimes get full-time personal assistants and cooks, massages, physical therapy, and 24-hour staffing — for 75 percent less than here at home. For more information on how to save money on good medical treatment overseas, see *Travel for treatment and save* in the *Straight talk about health insurance* chapter.

Take out a reverse mortgage. This can be a good option for people who can't afford a long-term care policy, yet have too many assets to qualify for Medicaid. You must be at least 62 years old to qualify.

Buy an annuity. Some of these investment tools include a long-term care benefit.

Consider a group policy. You may find cheaper long-term care insurance by buying it through your employer. Benefits may be less than with typical individual plans, but may be adequate.

Use Veterans' benefits. The Veterans Administration helps you save $1,000 or more a year on costs through a special pension fund. In addition, VA offers nursing home care and a variety of other long-term care services including adult day health care, respite care, and home-based primary care. For more information and details on eligibility, visit *www1.va.gov/health*.

Let your children pay and benefit. If your adult child pays for more than half of your care, he can claim you as a dependent and get a tax deduction. He can also use pretax money from a flexible spending account to pay for your care.

Check out charity. Programs through your long-term care center may help pay your bills if you run out of funds.

Turn to Medicaid. If you spend down your own money on care, this federally funded program may pick up the bill.

Respite care — welcome break for caregivers

Taking care of a family member with physical or mental disabilities has its rewards, but it's also challenging. Eventually you need a break. Respite care, or temporary relief for caregivers, can give you a chance to rest — both physically and mentally. But getting that break can cost big money. Respite adult day care at one facility in Wisconsin costs $45 to $60 a day, while overnight stays run to $230, depending on the type of care needed.

The good news is you can receive grants that will help pay for a professional caregiver or another family member to come visit and help out. You could also get a free stay for your relative at a nursing facility, either during the day or overnight. Contact these groups to see what help is available.

- National Family Caregiver Support Program. Get more information about this federal program at *www.aoa.gov*. Click on the "Elders & families" link.

- The Department of Veterans Affairs.

- Nonprofit agencies that cater to a specific disease. For example, if your loved one has Alzheimer's disease, you may qualify for a respite care grant from the Alzheimer's Association.

- Eldercare locator at *www.eldercare.gov*.

ALERT!

Draw up a formal contract — called a caregiver agreement — if you are paying a relative to provide care for you. It's a smart idea to prove you are spending down your estate as preparation for Medicaid benefits.

Insurance and annuity know-how

Your money or your life — test your insurance IQ

People are living longer and the number crunchers have noticed. That means the cost of life insurance has dropped dramatically in the past decade. So look at your policy to see if you can find a better deal. Here's the lowdown on the two basic types of policies: term insurance and permanent — or "whole life" — insurance.

Term insurance is temporary. Term life insurance covers you for a certain period of time, like 10 or 20 or 30 years. The extra cost for longer coverage is usually very small, so that 30-year policy may be worth it.

This type is a good choice if you want coverage only until your children are through college, for example. In this scenario, you're buying life insurance to be sure the kids would be able to finish their education in the event that you die unexpectedly.

Permanent insurance lasts your whole life. Permanent insurance covers you until you die, at whatever age. It's sometimes called "cash value life insurance." This type includes an investment component, since some of your money goes into an investment account — called the cash value — while some goes into an account for the insurance portion. You can drop the policy whenever you want and still keep the cash value.

Permanent insurance is a good option if you need coverage for longer than 30 years, if your heirs will need it to pay off expenses like estate taxes, or if your spouse won't receive any other financial benefits when you die. But it's more expensive than term. Experts say don't buy term insurance strictly for its investment value — most agree it's not the smartest way to build savings.

Conventional wisdom suggests you buy a policy that pays five to 10 times your annual income. You can determine how much coverage you need with the calculator at *www.foresters.com/calculator*.

Here's how you can save money by purchasing term life insurance, yet still leave enough money for your loved ones. Let's say a 30-year-old could either:

- pay $100 a month for a whole life policy that would pay out $125,000 or

- pay $7 a month for a 20-year term insurance policy and invest the remaining $93 every month in a good growth stock mutual fund.

If you get an 8 percent return on your investment over 30 years, you end up with more than $136,000 — even without taking inflation into account. That's more than the $125,000 policy would have paid. Plus if your term policy is still in effect, you're doubly insured.

Get lower premiums — health issues no hurdle

Don't assume you can't get life insurance or that you'll have to pay excessively high premiums if you aren't 100 percent healthy. Times have changed, and nowadays insurers look more carefully at individual situations rather than automatically turning down people with diabetes, asthma, or heart disease. If you had coverage at a higher rate or you weren't able to get coverage in the past because of a serious illness, you may get a better deal now.

Diabetes is not a deal breaker. If you aren't insulin dependent and your condition is controlled by diet or drugs, you can still get coverage — often at a lower rate than before.

Cancer not always a complication. If it's been three to five years since your previous cancer treatment, it's time to get a new insurance quote. Men who've battled prostate cancer may get standard insurance if they have certain Gleason and PSA scores. And women who have been treated for early stages of breast cancer may not have to pay extra.

Heart disease doesn't mean "no." Even if you've suffered a heart attack, you may still get affordable coverage. But don't ask for insurance quotes right after your heart attack. Wait one or two years, and you'll look like a better risk.

In all cases, you may need to provide detailed information from your doctor about your condition and how it's being controlled.

Smart tips lower your premium even more. Even if you don't have a chronic health condition, you can lower your rates with these tricks:

- Lose weight if you need to so you're in a more healthy category.

- Stop smoking, usually for one to five years.

- Lower your cholesterol.

- Control your blood pressure.

- Improve your driving record for at least three years.

- Shop for a policy just before your birthday or half birthday since the rates go up with age.

- Pay your annual premiums in a lump sum rather than monthly.

- Pay via automatic debit.

Save big bucks with a policy change

Times change, and so do your insurance needs. As you move into a new phase of your life, consider whether you should change or drop your life insurance policy.

Retire from work, retire your policy? Life insurance is intended to replace income that would be lost if you were no longer here. So after you stop working, you may be able to save money by dropping your policy. But first consider other reasons to keep it, like replacing lost Social Security income for your spouse, or taking care of a disabled child or parent.

Switch from term to cash value. If you've paid for the major expenses of life — your children are grown and out of school, your house is paid for, you're out of debt, and you have enough money invested to fund your retirement — it's time to reconsider term life insurance. You can probably drop that policy and save money. Another option may be converting it to cash value life insurance. You'll be able to extend your coverage and may not have to go through the process of completing questionnaires and undergoing physical exams.

6 easy ways to pay less

All life insurance is not created equal. Consider these factors as you compare policies, and you'll save money on good coverage.

Check the ratings. You want to be sure your insurance company will still be there when you need it, likely decades in the future. Several agencies analyze insurance companies based on their financial strength. Look for high ratings from these groups.

- Fitch Ratings (*www.fitchratings.com*)

- Moody's (*www.moodys.com*)

- A.M. Best (*www.ambest.com*)

- Standard & Poor's (*www.standardandpoors.com*)

- Weiss Ratings (*www.weissratings.com*)

Join the club. Look into group life insurance offered by your employer. Even if you have to pay for part of the cost, group insurance is often cheaper than an individual policy. But don't assume the group plan your employer provides as part of your benefit package is enough coverage — it's usually not.

Buy it before you need it. People who are older and those in poor health get stuck paying the highest rates for life insurance. That's why you should try to buy it when you're still healthy and fairly young.

Comparison shop. Various insurance companies set prices for similar policies differently, and have different rules for who gets the lowest rates. That makes it worthwhile to work with an insurance agent or broker who deals with several companies.

Look for discounts. Don't assume you'll automatically pay a higher premium for more insurance. Sometimes a discount kicks in when you reach a certain level. For instance, you could get $250,000 of insurance for less than the price of a $200,000 plan.

Read the fine print. Paying your insurance via installments throughout the year — fractional premiums — may be convenient. But be sure you won't be paying an extra charge for this privilege.

THE NEXT STEP

You can shop for cheaper life insurance online, just make sure you use a Web site that asks enough questions about your health and family history to give an accurate quote. Otherwise you may end up paying more after the application and physical exam process. These sites ask detailed questions to generate reliable quotes.

- *www.insure.com*

- *www.accuquote.com*

- *www.insweb.com*

3 surprising ways life insurance is worth the cost

If your kids are grown, your house is paid for, and your spouse can count on your investments, pension, and continuing Social Security, why do you still need life insurance? What can it do for you that justifies the continued cost? Here are three ways to make it useful to you.

Help your heirs pay estate taxes. Even if you have large investments, the cash value may not be readily available at your death. Your heirs may be forced to sell items like real estate or liquidate assets like a 401k at a loss to pay inheritance taxes. But if your heirs had the proceeds from an insurance policy to pay those taxes, they could keep the other assets without financial problems. And the good news is your heirs won't have to pay income tax on life insurance death benefits.

Stretch your pension. This is called a "pension maximization strategy." If your employer's pension plan makes you choose between getting a larger pension just for your own lifetime or a smaller pension that continues for your spouse after you die, it may be a good deal to pick the larger pension. Then you can cover your spouse's needs with your life insurance policy later. Crunch the numbers to see when each version lets you come out ahead.

Give the gift of independence. A life insurance benefit may be more than just money. It can act as a legacy for your children or grandchildren. That way when you die, your heirs receive money to let them live with greater financial independence.

Snoop out a lost insurance policy

Don't lose out if a loved one dies — even if nobody can find the life insurance policy. The Insurance Information Institute, a nonprofit group, suggests these steps to find a lost policy.

- Check the deceased person's bank safe deposit boxes for the policy.

- Search through personal files, bank books, and canceled checks to find the name and address of a possible insurer.

- Contact his financial advisor, who may have helped set up the policy.

- Examine applications for other insurance policies he may have taken out. They should refer to any previously purchased insurance.

- Check the database of life insurance state regulators that's maintained by the National Association of Insurance Commissioners. You can find this group online at *www.naic.org*. You'll get contact information for your state's department of insurance, which regulates insurance companies. Then you can work through that agency to contact the insurance company that sold the policy.

- If you know for sure there's a policy out there that will benefit you, hire a private search firm like the MIB Group, Inc. The price you pay for the search — around $75 — may be well worth it.

THE NEXT STEP

High ticket prices and worries about whether an airline or hotel will go out of business send many travelers searching for travel insurance. These policies can pay you back if your luggage is lost, your airline goes broke, or you need medical care overseas. The Web site *www.InsureMyTrip.com* lets you find the best deal on the coverage you want. Plug in your trip details, and you'll get price quotes from up to 19 insurance companies.

Take a bite out of dental care costs

You'd think paying premiums for health insurance would cover every part of your body. It often doesn't. Many health insurance plans don't include dental care, or you must pay extra to get your teeth taken care of. If you have the option of buying that extra care, it's probably worth it. Getting help with dental care now can save you money and pain later on, since dental insurance helps you keep small problems from getting bigger.

And don't think life gets simpler once you qualify for Medicare — it typically won't cover regular dental work unless it's related to a medical condition or other covered procedure.

So how can you pay for dental care if Medicare or your health insurance won't cover it?

Go back to school. Dental school, that is. You may be able to get inexpensive care from some very careful dental students if there's a school near you. The work may take longer, but you'll save big — perhaps 40 percent off the regular cost. Find dental schools listed by state at the American Dental Association's Web site, *www.ada.org*.

Ask for a better deal. Some dentists will give discounts of around 5 to 10 percent if you pay cash, are a senior, or even simply because you don't have insurance. Be sure to negotiate before any work is done.

Get a Medicare Advantage Plan. Some of these private options include dental care. Calculate the costs to see if it's a good deal for you.

Consider a discount card. A dental discount plan, such as CareIngton Dental & Vision Savings Plan or Aetna Dental Access, lets you pay a membership fee and get lower rates at participating dental centers. You'll want to investigate to be sure the $7 to $10 you pay every month is balanced out by your savings — but many plans claim you'll save up to 50 percent with their card. If you have a favorite dentist, just make sure he belongs to the plan.

Save with a tax-free account. With a flexible spending account (FSA) or health savings account (HSA), you can sock away pretax income to pay for unreimbursed medical or dental expenses later on. For more information on how to save money with a flexible spending account or health savings account, see *Plan wisely for tax-free savings* and *Best-kept secret about an HSA* in the *Straight talk about health insurance* chapter.

Healthy strategies for best injury coverage

Disability insurance pays part of your salary if you can't work because of illness or injury. That sounds great, and some people rush to buy it after they hear scary "what if" stories. But before you shell out money for a policy, consider these four points that should be critical in your decision-making process.

- Rates are high, maybe $2,000 a year or more.

- Many plans don't guarantee to pay benefits until you reach 65, when you would qualify for Medicare and perhaps Social Security.

- Disability payments don't replace all of your lost income. They typically cover no more than 70 to 80 percent. That's because insurance companies want you to have an incentive to return to work.

- You'll find strict limits on when a policy pays out. These could specify the severity of disability that qualifies, whether you're able to work in your own job as opposed to in any job, and so on.

But, of course, all disability coverage is not a waste of money. In 1999 some 14 million Americans were disabled, often from chronic conditions like arthritis, diabetes, or heart disease. If you decide you need it, pick a policy that works for you.

- Make sure the policy is noncancelable and guaranteed renewable. That means the insurance company can't drop you or increase your rates unexpectedly.

- Get guaranteed future insurability. This feature means you'll be able to increase your coverage in the future to keep up with your increasing salary — without having to pass another physical exam.

- Select the right waiting — or elimination — period before benefits kick in. You want it to be long enough so you can get a low rate, but not so long that you would run out of money before you get your first check.

- Find a policy with a benefit period that's long enough to meet your needs. One that lasts until you turn 65 years old would be ideal, but it will cost more.

- Ask for a cost-of-living rider so inflation won't sabotage your future. This rider could increase your premiums by up to 25 percent.

- Get a policy with an incontestable clause. That means the insurance company can't cancel the policy later if it's found you had a pre-existing condition.

- Include a Waiver of Premium so you won't have to keep paying them after you become disabled.

SuperSaver

Even if you purchased disability insurance while you were working, you can safely save money by canceling the coverage after you retire.

Get extra protection under umbrella coverage

Excess liability coverage — or an umbrella policy — is more useful the more assets you have. The longer you work and put away savings in your nest egg, the more you have to lose in a liability claim.

Augment your homeowner's coverage. Liability coverage is important to prevent losing your shirt in case of a lawsuit. Sounds farfetched, but it could happen if someone gets hurt at a party at your house or a delivery person trips on your front steps. Your homeowner's policy may cover you for $300,000 in damages, but even that might not be enough. Lawsuits are getting bigger, and damages sometimes include future earnings of the injured person. While experts say you should have an umbrella policy if you have a combined value of your home, investments, other assets, and future earnings equal to $1 million or more, this coverage is not only for the rich. An umbrella policy may be important if you:

- entertain often.

- have a swimming pool.

- own a dog that could bite.

- own a boat.

Feel protected when you rent. Having an umbrella policy in place may be more cost effective than the other choices of coverage when you rent a car. These options include carrying lots of liability insurance through your regular car insurance policy or buying supplemental liability insurance at the rental car counter for $7 to $14 per day.

Cover your teen. If you have a teenage driver on your car insurance policy, you may want the extra protection against the unexpected.

> Umbrella policy: This type of insurance coverage functions like an umbrella, sitting on top of your homeowner's insurance and car insurance to provide extra liability coverage. Also called excess liability coverage, it protects you from losses above the level that your other insurance would cover.

As insurance goes, an umbrella policy is cheap. For the price of a few hundred dollars a year, you can get a $1 million to $5 million policy — depending on where you live and what assets you have. Typical costs run $200 to $300 per year for the first $1 million of coverage and another $50 to $100 for each additional $1 million.

Say no to excess insurance

Some types of insurance are important to protect you from problems large and small. But other types are unnecessary, and buying them is a waste of money. Skip these insurance pitfalls and bank your savings instead.

Hospital indemnity insurance. This type of policy pays a certain amount for every day you stay in the hospital. Policies are relatively cheap, but they don't pay nearly as much as you'd need if you ever have a hospital stay. Instead, be sure your regular health insurance will cover a hospital stay.

Dread-disease insurance. These policies are sold to cover you in case you get a specific disease, most often cancer. They tend to be a waste of money since they duplicate coverage you already have through regular health insurance. Besides that, if you're known to be at high risk for a certain disease — like cancer if you smoke — you can't buy the coverage anyway. Instead, count on coverage from a good health insurance policy.

Life insurance for a child. Losing a child is a sad event, but you wouldn't be losing any income if it happened. Don't waste money on this insurance.

Extra rental car insurance. Don't throw away money duplicating coverage you already have through your regular auto insurance or from your credit card. Check your policy before you get to the rental car counter.

Credit card loss protection. If a thief steals your credit card and goes on a shopping spree, according to the Federal Trade Commission, your liability for unauthorized charges is limited to $50. This insurance is definitely a waste.

Mortgage insurance. This type of policy would pay off your mortgage if you die suddenly. But it's cheaper simply to buy enough life insurance to cover your mortgage. You'd pay three times as much to get the same coverage through a specific mortgage insurance plan.

Great reasons to think twice before buying

Annuities sound like a great deal, but appearances can be deceiving. These complicated investments, generally bought through an insurance company, guarantee either a lump sum payout or monthly income, depending on the type you choose.

Annuity salespeople target retirees, but these products are bad options for most older adults. Other investments offer better returns with lower fees and fewer strings attached. Experts say you should only consider buying an annuity if you:

- already set aside the maximum amount possible in a 401k, IRA, and Roth IRA. These retirement savings accounts offer a better deal, more flexibility, and lower fees than annuities. Plus, the interest earned from them gets taxed at a lower rate.

- plan to keep the annuity for at least 10 years. It takes that long for the tax benefits of even a cheap annuity to outweigh its fees.

- aren't planning for anyone to inherit it. Your heirs don't get a tax break on annuities like they do on stocks, bonds, mutual funds, or real estate.

- have other sources of retirement income. Don't stash all your money into an annuity. Many annuities don't let you access the extra cash in an emergency. Some experts suggest putting just 25 percent of your savings into one.

Instead of an annuity, consider tucking money into a retirement account, such as an IRA or 401k, and investing it in a safe mix of bonds and mutual funds. You can easily leave these assets to your spouse or heirs. Plus, you can generally tap the funds in a retirement account penalty-free after age 59 1/2.

Whatever you do, don't buy an annuity through your 401k or IRA. These accounts already grow your money tax-deferred, so owning a tax-deferred annuity in them doesn't do anything except tack on more fees.

Most people should also avoid variable annuities. Their fees are twice as high as the average mutual fund. In some cases, the fees offset any tax-savings you get, all the while exposing you to the whims of the stock market.

Know your annuities

Annuities come in two main types.

- Fixed annuities guarantee a certain return on your money for a period of one to 10 years. Unfortunately, that return rate is lower than what you'd get from stocks, thanks to expensive fees and commissions.

- Variable annuity payments depend on how well the stock market does. Your account balance could grow or plunge. Either way, you'll pay higher fees than with a fixed annuity.

Shop smart for best deal

Annuities and the companies selling them are not made equal. Choosing the wrong contract or insurer can cost you a bundle and eat into your life's savings. Become a savvy shopper with this simple buying guide.

Skip the bells and whistles. All the annuity add-ons can make your head spin, everything from accidental death insurance to so-called living benefits. Unfortunately, the more benefits you add, the more fees you pay. Death benefits alone can double your fees, while living benefits can boost them another 20 percent.

Stick with low-fee products. Although annuities are tax-deferred, it takes many years for those savings to offset all the fees. Speed up the process. Buy a low-fee annuity from a discount broker, such as

TIAA-CREF, Fidelity, Vanguard, and T. Rowe Price, and avoid buying them from financial planners who are paid by commission. A large portion of your annuity's purchase price will end up in the planner's pocket.

Shop for stability. Check the annuity company's finances before buying with them. If the company faces financial trouble, such as bankruptcy, your annuity payments could drop or even be seized by creditors. Only buy annuities from an insurance company with at least an A+ rating from A.M. Best's Rating Service, available at *www.ambest.com.*

Say no to surrender penalties. Most contracts lock you into an annuity for at least a few years. If you want out or need the money for an unexpected emergency, you'll pay a hefty surrender penalty of up to 15 percent, although the fee usually decreases the longer you hold the annuity. If you buy one, ask the salesperson to explain the surrender penalty, and be sure you know when it finally phases out.

Spot shady deals. Don't buy fixed annuities that promise high teaser rates of return. When those rates expire, the regular rate can be puny. View bonus credits with the same skepticism. The insurer selling the annuity may promise to kick in free money, but you'll end up paying higher fees on these investments than on those without the bonus.

SuperSaver

Mentioning your medical problems can net you a better deal on an annuity. Having health problems that reduce your life expectancy can earn you bigger monthly payouts. Companies may not ask about your medical history, so don't be shy about telling them and negotiating a better deal. You will need doctor and hospital records to prove your condition.

Break free from a bad annuity

Like marriage, annuities come with binding contracts, but they're even harder to get out of. Try these tricks to free yourself.

Take a look. Most states require annuities to offer a trial period of 10 or more days, called a "free look," during which you can cancel the contract without penalty and get your money back. Find out if your state has this trial period and make the most of it.

Read the fine print. Some annuities let you withdraw 10 to 15 percent of your principal without penalty under certain circumstances, for instance, if you become disabled, enter a nursing home, or develop a terminal illness.

Switch your investments. A variable annuity allows you to choose how the company invests your money. If you're unhappy with the returns, try changing how the money is invested. It may be cheaper and easier than trying to get out of the annuity altogether.

Try a 1035 exchange. It lets you move money from one annuity into another without owing taxes, and it can help you trade out a real stinker for a better one with lower fees, different payout options, or a wider variety of investment choices. Make sure you have owned the first annuity long enough to escape any surrender penalties.

Keep in mind, a new surrender period will start with the new annuity, so you may have to wait years before withdrawing money. For that reason, you may be better off keeping the old one, unless you plan to hold the new annuity for a long time. Also, have a financial or tax professional look over the exchange first to make sure you won't owe taxes on the cash you transfer.

Spot scams before falling victim

Seniors are a prime target for dishonest salespeople peddling risky, expensive annuities. Wise up with these tips.

- Resist high-pressure sales pitches. Shut the door on pushy agents who claim their deal is good for a "limited time only."

- Read the fine print. Read over the contract carefully before buying an annuity. The details, terms, and fees of each vary. Show the door to agents who won't give you time to research your contract or review other options.

- Ask questions. Have the agent explain any confusing contract terms or details you don't understand, like the fee structure.

- Don't fall prey to lawsuit fears. Salespeople often push annuities as a way to protect your retirement money from bankruptcy and lawsuits. But there are much cheaper ways to do that. Buying an umbrella liability insurance policy or keeping your savings in a retirement account, such as a 401k or IRA, will do the same thing for a lot less money.

- Check their license. Call your state's insurance commissioner to find out if the insurance company and agent are licensed to sell in your state. Also, ask the sales agent to show you his license and credentials. If he balks, walk out.

- Keep detailed records. Take notes during each meeting with the agent, and store them in a safe place along with any correspondence, payment receipts, contracts, and anything you sign.

Call your state insurance office right away if you think you've been scammed on an annuity, or if the insurance agent or company won't give you the answers you need.

Estate planning: safeguard your family's future

Foolproof planning for peace of mind

Estate planning sounds like something only rich people need to worry about. Yet, one thing's for sure. Everyone dies eventually, including you. That's why you should take some steps to ease your loved ones' burdens. Putting together an estate plan means making some tough decisions so your survivors don't have to. It also helps direct your assets to the people or organizations of your choosing and minimizes the amount of taxes, fees, and court interference that comes with settling an estate.

An estate plan consists of several components, including a will, living will, trusts, powers of attorney, and funeral plans. You will find out more about each of these components as you read further.

Take stock. Your first step is to take stock of your assets, which include your investments, retirement accounts, insurance policies, and any real estate or business interests. Then think about who you'd want to inherit them. Also, consider who you'd trust to handle your financial or medical decisions if you become incapacitated.

Get organized. Make it easy for your family members to follow your wishes. Take time to organize your information in a logical way.

- Make a list of important names and addresses. Include your attorney, anyone you have given power of attorney, all the people dependent on you for care or financial support, and anyone you want notified if something happens to you.

- Record your vital documents, such as your will, powers of attorney, medical records, funeral arrangements, insurance policies, birth certificate or citizenship papers, passport, marriage certificate, divorce information, and titles, deeds, and registrations for your home, car, and any property you own.

- List your financial accounts, including loans, credit cards, checking, savings, investments, retirement, and mortgage. Note where your tax records are located and the name of your tax accountant if you have one.

Store everything safely. It doesn't do you much good if your loved ones can't find your important information. Make copies of your important documents and place them in a binder. Store the originals in a fireproof safe or safe deposit box, and give an extra key to your spouse or someone else you trust. Make sure your attorney and family members know where to find everything.

> A living will is a legal document in which you state the type of life-prolonging medical intervention you want or don't want if you become terminally ill and unable to communicate.

While you can handle basic estate planning yourself, consider getting professional help to clear up any questions. Lawyers, certified public accountants, life insurance agents, bank trust officers, financial planners, personnel managers, and pension consultants can all contribute to forming an estate plan.

Know how to divide up your property

When taking stock of your assets, you should realize the difference between various types of property. That way, you'll be less likely to make a mistake when you divide up property in your will.

Real property. This means real estate, or land. If you hold any type of deed, lease, or mortgage, you own real property. Structures built on the land are part of the real estate and, therefore, real property.

Personal property. Everything else you own is considered personal property. Personal property can be divided into two main categories.

- Intangible personal property has no value in itself but represents a right to something else. A copyrighted song, an IOU, and a share of stock all qualify as intangible property.

- Tangible personal property is anything you can move or touch with inherent value. This includes cars, boats, furniture, jewels, clothing, and paintings. Collectable items also fall into this category. For estate purposes, a collection counts as one item.

Your property can also be divided into two other categories — probate and nonprobate. When you die, all your property — both real and personal — falls into one of these two groups.

Probate property. Any asset you own at the time of your death is considered probate property. If you're a partial owner of property, it must go through probate if the other person is not permitted to take your share.

- If you own real estate under a tenancy in common, your share must pass through your probate estate.

- If you're involved in a lawsuit before your death, the proceeds become part of your estate. If your death is caused by negligence, the executor can file a wrongful death suit. Part of the proceeds may be subject to probate.

- If you have a share in a partnership, it must be listed as part of your estate.

- Life insurance payable to your estate becomes probate property. Plus, any policy you own covering another person — the policy itself, not the proceeds — becomes part of your estate.

Nonprobate property. Anything you own that passes outside your estate by some other means is considered nonprobate property. For example, the contents of a living trust would not be disposed of through the will.

If you're worried about leaving property to a child too young to manage it, you can appoint a property guardian in your will. Other strategies include setting up a custodianship or a trust. Each of these steps lets you name a trusted relative or friend to manage the property until your child reaches a specified age.

Best place to stash your valuables

You want to keep your precious items safe. Rather than stuff them in your mattress or sew them into your drapes, keep your valuables secure in a safe deposit box at your local bank.

The contents of your box are private, so no one but you will know what it contains. The cost of the box depends on its size — and you can deduct the annual cost of the box on your tax return.

What might you want to store in your safe deposit box? Here are some suggestions.

- important papers, such as passports, birth certificates, and your mortgage

- gold and silver bullion or expensive jewelry

- collectables, like coins, stamps, or baseball cards

Don't keep your will or funeral arrangements in a safe deposit box. That makes it too hard for others to find these important papers after your death.

Avoid this problem by having the access card signed by someone trustworthy besides yourself so others — like your spouse and adult children — can get in if something happens to you. Check with your bank about its pricing and policies for safe deposit boxes.

Ins and outs of writing a will

Where there's a will, there's a way — to make sure you dispose of your property the way you want to. Without a will, the state decides who gets what. Besides distributing your assets, a will also lets you name a guardian for minor children and an executor for your estate.

Surprisingly, a recent AARP survey found that 41 percent of people over age 45 have not yet created a will. Millions of people die each year without one, leading to unnecessary legal costs and hassles for their survivors.

Act now. What are you waiting for? Draw up your will as soon as possible. You don't have to be in good health, but you must be of sound mind. No one likes to think about dying, but procrastinating won't do any good. Instead of dwelling on your death, think of your will as planning for your family's future.

Look it over. Once you have a will, make sure to review it periodically. Changes in your lifestyle or economic status could lead to changes in your will. If you lose your job, land a promotion, get married or divorced, have a child, or acquire additional properties or assets, you may want to update your will. You should also make sure the person you named as executor is still willing and able to carry out this responsibility.

Consider the cost. With an attorney's help, a simple, bare-bones will should cost around $100 or less. Including other estate planning tools, like financial and health-care powers of attorney and a living will, can boost the price to $200 or $300. More complex wills can cost $1,000 or more. If you have a large, complex estate, it's probably worth paying the steeper fees.

Weigh your options. Use special provisions to make sure your wishes are followed. Here are a few to consider.

- Prevent contesting of the will by adding an anti-contest, or noncontest, provision. If an heir contests the will and loses, he automatically forfeits any bequest made to him.

- Disinherit a child. You don't have to leave something to a child, but you should make it clear the omission is intentional. Make sure to mention all your children in your will, whether you bequeath them anything or not. And remember — you can't disinherit your spouse.

- Make a conditional bequest. You can attach a condition to any bequest, as long as it's legal, not against public policy, and possible to carry out. For instance, you can discourage an heir from getting married, prohibit an heir from converting to another religion, insist an heir give up a bad habit or addiction, or require an heir to dress a certain way, go into a designated profession, keep a surname, or avoid talking to a specific family member.

- Donate your entire estate to charity. Most states allow this, but some states limit the amount. And most states won't allow it if you have a spouse.

Know the limits. Wills do have some limitations. No matter how up to date your will is, it doesn't change provisions in other documents, such as the beneficiary on your life insurance policy. Wills also won't let you avoid probate. This process, while complicated and costly in some states, is not always as bad as it's made out to be.

While it may sound romantic, don't draw up a joint will with your spouse. These can lead to time-consuming and costly legal disputes and hassles. Better to prepare separate wills and avoid those problems.

Never include special burial instructions in your will. Put them in a separate document. The will is usually not read until after the funeral, so your heirs may discover you wanted to be cremated only after you've already been buried — or vice versa.

Skip lawyer fees with a no-frills will

Don't let lawyers siphon off your hard-earned estate. Draw up a do-it-yourself will that holds up in court. Instead of paying big bucks to lawyers, pay around $40 for computer software or online tools that guide you through the will-making process.

One valuable resource is legal publisher Nolo, which offers Quicken WillMaker Plus software and an interactive online will service. Just go to *www.nolo.com* to get started. You can also try other online resources, like BuildaWill at *www.buildawill.com* or LegalZoom at *www.legalzoom.com*. You won't spend much time or money, and you'll end up with a legally valid will.

If you prefer a low-tech approach, you can find good do-it-yourself kits and books to help you, too. Make sure whatever resource you use takes into account state laws, which vary.

These basic, no-frills wills work best for people with typical assets, such as a house, car, savings, and investments — especially if you're leaving your entire estate to one or two heirs with no strings attached. You also should be in relatively good health and not expect to owe estate taxes.

But do-it-yourself wills may not work for everyone. Sometimes it pays to have some professional advice. For example, if your assets are worth more than $2 million, your estate will be subject to federal estate tax. So you may want to look into tax-saving strategies.

If you have a complex family situation or own real estate in more than one state, you may want a lawyer's advice. You should also consult a lawyer if you need to set up a trust to provide for special needs children or expect your will may be contested.

5 must-haves to protect your estate

Experts say these are the five most important documents you should have for successful estate planning.

- will

- living will, also known as a medical directive or health-care directive

- revocable trust or living trust

- durable power of attorney for finances

- durable power of attorney for health care, also known as a medical or health care power of attorney or health care proxy

4 good reasons to change your will

Maybe everyone knows you didn't really mean to leave your ex-wife all your money, but if you don't update your will, that's exactly what you'll do. You may want to change your will for one of the following reasons.

- There's a major change in your family, like marriage, divorce, or the birth of a new child or grandchild.

- You acquire additional property or assets — or get rid of some.

- Your bank is executor of your estate and the bank is bought out. Find out who your new executor is and make sure you trust him. Also, see if the fees to carry out your will have changed.

- The federal estate-tax exemption changes. A higher exemption means you can leave more money to your heirs without paying taxes.

When changing your will, don't just cross out things or otherwise mark up the original document. That might not hold up in probate court. For minor revisions, you can add a codicil, a written amendment to your will that must be witnessed and signed with the same formalities as a will. For more extensive changes, experts recommend you write a new will.

Take care of your heirs with trusts

Keep Uncle Sam from taking more than his fair share of your estate. Here's how to ensure that your family will get what you want them to have. Trusts may sound like something for spoiled rich kids, but they come in handy when it comes to protecting your assets.

With a trust, you can set conditions on how and when your assets are distributed, avoid probate, and reduce estate taxes. While a trust costs more than a will to set up, it can save you money in the long run. That's because you don't have to pay probate costs — which can be 5 to 7 percent of your estate — later.

Types of trusts. Trusts can be complex, and there are several types to choose from. Talk to your estate planning lawyer before setting one up. Here are some helpful options.

- Bypass trust. Also called a credit shelter trust or AB trust, this lets couples bypass some estate taxes. Both spouses put their property into the trust. When one spouse — say the husband — dies, his half of the property goes to the beneficiary named in the trust, often the children. A condition is the wife can use that property for life, including any income it creates. When she dies, that part of the property goes directly to the children without being taxed in her estate. That means the wife's taxable estate is half of what it would have been if she had inherited directly from her husband.

- Dynasty trust. Also called a generation-skipping trust, this lets you transfer money tax-free to beneficiaries at least two generations younger than you. It's a great way to help your grandchildren. You can specify it should be used for health care, housing, or tuition bills. Just stay under the exemption amount — currently $3.5 million — to avoid a generation-skipping transfer tax.

- QTIP trust. A qualified terminable interest property (QTIP) trust lets you provide for both your current spouse and your children from a previous marriage. You decide how much of your estate should go into a QTIP trust after your death. These assets give your spouse income for life. After your spouse dies, the principal goes to your children.

- Irrevocable life insurance trust. This trust takes your life insurance out of your estate, allowing it to bypass taxes. You must surrender ownership rights, which means you may no longer borrow against it or change beneficiaries. But the proceeds from the policy may be used to pay any estate costs after you die and provide your beneficiaries with tax-free income.

Find a trusty trustee. You'll need to appoint a trustee to manage your trust. It can be yourself at first, but you should also name a successor trustee to handle things after your death. You can choose your spouse, an adult child, a friend, or your financial adviser. You can also opt for a professional trustee, like a bank and trust company. Just make sure whoever you choose is honest, organized, and able to deal with the duties and issues that come with the job.

Remember, you need to re-title your assets in the name of the trust in order to protect them. Otherwise, they may end up in probate court and not go to your intended heir. If you have a living trust — the kind that contains the majority of your assets — you should also have a "pour-over" provision in your will. That way, any property not mentioned in your will automatically becomes part of your trust and avoids probate.

Leave your pets one last treat

You love your pets, but what happens if they outlive you? Here's how you can provide for them after your death. First, calculate how much money it should take to look after them. Consider the average cost of food, litter, toys, treats, and veterinarian bills, as well as the pets' expected longevity. Then leave that amount to someone you trust if they agree to be the pets' guardian. You'll also have to will the pets to the guardian, since they are considered property.

---

5 vital tips for writing a living will

Imagine being in a vegetative state, kept alive only by machines. Without a living will, your life could be a living hell. Give some thought before the unthinkable happens.

A living will, also called an advance medical directive, states which life-prolonging medical interventions you want or don't want if you become terminally ill and unable to communicate.

You might think your loved ones would know and respect your wishes in that situation, but if you don't make those wishes clear, things could get ugly. Just think of the recent high-profile case of Terri Schiavo, the Florida woman whose husband and parents argued very publicly over whether to keep her on life support.

Avoid that heartache by drafting a living will. Follow these tips for greater peace of mind.

Be specific. State your wishes clearly. You'll need to consider several issues, but you must include these three things.

- Artificial respiration. If your breathing is labored or ceases, do you want to be kept alive with a ventilator or respirator?

- Intravenous feeding. If you are unable to eat, do you want a feeding tube or intravenous line inserted, or do you want food and water withheld? What about other life-sustaining treatment?

- Pain relief. Do you want pain relievers, and if so, how often?

Also, specify your stance on cardiac resuscitation, major surgery, blood transfusions, and antibiotics to treat life-threatening infections. You need to decide which emergency measures you want to include in your living will, and under what circumstances. For example, you may want the hospital to use all possible means to revive you as long as there is hope of survival. Or you may want them to try a given treatment for a specified period of time, then withdraw it if you show no improvement.

Appoint an agent. Get added protection with a health care proxy, or health power of attorney. Similar to a financial power of attorney, this legal document lets you appoint someone to make medical decisions on your behalf when you are unable to make them yourself. Choose your health care proxy wisely. This person must understand important medical information and manage the stress of making difficult decisions, while keeping your wishes and best interests in mind.

Distribute it. You don't want your family and doctors playing hide-and-seek to discover your living will. Make sure it's easy to find. Besides giving copies to trusted family members, give one to your primary care doctor. Make sure a copy is on file at the hospital where you will most likely be treated. You can even keep an extra copy in your wallet or car in case of emergency.

Talk about it. Don't just hand your family a legal document. Discuss your wishes with family members, doctors, and your health care proxy. Explain the reasoning behind your decisions, and make sure everyone respects them, even if they don't agree with them. This can help minimize fighting later.

Get professional help. Requirements for living wills vary from state to state, so you may want to have a lawyer prepare your living will. Many lawyers who practice estate planning include a living will and health care power of attorney among their estate planning documents. You may also want to talk with your doctor about life-prolonging options so you understand what each involves.

THE NEXT STEP

Check out the U.S. Living Will Registry at *www.uslivingwillregistry.com* for more information about living wills. Besides helpful information and resources, this site lets you download forms and register your living will online. You can also call 800-548-9455 or write to the following address for more information.

U.S. Living Will Registry
523 Westfield Ave.
P.O. Box 2789
Westfield, NJ 07091-2789

Why you need power of attorney

You may not always be able to make important financial decisions. Fortunately, you can decide who can make them for you. That's why power of attorney, a legal document recognized in all 50 states, is an important estate planning tool.

Pick a power. You have two main options when it comes to power of attorney. Consult an attorney to help you decide which type would work best for you.

- Springing power of attorney goes into effect only when you become disabled or incapacitated by illness. You must specify the circumstances that would trigger this, such as being admitted to a nursing home. Often, your doctor must declare in writing that you are unfit to handle your affairs.

- Durable power of attorney goes into effect immediately. Your agent does not need to prove you are incapacitated in order to sign your name.

Designate an agent. Power of attorney lets you designate an agent to act on your behalf. This agent can pay your bills, manage your investments, and perform the following duties.

- Sign checks you receive, enter into contracts for needed services, and buy or sell property, such as your house or car.

- Deposit or withdraw funds from your accounts and enter safe deposit boxes to remove or add to their contents.

- Run your business and create trusts for you.

- Make financial health-care decisions or make gifts and other transfers of property.

Because of the tremendous power that comes with power of attorney, only appoint someone you absolutely trust. A shady agent could use power of attorney to wipe you out. You can choose your spouse, an adult child, a relative, or trusted friend. You can also turn to a bank or lawyer, in which case you'll have to negotiate compensation. If you become incapacitated without power of attorney, a court will appoint a guardian for you. This may be costly — and may not be the person you would have chosen.

Set up safeguards. While your best move is to simply grant a trustworthy person power of attorney, you can take some additional steps to protect yourself. For instance, you can appoint co-agents. While this gives you some checks and balances, it will also slow things down because every transaction will require two signatures. You can also require your agent to provide regular accounting statements to your family or attorney. Spell out exactly which powers you want your agent to have, limiting his ability to give your money to himself. Another option is to set up something called a living trust and appoint a trustee to manage it.

If your family suspects your agent of foul play, they can petition the court to name a guardian, who can sue the agent to recover funds. Any wrongdoing should be reported to the district attorney's office.

Laws and regulations regarding power of attorney vary from state to state, so make sure to consult an attorney before signing any documents.

Save your estate from con artists

You can't teach an old dog new tricks — but con artists always find new tricks to use on older people. In fact, a whopping 70 percent of all fraud is targeted directly at seniors. Still, you and your family don't ever have to be victims.

Once a con artist earns your trust, it can have disastrous consequences on your finances. Maybe the scoundrel will "borrow" money, run up credit card debt, or wipe out your savings. He may even talk you into changing your will or putting him in charge of your finances. All the while, he will probably try to isolate you from friends and family who could protect you.

Beware of anyone several decades younger who shows a romantic interest in you. While it may be flattering, it can also be a scam. By the time you realize you've been taken advantage of, you may be too embarrassed to tell anybody about it. Swallow your pride and speak up right away so the authorities can catch the crook.

Watch out for caregivers who can weasel their way into an older person's good graces and take advantage of them. Conduct a thorough background check before hiring a caregiver and steer clear of anyone with a history of financial problems. Don't let caregivers handle your bills. Choose a trustworthy family member instead. Of course, not all relatives can be trusted. Even your own son or daughter could swindle you for financial gain.

Protect the older people in your life by staying in contact with them. Check on them often, and be on the lookout for any shenanigans. Report any suspected scams immediately.

6 steps to avoid ill will

Your will shouldn't include harsh surprises. Avoid conflicts and settle disputes by talking to your heirs about your wishes, as well as theirs. Parents and children often don't discuss money ahead of time, but doing so can lighten the load of your passing and help your children plan their own estates. Take solid steps now to make sure your wishes are honored and your children are left with fond memories.

Divvy up now. One option — divide your belongings now, at least verbally. Let your children ask for things they each want most. Avoid playing favorites. Instead of giving the eldest first choice, draw names randomly. Once everyone has chosen their first item, reverse the order or draw again for the next round.

Be fair. It's hard if not impossible to divide everything equally, but you can strive for fairness. If one child gets something worth a lot more money than the other, make up the difference with cold, hard cash.

Get creative. Consider a family auction, especially if you own many valuables. Have everything appraised beforehand. Add up the total value, and divide that by the number of children or "bidders" you have. Hold a family get-together, explain in advance how the system will work, and give each heir the same amount of "money" to bid on items.

Ask before giving. You think your mother's china should go to your oldest daughter. What if she doesn't want it, but your youngest one does? Ask people if they want an item before you bequeath it to them. If you do wind up leaving specific gifts to people, have an attorney look over your instructions to make sure they are legally binding.

Explain yourself. Whether you do it now or in a posthumous message, tell your heirs why you decided to leave each item to the people you did.

A personal note or video of you explaining your wishes can go a long way toward soothing hurt feelings and standing up to legal challenges.

Take care of contested items. Siblings tend to squabble, no matter their age. Create a "time out" shelf for items your heirs can't agree on, and put them there until everyone cools down. If that doesn't work, consider selling the item and donating the money to charity or dividing it among your heirs.

Save lives after death

Some of your most valuable assets aren't in your bank account or stock portfolio — they're in your body. Become an organ donor and help save a life after you lose yours. Don't worry about being too old or too sick to be a donor. People of all ages and medical histories can successfully donate their organs and give another person a second chance at life.

The key is to make your wishes known so doctors don't waste precious time trying to find out. Each state has different requirements for organ donation. Here are three ways to give the gift of life.

- Sign up as an organ donor when you get or renew your driver's license or state ID. Call your Department of Motor Vehicles to see if your state participates in this program.

- Register online to become a donor. More than half the states have online donor registries, and more states are creating their own registries every year.

- Make organ donation part of your estate plan. Specify what you want done in a letter and give it to your executor and immediate family members. Many hospitals require relatives to sign a consent form authorizing organ donation, so it's important they know where you stand.

Visit Donate Life America at
www.donatelife.net for more information
about organ donation. You can also call
804-782-4920 or write to them at the following address.

Donate Life America
700 N. Fourth Street
Richmond, VA 23219

Excellent tips for executors

Where there's a will, there's an executor. You may one day be asked to serve as one for a friend's or family member's estate, or you may need to choose an executor for your own. Executors are responsible for:

- notifying family, friends, clergy, and professionals, such as financial planners or insurance agents, when the person dies.

- taking care of the physical and financial arrangements for dependents.

- making the funeral arrangements, including any special requests the person made in their will.

- tracking down all of the person's important documents and a death certificate.

- filing the will in probate court.

- creating a list of the person's assets and hiring an appraiser to value them.

- keeping all the assets safe until they get distributed, including protecting them from theft by family members.

- settling all the person's accounts, such as utility bills, property taxes, credit cards, pension, life insurance, social security payments, and income taxes.

With such important duties, you can be sure there are just as many pitfalls. Follow this advice for a smooth stint as executor.

Don't mix money. As soon as the executor takes over, he should open a separate checking account, transfer all the deceased person's funds into it, and close the old ones. Pay all of the estate's bills — property taxes, credit card payments, and so on — from this account. Keep a receipt for every transaction.

Never pay the estate's bills out of your own pocket. The executor is not responsible for the deceased person's debts, even if the estate runs out of money.

Remember to pay yourself. Executors are entitled to about 2 1/2 percent of the money they collect and redistribute for the estate, although the amount varies by state.

Hold off hiring a lawyer. You may be able to settle the estate without help from a lawyer, especially if the probate court prints instructions for executors.

> An executor is the person responsible for presenting the deceased's will to the court, making an inventory of the estate's assets, paying its bills, and dispersing what's left as directed by the will.

Stay strong. Executors must remain objective and guard against making emotional decisions, even if they were close to the person who died. If you are worried you won't be able to do this, ask the person to designate a different executor.

Give more to your kids — less to Uncle Sam

You don't have to wait until you're dead to give money to your children or grandchildren. Take advantage of tax loopholes to help them now. Just don't help too much.

If you expect estate taxes to slash the amount of money your heirs inherit, giving money to your kids now can reduce the size of your estate — and the estate tax. Loopholes in estate tax and gift tax laws make this possible.

For example, in 2009, a single person could give up to $13,000 per recipient to any number of people without paying gift taxes. Couples could give up to $26,000 per recipient. Best of all, recipients paid no taxes on the money received. That's much better than paying a 45-percent estate tax. For more information about how much you can give, visit *www.irs.gov* or call 800-829-1040.

If you need to give away more money than the limits allow, you can pay an unlimited amount for current — not future — tuition expenses or medical expenses. You can also give money to your heirs through trusts, such as irrevocable life insurance trusts and charitable annuity trusts. Talk to a financial professional to learn more.

Consider the circumstances carefully before you give. Helping adult children with a house down payment, credit card balance, or student loan can be good, but many financial experts say giving too much may keep children from becoming financially independent. What's more, cash gifts to your children can leave less money available to fund your retirement. Thanks to greater life expectancies, your retirement could last longer and cost more than you expect. Keep this in mind when planning cash gifts for your heirs.

ALERT!

You want to consult an expert when making an estate plan — but be careful who you choose. Many promoters of estate planning services may just be after your money. Some people who call themselves "trust specialists" or "certified planners" just want to sell you annuities or other commission-based products. Look closely into a person's qualifications and beware of high-pressure tactics. Don't be pressured into buying any products or services or giving out detailed information about your assets and finances.

What your heirs should never do

What happens if you die owing money to your credit card company? Will your family have to pay your debts? The credit card company would certainly like them to — and may even pressure your survivors with phone calls. But your heirs have no legal obligation to pay your debts.

In spite of this, your heirs could still be affected. That's because creditors must be paid from your estate before anything goes to your heirs. So they may end up with a smaller inheritance. However, if the assets in your estate can't cover your debts, your estate is declared insolvent and your bills can remain unpaid.

Unless a family member is a joint account holder or cosigned a loan for you, any debt should be canceled with proof of your death. In some states with community property laws, your spouse may be liable for your debt. Make sure you know the laws for your state.

If one of your relatives dies with debt, beware of shady tactics. Creditors and collection agencies may try to coax you into paying your deceased relative's debt. They'll use empathy, persuasion, misleading statements, and outright lies to get your money. Do not agree to anything. Check with a lawyer before making any payments.

Rest in peace with a funeral plan

It's a good idea to make your own funeral arrangements while making your estate plan. That includes letting your survivors know exactly what you want so they don't waste money on extras.

You could even prepay for your funeral with prepaid burial or pre-need insurance. This insurance lets you plan and pay for your funeral ahead of time. You and your pre-need insurance agent, often a funeral director, can design a policy that includes such things as your burial plot, casket, grave liner, grave marker, flowers, and the digging and filling of the grave. This can be expensive, so use these tips to help save money — and avoid scams.

- Make sure the policy is very detailed. It should specify the style, type, and material of your grave marker and the location of the grave site by section, row, and plot number.

- Ask whether you'll pay penalties if you get your grave marker or casket from another seller. For example, you might buy a casket from a discount supplier you find in the Yellow Pages. If you're a veteran, you can also contact the Department of Veterans Affairs to get a free grave marker — no matter where you will be buried.

- Learn about your state's laws on pre-need insurance and check the license of the company, funeral director, or agent writing your policy.

THE NEXT STEP

Visit the Funeral Consumers Alliance at *www.funerals.org* for reliable information to help keep funeral costs down.

Scam-proof a prepaid funeral

They say you get what you pay for. Yet, when it comes to prepaid funeral plans, that's not always the case. Prepaid, or pre-need, funeral policies are supposed to let you choose and pay for your funeral and burial plot ahead of time.

When the policies work, the money is held in trust fund investments until needed. Funeral policies that deliver less than promised — or even nothing — are becoming widespread. Funeral companies may break these contracts due to new ownership, going out of business, or because they raided the pre-need trust fund. If you choose to sign a pre-need contract, take these precautions.

- Read the contract carefully to learn which parts of the funeral are included and which are not.

- Ask whether the policy can be canceled or moved to another funeral home. Determine whether you'll get a refund or pay penalties for doing this.

- Find out how the funeral home will invest your funds and whether that's a risky investment.

- Ask what happens to your policy if the funeral home changes hands.

- Inquire about substitutions if something you've chosen is no longer available.

- Sign the contract only after your lawyer has reviewed it.

SuperSaver

Don't forget these little-known ways to limit burial or funeral expenses.

- Take advantage of veterans' benefits. Veterans and their spouses are entitled to free burial plots in a nearby national cemetery. Contact the Department of Veterans Affairs at 800-827-1000 or visit *www.va.gov* for details.

- Help advance medical science. Arrange to donate your remains to a medical school.

8 common estate-planning errors

Nobody's perfect — but if you care about your family and friends, avoid making these common mistakes.

- Having no will. If you die without a will, state law decides how your assets are divided among your heirs. That may differ drastically from what you wanted.

- Failing to update important documents. Review and update both your will and the beneficiaries on your insurance policies, retirement accounts, point-of-death accounts, and other estate-planning documents once every three years. Also, consider updating after births, deaths, divorce, and when you buy or sell property.

- Focusing only on taxes. Take steps to prevent family squabbles and high probate fees.

- Keeping unorganized paperwork. Organize such documents as life insurance policies, financial records, and important documents so your executor can easily find and use them to settle your estate and pay your bills.

- Putting your child's name on your house's title. Your child must report this as a gift, pay taxes on their portion of the home's value, and possibly pay extra taxes if the home is sold.

- Making an heir joint owner of your bank or brokerage account. This could prevent other heirs from inheriting their share no matter what your will says. Use durable power of attorney instead.

- Assuming your estate is small. Home ownership, life insurance policies, or retirement accounts may boost your estate size so your heirs must pay taxes. Find out your estate size so you can plan ways to reduce estate taxes.

- Not coordinating advisers. If you use a tax advisor, financial planner, estate planning attorney, or similar professionals, tell these advisors about one another so they can work together.

Stretch your dollars in retirement

3 extra ways to meet your nest-egg goal

You've done your retirement calculations, and you know you won't have enough money to last. You're already saving extra dollars, but it's just not enough. Before you give up hope, consider these options.

Work a little longer. If you haven't retired yet and you're in good health, consider working a couple of extra years. Doing this will let you save more money while you delay taking cash out of your retirement funds.

Delay Social Security. Moving back the age you start taking Social Security benefits means you will get a bigger paycheck later. You can delay benefits as late as age 70.

Downsize. Consider moving to a less expensive home. If you can use the money you make when you sell your current home to pay for a cheaper house, you could soon be done with mortgage payments. That will free up money that can be saved for retirement, or you can at least lower your expenses during retirement. Run the numbers to be sure the trade-off is a good deal.

SuperSaver

If you move to a smaller house and choose the same amenities you had in your big house, like granite countertops or a jacuzzi tub, you'll pay top dollar up front. But in the long run, you'll still save on maintenance, energy costs, and property taxes by living in a smaller space. Keep it simple to save the most.

Rescue your retirement the fun way

You can retire on a shoestring and still have fun when you make money from a hobby or part-time work. At last, you can work for both fun and funds, and it may save your retirement from a bad end.

Maybe you've always dreamed of working for a jeweler, teaching quilting classes, or becoming a golf pro. Your dream job didn't pay enough to tempt you away from your career, so you put those wishes on the back burner. Now may be the time to bring them out into the open.

Many older adults are happy to partially retire, meaning they stop working full time at their regular jobs and switch to fun-oriented work. Don't feel limited by what you've done in the past. Consider working part time at your old job, joining up with a new employer, working for yourself, starting a home business, becoming a consultant, or even working for a temporary agency.

The new challenges will make your days more fun and interesting after you retire. You may become fully absorbed in what was once just a weekend hobby, and you'll benefit from social activity and having a daily routine. Best of all, it will help you avoid running out of retirement money too soon.

4 good reasons to work longer

Even if you don't need the money a job can bring in, there are plenty of other reasons to keep your finger in the workplace pie — maybe long after traditional retirement age.

Stay active and connected. There's only so much golf you can play, fish you can catch, and birdhouses you can build. Eventually your hobbies may not really fill your time — or your life. That's when you may start missing those interesting people you used to spend your work days with. Nobody wants to spend all their time at home alone.

Keep yourself busy. If you like what you do and find it challenging, you may miss it if you quit. Without something to keep you busy, every day can turn into a long stretch of boredom.

Extend your health insurance. Early retirement may sound like fun, but not if you have to cover high health-care costs before you qualify for Medicare at age 65. Even if your former employer offers you health insurance coverage until you're 65, you can still expect to pay around $10,000 a year for a family, or $3,600 for just one person.

Some employers even offer health insurance for part-time workers, typically those who work at least 20 hours a week. These include Target, Starbucks, Lowe's, J.C. Penney, and Barnes & Noble. So don't assume you won't have benefits if you don't work full time.

Maintain your health. You may stay healthier longer if you keep working. A recent study found that people who retire when they're 55 years old are 89 percent more likely to die during the first 10 years of retirement than people who wait and retire at 65. Early retirees are also more prone to depression. So do your body and brain a favor — get out of the rocking chair and back to work.

MAKING IT WORK

Here's how you can benefit from working part time after your official retirement date.

Let's say you've saved $150,000 for retirement, and you expect another $4,000 a year from Social Security benefits. Divide $150,000 by 30 years of retirement, and you'll get about $5,000 per year. Even added to Social Security, that's only $9,000 per year — not much to live on.

But if you spend your first five years of retirement working a part-time job that pays $12,000 a year, you may be able to leave your retirement savings untouched. This could give your retirement investments a chance to grow. If your $150,000 grows at a rate of 6 percent, it could reach $202,327 by the end of that five years. That gives you $6,744 every year for 30 years or $8,093 a year for 25 years.

If you still receive $4,000 a year in Social Security, your total would be either $10,744 for 30 years or $12,093 for 25 years. But delaying Social Security for five years while you work could lead to a higher monthly check as well.

Have top-notch skills and no place to spend them after retirement? Consider becoming a volunteer consultant through the National Executive Service Corps. This group pairs former business executives and seasoned professionals with nonprofit groups that need help. You get the pleasure of helping out your community, while the nonprofit group benefits from your experience. Get more information at *www.nesc.org.*

Get a foot in the door through AARP

A head covered in gray may be your ticket to an interesting new job — if you find an employer who appreciates your years of experience. Dozens of employers are begging for experienced seniors. Even the biggest employer in the country, the federal government, is eager to hire you. So if you're a senior looking for part-time or full-time work, you're in luck. Here's help finding your next job.

The American Association of Retired Persons (AARP) screens employers to find out how friendly they are toward hiring older workers. Companies answer questions about their hiring practices, benefits, types of positions available, work hours, and so on. The idea is that these employers are more than willing — even eager — to hire older-than-average workers. Employers that make the cut can join the AARP's National Employer Team.

You can see the AARP's list of National Employer Team members at *www.aarp.org/employerteam*. Check out details of each possible employer, and search and apply for job openings through this one online site. You'll find openings in retail, health care, communications, financial services, the travel industry — and yes, the federal government. Uncle Sam is recruiting for the IRS, the Office of Disaster Assistance, and the Peace Corps. Remember — Peace Corps workers are called volunteers, but they actually earn a small salary and living expenses. And there's no upper age limit on joining, so 5 percent of workers are older than 50.

THE NEXT STEP

Check these Web sites for topnotch help in finding a job.

- *www.experienceworks.org* — helps train seniors in new skills

- *www.workforce50.com* — provides job listings and advice

- *www.dinosaur-exchange.com* — lists employment around the world

- *www.seniors4hire.org* — for 50+ workers in the job market

- *www.retiredbrains.com* — includes search tools and advice

Pick a great second career

You're ready to retire from your long-term job, but you're not eager to leave the work world. Consider a career change. These 10 later-in-life careers can earn you anywhere from a few thousand dollars up to $200,000 a year. Many require little or no training, and some can be done in the comfort of your home.

- Vendor on eBay. Join the folks making good money by selling all kinds of items through *www.eBay.com*. First check out the hour-long training video available through eBay University at the Web site's help section.

- Fund raiser. Charities need a go-getter who can raise money for a good cause. Pick your favorite nonprofit, and you'll feel that you're doing some good every workday.

- Librarian. These information technicians have joined the electronic age — now they help out in schools, universities, museums, and corporations as well as in public libraries.

- Home health aide. You'll probably need state certification in the form of an associate medical degree. Then you can make $20,000 a year working part-time for an agency or directly for clients.

- Graphic designer. Work in the comfort of your home, and you can make more than $35,000 a year. You may need a degree, and you certainly need some experience.

- Personal chef. Keep it simple by cooking for just a few clients. You'll need credentials from a culinary school.

- Social worker. People who've made the switch to this rewarding job find the personal fulfillment more than balances out a salary drop.

- Massage therapist. Get the license or certificate required in your state, and you can start a new career helping one person at a time.

- Teacher. Work — but have your summers off. If you're a professional in another field, you may be able to get into teaching quickly through special programs like Teach for America. Your current employer may even foot the bill.

- School crossing guard. This job, requiring little training but lots of goodwill, is a common choice for older people.

If you think you've been discriminated against due to age, you may want to contact the EEOC (Equal Employment Opportunity Commission) at 800-669-4000 or *www.eeoc.gov*. The 1967 Age Discrimination in Employment Act makes it illegal for a company to fire, refuse to hire, or discriminate in any way based on age.

Rework your resumé to fit the new you

Searching for work in a new field means you probably need a new resumé. That's because a good resumé needs to show you can fill the bill for the new job — even if you haven't actually done the work before.

You can hire a professional to help you update your resumé, but that will cost you. For a do-it-yourself approach, follow this advice from an experienced career coach.

- Include highlights of your job history on the resumé, and save the small details for an interview. Don't try to explain all your experience in one document.

- Show how you would fit in. Although you're moving between career fields, demonstrate how your experience can relate to the new position.

- Choose the right keywords for your new chosen field. Nowadays, computers often sort through a stack of resumés before people see them. If your resumé doesn't include the specific words and phrases an employer thinks are important to the job, it won't make the cut.

- Create multiple versions of your resumé, one for each type of job you're interested in. Your computer makes it easy to update and alter documents.

- Skip a listing of your education, unless it's truly impressive or relevant. But retain details of your education on the resumé if they're related to the job you want.

- Aim for perfection. Typos, spelling errors, and grammar slip-ups make you look careless.

THE NEXT STEP

You can get free job training if you're 55 or older and low income. The Senior Community Service Employment Program (SCSEP) pays older Americans to learn a new job that helps a local nonprofit or community service group. You get paid while you train, then you continue to work either part time or full time. Find out what this U.S. Department of Labor program offers in your community at *www.doleta.gov/SENIORS*.

Get paid to shop

An estimated 1 million Americans earn extra cash as mystery shoppers. All kinds of companies and stores want to know how they're doing, so they hire marketing firms to find out. That's where secret shoppers come in.

Mystery shopping, or secret shopping, involves working as a kind of undercover agent to shop at a store, stay at a hotel, or eat in a restaurant. Marketing firms hire secret shoppers, then report to the store about how things are running. Writing a report or completing a survey is part of the job.

You won't get rich as a mystery shopper, but you can make between $10 and $50 per assignment. You may also get free groceries or restaurant meals when you're reimbursed for making a required purchase.

Work within the guidelines. To be a successful mystery shopper, you need to follow certain rules.

Do:

- get names and descriptions as you go rather than trying to remember the details later.

- give clerks and associates the chance to do their jobs right. Don't trap them.

- be thorough, fair, and accurate when you write your report.

Don't:

- be afraid of going into a store or restaurant.

- rush or skip important steps in the job.

- announce that you are a mystery shopper or get caught taking notes in the store.

- miss your deadlines.

- do sloppy work.

Sort out the scams. Don't be fooled by mystery shopping offers that seem too good to be true. You shouldn't have to pay fees to be trained or signed up as a mystery shopper. If you want to pay for cer- tification through the Mystery Shopping Providers Association (MSPA), you can. But you don't need this credential to get work. Also, don't expect to work from home as a mystery shopper. You need to visit the stores. Finally, be sure your assignment comes from a reputable marketing firm. Big names in the business include BARE International and Market Force Information.

Create your own dream job

You enjoyed working before you retired, but you didn't enjoy answering to a boss. Become the boss by running your own business. It can be a risky venture but can also reap you great rewards.

Understand the pros and cons. One great thing about starting your own business is the chance to be your own boss and make your own decisions. You also may have the opportunity to become financially independent — a sometimes iffy prospect if you work for someone else. Perhaps best of all, you get to do exactly what you want to, whether it's taking your old career out for an independent test drive or turning your longtime hobby into a business.

But running your own show is not all wine and roses. New businesses have a high rate of failure. Some 20 percent close within the first year of opening, while another 20 percent fail during the second year. Problems that can lead to failure include bad planning, poor management, too little capital, and lack of marketing — especially for inexperienced business owners.

Plan ahead. Before you jump into self-employment, consider your answers to these questions.

- How will you get funding? One option may be a microloan from the Small Business Administration to help with startup costs. The maximum limit for this type of loan is $35,000.

- What is your niche? Who will your customers be? No matter how great your product or service is, your business will fail if nobody is willing to pay for it.

- How much time and energy do you want to commit to the project? It will take a lot of both — probably more than you think.

- Do you have the needed basic business skills?

- How long will you keep trying before you throw in the towel? It's good to persevere, but don't let a failed venture eat up your retirement money.

The U.S. Small Business Administration (SBA) offers advice, tools, resources, even free online training courses — all for people like you who want to start a small business. Check out what is available at *www.sba.gov,* or call the SBA Answer Desk at 1-800-U-ASK-SBA (1-800-827-5722).

The scoop on working and Social Security

One great reason to work after you've officially retired is to delay taking Social Security benefits until later. Doing that can increase the amount of your Social Security check once you begin taking it — by age 70, for sure. But if you've already started taking those benefits, Uncle Sam is not going to be as generous.

Expect a reduced check. Working after retirement affects your Social Security benefits in two main ways.

- Size of the benefit checks. If you started taking Social Security before your full retirement age — between 65 and 67 years old, depending on your year of birth — your check will be reduced by $1 for every $2 you make. That's assuming you earn more than $13,560 as of 2008. But once you reach your full retirement age, you can earn income without losing Social Security benefits.

- Taxes. If your income plus Social Security is above a certain level, you'll pay income tax on Social Security benefits.

For more details on how Social Security benefits are affected while you're still working, see the story *The truth about earnings limits* in the *Social Security simplified* chapter.

Make the most of Medicare. The good news is that having an income from working won't directly affect your Medicare benefits.

But if you are not yet eligible for Medicare, you may need to stay employed — or get a new job — to prolong your health insurance.

Use caution when you reverse your mortgage

You've paid off your house and have a lot of equity, but you're a little short on cash. You've heard a reverse mortgage would allow you to live in your home while it pays your bills. Should you take the leap? Here are some things you should consider before jumping in.

Understand the basics. When you get a reverse mortgage, you trade the equity you have in your home — some or all of it — for ready money. You can choose a lump sum, monthly payments, or a line of credit. You still get to live in your house until you decide to sell it or until you pass on. Then your heirs likely will sell your house to pay off the note.

You can use the money to supplement your retirement income, pay property taxes, make home improvements, or pay for in-home health care. The safest option is a home-equity conversion mortgage (HECM), which is insured by the U.S. government.

Know the rules. Only homeowners 62 and older can qualify for a reverse mortgage. If you and your spouse are joint owners, both of you must be at least 62. The house has to be your primary residence, and it must be all or nearly all paid off.

A reverse mortgage is most helpful for someone with a low income but lots of value in a home. It may be a good choice for older retirees, say people in their 70s and 80s, since they would receive more money from a reverse mortgage. In contrast, someone in her 60s could outlive the money from a reverse mortgage.

Beware the dangers. A reverse mortgage is not for everyone. Consider these drawbacks before you sign on the dotted line.

- High closing costs could easily run $15,000 or more. That would only be worthwhile if you plan to stay in the house for at least five years.

- Taking a larger sum up front means you pay more in interest. Instead, take only what you need, then reserve the rest in a line of credit or monthly payments.

- You're stuck living in the house, even if things change. Think about whether you'd want to stay in the house if your children moved across the country or your husband had to enter a nursing home.

- There will be little or no equity left in your home to leave your heirs.

Get good advice. Federal law requires that you consult with a HUD-approved counselor before you take out a reverse mortgage. That's good, since it will help you understand what you're getting into and what the possible costs may be.

Tap home equity for extra cash

A reverse mortgage may not be the answer for you, but there are other ways to get cash out of your home's equity. Any homeowner with the right credit may qualify for a home equity loan or home equity line of credit. But again, know the downside.

> Home Equity Loan — A loan to homeowners based on the amount of equity you have in your home. Your house is collateral.

Investigate the risks. This type of loan is based on the equity you have in your house. For example, if your house is worth $250,000 and you still owe $100,000 on your mortgage, you have $150,000 in equity. You can tap up to about 80 percent of your home's value, or $100,000 in this case.

Obviously, that would take a big chunk out of the equity in your home. If times get tough and you can't make the loan payments, you risk losing your home. Taking out a home equity loan or line of credit was a popular

> Home Equity Line of Credit (HELOC) — Similar to a home equity loan, it's a line of credit you can draw on as needed.

move when home values were constantly rising. Then people could rely on a higher home value to ensure they'd have some equity when they decided to sell the house. But the housing market is no longer that reliable, so this strategy can backfire. You don't want to try to sell your house, only to find you owe more than it's worth.

Even worse is the idea of taking out a home equity loan to pay off a credit card balance. This can seem like a quick solution to a big problem, but it can lead to more debt. Many times people pay off the credit card with loan money, then continue to use the credit card. A year later they have the home equity loan to pay, plus they're back in debt to the credit card company.

Exercise your options carefully. A home equity loan might be the right move in certain cases. If you're struggling with high-interest debts, it may let you pay those off with a new lower-interest loan. You can save on taxes since the interest may be tax deductible. And if you use your home equity loan to consolidate debt, your FICO score — credit rating — may go up. Another possibly worthwhile use for home-equity-loan money includes paying for home improvements that will increase the value of your home.

Planning guide for home maintenance

You've worked hard and paid off your mortgage, so now your home is all yours. That's great — except you're not done paying for it. Wear and tear on the materials used to build your home, from the linoleum floor in your kitchen to your water heater, means you still need to budget for replacing items. Plan ahead so you're not left with a tumbledown house and no money to spare.

A major bank that offers home equity loans did a study to find out how long items in your home should last. Average lifespans vary because of differences in use, quality of materials, climate, and so on. Besides that, sometimes homeowners replace kitchen cabinets or bathroom fixtures simply to keep up with decorating trends. But here's what you can expect.

Lifespan	Household item
6–10 years	microwave, dishwasher, trash compactor carpet electric or gas water heater smoke detectors, security systems
15–20 years	faucets, fixtures, shower doors gas range electric or gas furnace aluminum windows garage door interior and exterior paint wood deck asphalt driveway
20 years to a lifetime	toilets kitchen and bathroom cabinets wood, linoleum, and granite flooring wood windows walls, ceilings, and doors roofing materials

Practical way to help pay the mortgage

George Bailey's mother turns the family home into a boarding house to make ends meet in the classic movie *It's a Wonderful Life*. That's one of the most heartbreaking moments in the film, but taking in renters doesn't have to be a nightmare. You can lower your cost of living while you get help paying bills by carefully planning your life as a landlord.

If you have a little money, energy, and ambition, you could buy a house or duplex and rent it out. Becoming a landlord can be a good investment if you're careful and plan right. Experienced owners say you should buy property that's cheap — even a fixer-upper — but in an up-and-coming neighborhood. And get help from experts, including a good Realtor, property-management company, banker, and attorney.

A simpler plan that lets you use what you already have is to rent out extra space in your own home. Renting out a furnished room brings in roughly $400 to $550 a month for homeowners. That's not peanuts, for sure. If you've been living alone, you may enjoy the company of a housemate. You may be able to get help with lawn care or housework if you work it into the rental agreement. And if worst comes to worst, there will be someone around to help if you become ill or suffer a fall.

Follow these three steps for success.

Remodel. You can turn part of your home into an apartment just by finishing a basement or splitting the house into a duplex. Check zoning rules in your area to be sure you can make the changes you desire. Then hire a licensed contractor to do the work, and be sure he gets the correct work permits. Installing a separate utility meter for the new apartment can prevent disputes.

Find the right tenant. Like a comfortable marriage, a good roommate relationship requires compatible people. You're in the driver's seat, because you own the house. Look for a tenant who is financially stable, with enough income and a steady job. If possible, drive by her current residence to see how it's being kept. Most importantly, when you find a good tenant, keep her. You can do that by keeping the space maintained so it's a great place to stay. Also consider offering a discount after a year of on-time rent payments.

Get everything in writing. A strong lease makes the details of your agreement clear and follows the laws of your state. Get contact information to find out about those laws at *www.hud.gov/local*. Your property-management company can also help you create a good lease.

Then there's the little matter of rent. You need to charge enough to make the deal worthwhile — but not too much. Jody Kell, an Atlanta Realtor, specializes in real estate investing. He suggests investigating local rental rates to find out how much to charge.

"Look at current rental comps in the area to see what similar properties are renting for," Kell advises. "Remember, rents are constantly changing, so make sure that you keep abreast."

Try listing your available rooms through one of these online matching services.

- *www.homestore.com*

- *www.apartments.com*

- *www.rent.com*

- *www.apartmentguide.com*

You can also get help finding a roommate from the National Shared Housing Resource Center at *www.nationalsharedhousing.org*.

Great gardening on the cheap

Attractive landscaping can increase the value of your house, and gardening is a great healthy hobby. But you can spend almost as much on the outside of your home as on the inside. Try these tricks to keep your yard and garden looking great for next to nothing.

Divide and multiply. Don't buy more greenery when you can divide your perennial plants and move some to new ground. Doing this helps plants that tend to form crowded clumps stay healthy. It works well with hostas and day lillies. Do your dividing in the spring.

Make acidifier for free. Save the juice that's left in a pickle jar, mix in lots of water, then pour around flowering shrubs. The liquid will increase the soil's acidity and encourage flowers to bloom.

Mark your rows. Spend pennies on old wooden mixing spoons and spatulas at yard sales. You can write the names of flowers or veggies on the spoons, then use them to mark rows in your garden.

Start small. Buy six-packs of the plants you want rather than a single larger plant. You'll pay less and — depending on how green your thumbs are — end up with six times the greenery. If you're really patient, start plants from seeds and grow a whole crop for pennies.

Scrounge for mulch. Don't overpay for this garden necessity at a home improvement store. You may be able to get it for free from a local tree trimmer or your city's public works department. Call to see if workers can dump a load of wood chips at your house, or find out where you can pick some up.

DIY drip irrigation. Plants love this type of slow, deep-soaking system — but it's expensive to have installed. Instead, save up empty 2-liter plastic beverage bottles or large milk jugs. Punch a small hole in the bottom of each, fill with water, and stand one up next to each plant that needs water.

Save on sod. Do your yard in a patchwork job. Buy scraps — odd-sized roll ends — of sod at your local sod farm. It will take some time to patch these together to cover the ground you need, but you'll save money. If you like working puzzles, this will be fun.

Save big on cleaning supplies

Stop shelling out money for specialty cleaners to keep your house spic and span. You can do the job with simple products you probably already own.

Stop buying this:	Use this instead:	Example of how to use it:
silver cleaner	baking soda	Line a glass or plastic container with aluminum foil, add tarnished silverware, sprinkle on baking soda, then pour in hot water. A chemical reaction transfers tarnish from silver to the foil.
kitchen cleanser	baking soda	Dissolve one-half cup baking soda in one-half gallon warm water. Use on a sponge to clean and deodorize surfaces.

Stop buying this:	Use this instead:	Example of how to use it:
spray mildew remover (like X-14)	bleach	Spread shower curtain in bathtub and fill tub with cold water and bleach. Weigh the curtain down if it floats. Soak overnight, then rinse.
soft-scrub sink cleanser	bleach	Fill stained porcelain sink with warm water. Add a few ounces of bleach, and let stand for one hour. Rinse.
oven cleaner	ammonia	Warm up oven, then turn it off. Place a small bowl of ammonia in the oven and close it. Let it sit overnight, then wipe the oven clean.
spray household cleaner (like Formula 409)	ammonia	Remove crayon marks from walls with a cloth soaked in ammonia.
carpet cleaner	distilled white vinegar	Remove stains on carpet or wood floors with a vinegar-water solution.
toilet bowl cleaner	distilled white vinegar	Pour a cup undiluted white vinegar into bowl, let stand five minutes, flush.
floor cleaner	liquid dishwashing detergent	Add dish detergent and a cup of lemon juice to a bucket of hot water, then mop your floors.
grease remover	liquid dishwashing detergent	Soak greasy tools in mixture of dish detergent and warm water. The soap will cut right through grime.

SuperSaver

Better than cheap — get the things you need for free.

- *www.freecycle.org* — Join freecycle, and you'll be alerted when someone in your area is giving away something they don't want. All you have to do is claim an item you can use and go pick it up.

- *www.heyitsfree.com* — This site is known as one of the best. It's updated daily with offers for free product samples, shipping discounts, maps, and more.

Web sites that can save you 1,000s

It used to be you had to spend lots of time, energy, and gas money to find the best prices on items for your house. No more. Now you can grab bargains from the comfort of your own home. If you're computer savvy, shopping via the Internet may net a better deal than you'll find in any store. Here's how to use your computer to save money.

Read the reviews. First, head to a Web site like *www.buzzillions.com* and check out product reviews of the item you want to buy. These opinions come from other customers who share information about things they've bought. A good strategy is to start by reading the lowest rated reviews. That way you'll know what models to avoid buying.

Compare prices. You could navigate to various store Web sites and compare prices on that coffee maker you want. That takes time — and you may miss the best deal. Instead, let a special type of search engine do the legwork for you. Sites like *www.pricegrabber.com* and *www.bizrate.com* show you a list of stores and prices on the exact item you want.

Go to the discounters. For electronics and computers, check out sites like *www.tigerdirect.com* and *www.newegg.com*. You're likely to find lower prices than general retail sites offer. And these sites, in particular, have good reliability records with buyers.

But if you need to buy things like furniture and housewares, try out *www.overstock.com* or *www.graveyardmall.com*. You never know what you'll find, since they're often items on clearance from other stores. But if they have what you want, the deals can be great.

Avoid extra costs. Don't let high shipping costs derail your online deals.

- Get help. Before you shop for the best price, shop for the cheapest shipping at *www.freeshipping.org*. You select a product type like "furniture," then scroll down the list to find free or discounted shipping at more than 800 retailers. Much better than a nasty surprise during checkout.

- Make it seasonal. You can often find free shipping offers during the Christmas shopping season, when retailers are especially eager to bring in customers.

- Form friendships. Find an online store with policies and products you like, and stick with it. For example, shoe store *www.zappos.com* always offers free shipping — both sending merchandise to you and for returns. All purchases from *www.overstock.com* ship for $2.95 each. And *www.amazon.com* offers free shipping on qualified orders of $25 or more. Some retailers offer free shipping to repeat customers who sign up to receive e-mail offers.

You may even avoid paying sales tax for online purchases. Laws can change, but companies currently don't have to collect sales tax on a purchase you make online if the store doesn't have a brick-and-mortar presence in your state.

Creative housing:

living on less

Take steps to stay in the home you love

You don't want to move out of your home, but as you get older, you may find it harder to manage. Steep stairs, hard-to-reach cabinets, and slippery bathrooms are just some of the obstacles you may face. Instead of moving, modify your home. Called aging-in-place, this approach ranges from a few simple changes to major remodeling projects.

Make sure you consider the cost and how much you can afford to spend on the project. It might make more economical sense to move. You should also consult a Certified Aging-in-Place Specialist. These builders or remodelers are qualified to make these types of home improvements. Before deciding on one, get recommendations from friends, check up on the company, and ask for a written estimate. These helpful modifications will make your home senior friendly.

- Install handrails along stairs or add ramps.

- Secure throw and area rugs with double-sided tape.

- Put nonslip surface on steps.

- Replace door knobs with lever handles.

- Enlarge lamp switches.

- Modify windows with easy-to-grip and easy-to-reach handles and locks.

- Adjust kitchen countertop heights.

- Increase access to high cabinets or low storage spaces with adjustable shelving or pull-out units.

- Install bath, shower, and toilet grab bars.

- Get an adjustable-height shower head.

- Elevate toilet with portable seat or pedestal.

- Put nonslip strips in tub or shower.

- Use a side bed rail and chairs with armrests.

- Put lights and adjustable rods and shelves in closets.

- Link a flashing light or sound amplifier to the doorbell if you have vision or hearing problems.

- Move your bedroom and bathroom downstairs.

- Install an elevator.

Aging-in-place strategies don't end with renovations. Need help around the house? Just pick up the phone and call 800-677-1116 for free handyman services for seniors. You'll reach the Eldercare Locator, a public service of the U.S. Administration on Aging.

You can also visit the Eldercare Locator Web site at *www.eldercare.gov*, where you can search for local resources by ZIP code, city, or county. You'll find all sorts of services, including home repair. Volunteers might come to your home to patch a leaky roof, repair faulty plumbing, or insulate drafty walls. Their goal is to help older people keep their homes in good condition by fixing minor problems before they become major ones.

At the Web site, you'll also find information about local, state, federal, and volunteer programs that provide special grants, loans, and other assistance for home modification. Check for programs in your area that help seniors stay in their homes. Ask about rides to the grocery store, access to health care, home delivery of meals, and other services.

For more information on aging-in-place strategies and programs, contact these organizations.

National Association of Home Builders
1201 15th Street NW
Washington, DC 20005
800-368-5242
www.nahb.org

Rebuilding Together, Inc.
1899 L Street NW, Suite 1000
Washington, DC 20036
800-473-4229
www.rebuildingtogether.org

Stay safe in your own home

Renovations and modifications make your old home more comfortable. They also make it safer by reducing the risk of falls. But there are other steps you can take to stay safe — especially if you live alone.

Know your neighbors. It's important to have people nearby who can help you during an emergency. After the heat wave of 1995 killed hundreds of people in Chicago, experts pointed to the isolation of seniors in some neighborhoods as one reason why so many people died. Nobody checked to see if these people were keeping cool, and a lot of them weren't. People with fewer friends and relatives nearby were more likely to suffer and die.

Of course, having friends nearby also makes life more fun. Check out your local senior center. It's a good place to meet new friends and participate in activities, like shopping trips, bowling, creative writing, and line dancing. It may also offer free health screening, nutrition classes, and other services.

Stay healthy. Even though nobody's there to make sure you eat your vegetables and go for a walk, do it. You're more likely to live a longer, healthier life if you take good care of yourself. Stick to a healthy diet, exercise regularly, get plenty of sleep, and take your medication.

Get organized. You may not have anyone around to remind you to take your pill or get to your doctor's appointment, but that doesn't mean you're on your own. Use handy tools, like calendars, date books, pill sorters, and alarms to keep track of your life.

You may even want to stock up on supplies in case of emergencies. Flashlights, batteries, blankets, candles, and matches come in handy during power outages. Having a well-stocked freezer, extra canned goods, paper products, and bottled water lets you stay safely indoors during winter storms and other bad weather.

Step up security. Don't forget about standard security measures, like changing the batteries in your smoke detectors, installing reliable locks, or getting a security system. You may want to look into a monitoring service for seniors. Many older people wear emergency pendants that can signal for outside help if you fall or need medical help.

While you can't eliminate all risks of living alone, you can certainly reduce them. Staying connected, healthy, organized, and safe will help you stay in your home longer. That's less time — and money — spent in assisted living, nursing homes, or other facilities.

Stretch your savings by downsizing

Moving from your big house to smaller quarters — whether it's a smaller home, condo, or apartment — can help you save money and avoid hassles. You'll likely end up with a smaller mortgage and spend less on insurance, taxes, and upkeep. You may not have as much room when your grandchildren visit, but you'll free up more money to put toward your retirement.

Choose a condo. When you move into a condominium, you get more bang for your buck. That's because these developments come with all sorts of extras, like a clubhouse, gym, swimming pool, hot tub, tennis courts, and sometimes even a golf course. You'll have plenty of time to enjoy these amenities because management hires grounds-keepers and maintenance crews. Of course, you must pay maintenance fees, but it's cheaper and more convenient than owning a home. You can even find condominium developments for those over age 55.

Opt for an apartment. Sometimes, it makes more sense to rent. Apartments offer convenience, flexibility, better access to your wealth, and the freedom to travel without worrying about your property while you're gone. Selling your home and moving to an apartment frees up equity that can be invested. It also frees you from mainte-nance and gardening chores.

You can find age-restricted apartments that fit every budget. Some senior apartments even include meals and transportation services. Consider parking, lighting, storage space, stairs, amenities, security, management, and the distance to health care, shopping, and family when looking for an apartment complex.

Of course, you don't need to limit yourself to senior apartments. You shouldn't have trouble finding an apartment or house to rent. Landlords tend to prefer older tenants because they're more reliable and less likely to trash the place.

ALERT!

New condominium developments may come with sparkling new appliances and amenities — but they also come with unpredictable maintenance fees. If you rely on the estimates of the developer or broker, you may be in for an unpleasant and costly surprise when you get the bill. You may prefer to move into a develop-ment that's been around a few years. They generally have more predictable and stable maintenance fees.

Visit permanently. As a last resort, you can always move in with one of your adult children. Statistics show this is becoming more common. In fact, the number of parents living with adult children increased by 67 percent from 2000 to 2007. Besides saving money, this option lets you spend more time with your children and grandchildren. And you won't be alone in case of an emergency. Nevertheless, to make the arrangement work, everyone needs some privacy. You also need to hash out the rules, boundaries, chores, and expenses.

Escape the costs and hassles of home ownership

Fly the coop and buy into a senior cooperative, or co-op. With senior co-ops, residents own both the building and the land. Buildings can be townhouses, high-rises, or single-family homes.

Think of the co-op as a corporation, with stock owned by residents. The size of your home determines the value of your stock. Like a corporation, the co-op elects a board of directors to make policy decisions. Each co-op unit is individually owned.

Best of all, there are group facilities and events, so you get a mix of individual and communal living. While some co-ops include light housekeeping or meal service, most likely you'll take care of your own place and cook your own meals.

Senior co-ops have age requirements. Usually, you need to be at least 55 years old or married to someone who is. Some co-ops are designed specifically for low-income seniors, while others are considerably pricier. They typically range from $50,000 to $180,000, with monthly charges from $300 to $2,000 depending on the age of the building, unit size, and type of financing. It's a good alternative to renting and the high cost of assisted living.

Some residents say cooperatives combine the best of renting with the best of owning. For instance, you get homeowner tax advantages because you can deduct mortgage interest and real estate taxes from your state and federal taxes. You also enjoy lower maintenance costs, a supportive and safe community, social activities, and services — such as landscaping, housekeeping, transportation, and shopping assistance.

While senior co-ops may sound like a good idea, you may have a hard time finding one. They are very common in Minnesota and other parts of the upper Midwest, like Iowa, Michigan, and Wisconsin. But cooperatives are few and far between in other parts of the country. That may change, so keep your eyes open.

THE NEXT STEP

Contact the Senior Cooperative Foundation for more information about senior co-ops.

Senior Cooperative Foundation
909B Selby Avenue
St. Paul, MN 55104
651-310-0225
www.seniorcoops.org

Affordable housing worth considering

You want to be close to your adult children, but you hate the idea of being a burden or losing your privacy. One unique option is ECHO, or Elder Cottage Housing Opportunities. A concept that started in Australia, ECHO gives you the best of both worlds. You're close to your family, but you also maintain your privacy. As you get older, you have the support you need without spending big bucks for private care.

An ECHO housing unit is a manufactured home set on a family member's property. You can choose a studio or one-bedroom unit. It's small — 700 square feet or less. Prices vary depending on where you live, but expect to pay about $25,000 for a 500-square foot one-bedroom unit. If you currently own your own home, consider renting it to finance the ECHO unit. It's a good way to earn income and build equity. You may also be able to lease an ECHO unit.

Like any housing option, ECHO has its pros and cons. ECHO units are designed to be temporary, so they can be removed and reused once they're no longer needed. It's easy to get help in an emergency, since your family is right next door. You get to spend more quality time with your grandchildren, help with household tasks, and avoid — or at least delay — moving into assisted living or a nursing home. Because your family is nearby, you're also less vulnerable to criminals and con artists.

On the other hand, there are some obstacles. First of all, zoning codes may not allow an ECHO unit in your area. Or, it may need to be attached to the home, rather than freestanding. Look into your local laws. Even if it's legal, your family's neighbors may not appreciate a mobile home in your yard. Discuss it with them first.

Consider cost and space issues, too. An ECHO unit may be too cramped for you, especially if you're used to a big house. You also need to make sure there's enough room on your family's property for an extra dwelling. While the unit itself may be cheap, consider the cost of utility hookups and pouring a foundation. It may also be harder — and costlier — to remove than you think.

Clever way to cut living expenses in half

You want to stay in your home, but it's getting hard to make ends meet. Consider shared housing. This simple arrangement means you invite — and charge — someone to live with you. You get companionship, help around the house, and a financial boost.

In a shared housing arrangement, most of the home or apartment, including the kitchen, living room, and dining room, is shared space. Yet, each person has a bedroom for complete privacy.

Check out the benefits. The main benefit of shared housing is shared expenses. You can cut your monthly mortgage payment and utility bills in half if you and your new housemate split everything down the middle. Shared housing offers other benefits, too.

- Lessen loneliness. You'll have someone to spend time with. If you're widowed or divorced, shared housing can help you find companionship and friendship.

- Keep up with upkeep. An extra set of hands can really help with cleaning, cooking, gardening, and repairs.

- Strengthen your weaknesses. If you don't like to cook, choose someone who does.

- Beef up security. Having someone else in the house can make you feel safer.

- Spread your wings. A housemate may provide transportation if you no longer drive.

Make it work. Shared housing isn't for everyone. You must be both assertive and flexible enough to share your space with someone else. There's also the matter of finances. You can negotiate a straight 50/50 split or your housemate can pay less in return for providing other services, like yardwork or transportation.

You may want to enter a shared housing arrangement on a trial basis to see how it works. Most important, screen any potential housemates.

Find a match. One good way to find a housemate is through the National Shared Housing Resource Center. Visit the Web site *www.nationalsharedhousing.org*, which features a directory by state so you can find information and match-up programs. Along with home providers and home seekers, the directory also lists shared living residences. That's when a number of people live cooperatively as an unrelated family in a large dwelling. Other possible resources include community or church groups and your local senior center.

Cost-effective alternative to assisted care

Something may be rotten in the state of Denmark — but it's not cohousing. This semicommunal living arrangement, which originated in Denmark in the early 1970s, is relatively new in the United States. You can currently find cohousing communities in 19 states, and they are most common in California, Colorado, and Massachusetts.

A cohousing community may be a less-expensive alternative to assisted living or nursing homes. It consists of separate, individually owned units arranged around a "common house." The common house usually features a kitchen, dining area, and space for gatherings and activities. It may also include a library, exercise facilities, a laundry room, and a workshop. Smaller than other group living arrangements, cohousing usually includes between 20 to 40 units. You may even be able to rent, rather than buy, a unit.

The idea is to foster a true sense of community among residents who share meals and chores and help when a fellow resident gets sick or injured. Like co-ops, cohousing communities feature group meetings and decision making. However, there are no elected leaders and decisions are made based on consensus rather than voting. Residents also help design the community. This process involves meeting with a developer and architect and is a key part of cohousing. Unfortunately, it may take more than two years to complete a project.

THE NEXT STEP

Contact the Cohousing Association of the United States for more information about cohousing.

Coho/US, #1445
22833 Bothell-Everett Highway, #110
Bothell, WA 98021
866-758-3942
www.cohousing.org

4 things to consider before relocating

Moving to an area with a lower cost of living is worth considering, even if money isn't an issue right now. Not only will your money go further, the savings will come in handy in case of an unexpected illness or other emergency. To help you make a decision, keep these things in mind.

Calculate the cost. Obviously, you'll need a place to live in your new location. Look beyond home prices and property taxes when figuring out an area's cost of living. Consider the cost of groceries, transportation, and heating and cooling bills, as well as sales tax.

Your computer and telephone can help you figure out these numbers. Go online to find helpful tools that let you compare the cost of living in different cities. Contact chambers of commerce, tourism boards, housing offices, and other organizations in the area. Browse local newspapers, which you can probably find online. Call utility companies to get a handle on their rates.

Look at the lifestyle. An area may be dirt cheap for a reason — no one wants to live there. When scouting a new location, take into account other factors besides cost. The climate, crime rate, quality of health care, convenience, and culture could help determine if a place is right for you.

Branch out. Relocating doesn't necessarily mean moving to a retirement community in Florida or Arizona. Think outside the box, and you'll find some great spots to spend your golden years.

- College towns aren't just for college students. As a retiree, you can also take advantage of well-stocked libraries and cheap concerts and sporting events. You may even be able to sit in on classes. As an added bonus, you can supplement your income by renting rooms to students or faculty.

- Think small. Smaller communities often feature lower housing expenses.

- Become a city slicker. Urban areas offer culture and convenience for retirees. While some things may be pricey, you can do without a car — and all the maintenance, fuel, and insurance costs that come with it. You can use public transportation or even walk to shops, restaurants, and entertainment.

Proceed with caution. Don't rush into your move. Test out the new location first. You may want to rent a place for a while to get a feel for the area. Sample the restaurants, shops, and transportation, and talk to some of the locals. Often, that's the best way to get a feel for a place. Visit in different seasons to get a complete picture. Seek out any drawbacks about the area. Always consider worst-case scenarios, like soaring property taxes or natural disasters, and make sure you'll be able to handle them.

THE NEXT STEP

Check out these helpful Web sites when choosing the best place to live. Sperling's BestPlaces at *www.bestplaces.net* lets you research the cost of living in different cities. Just enter the city, town, or ZIP code to find out how the cost of living compares to the U.S. average. You'll also get average home costs, population statistics, and unemployment rates.

You can compare the cost of groceries, housing, utilities, transportation, and health care in your current location to another city at CNNMoney.com. Just go to *cgi.money.cnn.com/tools* and click on "Compare the cost of living."

Spend your retirement on the road

Recreational vehicles (RVs) are great for vacations. Fortunately, you can reap the same benefits by making your RV your full-time home.

Mix convenience and comfort. With an RV, it's easy to visit family. And you won't overstay your welcome because you have your own lodging. In fact, you can travel anywhere, anytime. No need to book flights or hotel reservations. Be spontaneous and hit the road.

You get the comforts of home with fewer hassles. No more shoveling snow, mowing the yard, or paying property taxes. You'll have less space to clean and more time to bond with family and meet new friends at campgrounds. Traveling by RV is also a good way to scout out areas where you might want to settle down.

Trim costs. Best of all, you save money with an RV, which can cost anywhere from $15,000 to $100,000. You don't have to pay for multiple cars, a home, maintenance of your yard and house, and usual travel expenses, like airfare, rental cars, and eating out. In one informal poll of RVers, half of those surveyed said they live on less than $2,000 a month and 11 percent said they get by on less than $700 a month.

Most RV communities offer affordable daily, weekly, monthly, or even annual rates. Save even more money by spending some nights in Wal-Mart parking lots or "boondocking" — camping without hookups — on Bureau of Land Management Property for little or nothing.

Consider the cons. Of course, there are some drawbacks to living in an RV. You may find it difficult to go from a big house to a small space. And there's no escape from the person you're living with. What's more, as you get older, you may find an RV difficult to drive. You also have to take into account maintenance and repair costs, as well as the high cost of fuel. And unlike a regular home, your mobile home won't appreciate in value.

Enjoy retirement at sea

Swap your home for a boat and get ready for a great adventure. You'll never get bored with your surroundings, and you can't beat the view. You'll also have much more freedom. Keep in mind, you'll have to adjust to a smaller living area. That means fewer possessions, less storage space, and smaller appliances. You'll also have to get used to the rocking and lack of privacy onboard.

Living on a boat is cheaper than buying ocean-front property, plus you'll have fewer bills. But don't forget the cost of maintenance, repairs, and docking at marinas. These expenses may be higher than you expect. Make sure you know how to handle a boat and follow all appropriate regulations. To save money, you should also know how to make some repairs yourself. Living on a boat isn't for everyone. If you're considering it, live aboard a docked vessel for a trial period first.

Think globally to shrink expenses

Don't limit your retirement options to the United States. More and more retirees are living abroad to stretch their retirement dollar. Popular retirement destinations include Mexico, Costa Rica, Guatemala, Panama, and Belize. Lately, countries like Bolivia, Croatia, Thailand, Turkey, and Uruguay have also lured American retirees.

Temperate climates and low-cost housing, along with favorable income and property tax systems, make these countries attractive. Your money goes further there, which helps when you're on a fixed income. You can afford to live a more luxurious lifestyle. In most cases, you can still collect your Social Security benefits.

When living abroad, you may need to learn a new language and get used to a whole new culture. This often means adjusting to a new pace of life. Don't expect your new country to be as efficient as the United States when it comes to banking, Internet connections, and other aspects of daily life. Know what you're getting into with health care, too. Medicare will no longer cover you, so you'll need to get private insurance or participate in the local health-care system, which could be wonderful or woeful.

Consider the safety, political stability, infrastructure, and exchange rate of the country, as well. And don't forget you still have to pay U.S. taxes. You may want to consult tax experts both in the United States and your new country.

Do some research before you make the move. Contact the U.S. embassy in the country you're considering. If you know people who have retired abroad, get advice from them. You can also communicate with expatriates over the Internet at *www.liveabroad.com.* Another good resource is the Web site *www.internationalliving.com,* which provides information about living and buying property overseas. Consider renting a place overseas for a few months to see if things work out. Remember, you can always return to the United States.

Index

Index

1035 exchange 327
12b-1 fees 141, 186
4-percent rule 217
401k plan 136-137
  broker fees 140
  cashing out 115
  company match 138
  individual 143
  rollovers 143-144
  Roth 139
  tax savings and 137
  unclaimed benefits 135

A

Abroad, retiring 389
Advance medical directive. *See* Living will
Adviser, investment 205, 222
Aging
  discrimination 360
  in place 113, 376-378
Aid, financial 105-106
Aide, home health 359
Air conditioner (AC) 38
Airlines. *See* Flying
Alert, fraud 231
American Association of Retired Persons (AARP), employment and 357
Ammonia 372
Annual gift exclusion 263
Annuity
  buying 324-326
  canceling 327

pension, choosing 133
scams 327-328
types of 325
Appliances, Energy Star 33-35
Asset allocation 220
Assisted living 302
ATM (Automated Teller Machine) 3
Auctions, online 11, 79
Audit, energy 37
Automobile. *See* Car

B

Baking soda 371
Ballpark Estimate 118
Banking
  errors 6
  hidden fees 2-4
  online 6
Bankruptcy, assets safe from 142
Bargains
  clothing 77-79
  furniture 76-77
  negotiating 72
  online 373-374
Benefits
  checkup 288
  educational 104-106
  pension 133-135
  survivors 166-168
Bequest, conditional 334
Bills
  paying automatically 12
  paying online 5
Bleach 372
Bond fund 184

L

Landlord 368
Landscaping 47, 370
Large-cap fund 189
Late savers, advice for 121
Leaks, plugging 36
Lease 369
Librarian 359
Life expectancy 132, 219
  Social Security and 152-154
Life insurance
  finding online 316
  health issues and 313-314
  policies 314-316
  types of 312
Life-cycle fund. *See* Target-date
  fund
Lifestyle, and retirement
  109-110
Lighting, and home sale 45
Living will 331, 339-341
Loan
  car, refinancing 90
  home equity 366
  home, refinancing 247
Long-term care
  comparing 303
  insurance for 307-310
  Medicaid and 304-306
  overseas 309
  premiums, deducting 241
  types of 302
  veterans and 309
Look-back period, and
  Medicaid 305
Luggage 100

Lump sum, and pension payout
  132

M

Mail-order pharmacy 283
Maintenance
  car 91-93
  home 367-368
Margin of safety 198
Massage therapist 359
Meals on wheels 302
Meat, storing 27
Medicaid 300
  long-term care and 304-306
Medical
  bills, errors in 279
  expenses, lowering 275
  fees 273
  retirement costs 114
  services, free 288
  tax deductions 238-241
  tourism 276
Medicare
  Advantage plan 296
  fraud 291
  prescription drugs and
    297-299
  program overview 285-288,
    300
  scams 290
  shortcuts 289
  therapeutic shoes and 81
  veterans benefits and 292, 299
Medication. *See* Drugs
Medigap 293-295

T

V

Vacations, cheap 96, 103-104
Vaccine, for shingles 299
Valuables, storing 332-333
Value fund 184
Value, intrinsic 198
Variable annuity 325
Vehicle. *See also* Car
  certified preowned 88
  demo 89
  recreational 387-388
Vendor, eBay 358
Veterans
  educational benefits 106
  funeral costs and 351
  long-term care and 309
  Medicare and 292, 299
  pensions and 134
Vinegar 372
VIPPS (Verified Internet
  Pharmacy Practice Sites) 284
Vision. *See* Eye care
Volunteer Income Tax
  Assistance (VITA) 258
Volunteering 61

W

Water
  bills, lowering 39-41
  bottled 30
  heater, tankless 41
  leaks 39

Weatherization Assistance
  Program 36
Web sites. *See* Online
Weight loss, as tax deduction
  240
Whole life insurance 312
Widows, tax break for 251
Will
  executor for 346
  living 331
  pour-over provision 339
  writing 333-336
Work credits, and Social
  Security 147
Working, after retirement
  354-363
  Social Security and 364

Y

Yard sale 10
Yard, landscaping 47, 370

Z

Zero-coupon bonds 210
Zero-percent offer 13-14